Lecture Notes in Artificial Intelligence   5683

Edited by R. Goebel, J. Siekmann, and W. Wahlster

Subseries of Lecture Notes in Computer Science

W0090815

Gennaro Di Tosto   H. Van Dyke Parunak (Eds.)

Multi-Agent-Based Simulation X

International Workshop, MABS 2009
Budapest, Hungary, May 11-12, 2009
Revised Selected Papers

 Springer

Series Editors

Randy Goebel, University of Alberta, Edmonton, Canada
Jörg Siekmann, University of Saarland, Saarbrücken, Germany
Wolfgang Wahlster, DFKI and University of Saarland, Saarbrücken, Germany

Volume Editors

Gennaro Di Tosto
Istituto di Scienze e Tecnologie della Cognizione - CNR
Via San Martino della Battaglia 44, 00185 Rome, Italy
E-mail: gennaro.ditosto@istc.cnr.it

H. Van Dyke Parunak
New Vectors division of TechTeam Government Solutions, Inc.
3520 Green Court, Suite 250, Ann Arbor, MI 48105-1579, USA
E-mail: van.parunak@newvectors.net

Library of Congress Control Number: 2010928261

CR Subject Classification (1998): I.2, I.2.11, C.2.4, D.2, H.4, H.3

LNCS Sublibrary: SL 7 – Artificial Intelligence

ISSN   0302-9743
ISBN-10   3-642-13552-8 Springer Berlin Heidelberg New York
ISBN-13   978-3-642-13552-1 Springer Berlin Heidelberg New York

springer.com

© Springer-Verlag Berlin Heidelberg 2010
Printed in Germany

Typesetting: Camera-ready by author, data conversion by Scientific Publishing Services, Chennai, India
Printed on acid-free paper   06/3180

Preface

This volume contains a selection of the papers presented at the 10th International Workshop on Multi-Agent-Based Simulation (MABS 2009), a workshop co-located with the 8th International Conference on Autonomous Agents and Multiagent Systems (AAMAS 2009), which was held during May 10-15, 2009, in Budapest, Hungary.

The MABS Workshops Series continues to represent an important event that brings together researchers from the multi-agent systems community and the social simulation one. There were 43 submissions for the 2009 edition, each one reviewed by at least three Programme Committee members, and 16 were accepted for presentation during the workshop. All of them underwent a second review phase, and 12 papers were selected and are collected here, grouped into four general thematic areas.

We would like to thank all the authors who considered MABS as a venue to share their work and all those who attended the workshop for their active participation and lively discussion.

March 2010

Gennaro Di Tosto
H. Van Dyke Parunak

Organization

The 10th International Workshop on Multi-Agent-Based Simulation (MABS 2009) was organized by the *Institute of Cognitive Sciences and Technologies – CNR*, Italy, and *NewVectors division of TechTeam Government Solutions Inc.*, MI, USA. Gennaro Di Tosto enjoyed funding from the European Science Foundation under the EUROCORES initiative "TECT: the Evolution of Cooperation and Trade".

General and Programme Chairs

Gennaro Di Tosto H. Van Dyke Parunak

Programme Committee

Diana Francisca Adamatti
Frédéric Amblard
Luis Antunes
Joao Balsa
Riccardo Boero
Tibor Bosse
Sung-Bae Cho
Helder Coelho
Nuno David
Paul Davidsson
Gennaro Di Tosto
Alexis Drogoul
Nigel Gilbert
Nick Gotts
David Hales
Rainer Hegselmann
Cesareo Hernandez
Marco Janssen
Satoshi Kurihara

Jorge Louçã
Adolfo López-Paredes
Maria Marietto
Ruth Meyer
Emma Norling
Paulo Novais
Mario Paolucci
H. Van Dyke Parunak
Juan Pavón
Juliette Rouchier
David Sallach
Keith Sawyer
Carles Sierra
Elizabeth Sklar
Oswaldo Terán
Jan Treur
Klaus G. Troitzsch
Harko Verhagen

External Reviewers

Azizi Ab Aziz
Fiemke Both
Marco Campennì
Robson França
Ken-ichi Fukui
Charlotte Gerritsen
Johan Holmgren
Andreas Jacobsson
Sindhu Joseph
Zulfiqar Memon

Dawit Mengistu
Robbert-Jan Merk
Koichi Moriyama
Emerson Noronha
Nardine Osman
Kai Petersen
Alexei Sharpanskykh
Paulo Urbano
Rianne van Lambalgen

Table of Contents

Urban and Environmental Modelling

Simulation of Economic Behaviour

Methods and Methodologies

Modelling of Social Phenomena

Cumulative Effects and Emergent Properties of Multiple-Use Natural Resources

Scott Heckbert[1], Wiktor Adamowicz[2], Peter Boxall[2], and Daniel Hanneman[3]

[1] CSIRO Sustainable Ecosystems, Townsville, Australia 4814
scott.heckbert@csiro.au
[2] University of Alberta, Dept of Rural Economy. GSB 515, Edmonton, Canada T6G 2R3
[3] pixelStorm Inc. 850 Barnes Link, Edmonton SW, Canada, T6W 1G7

Abstract. Quantifying cumulative environmental impacts (cumulative effects) is challenging due to complex dynamics of natural and human systems interacting. Cumulative effects in social-ecological systems are examples of emergent properties of complex systems, which arise from interactions between multiple resource users. The article presents a multi-agent-based simulation model designed to quantify cumulative effects in the case of interactions between forestry and hunting. The specific contributions of the paper are a) quantification of emergent properties in natural resource management systems, b) evaluation of different road decommissioning policies and the effect on game population sustainability, c) calibration of agent behaviours from numerous empirical studies. Preference weightings in the utility function of hunter agents are calibrated from stated and revealed preference studies of Canadian hunters. Simulations explore moose population sustainability under various forestry access management policies and with different hunter preference parameter configurations. Contrary to the intent of access management, earlier road decommissioning is found to negatively impact overall sustainability of game populations due to cumulative effects of aggregate hunter behaviour. Altering agents' preferences for travel cost, game populations, and hunter congestion result in dramatically different spatial outcomes for where game extirpations occur. Certain preference parameter settings create resonance between hunting pressure and game population growth, forming self-organized and persistent spatial resource use patterns.

Keywords: Cumulative environmental impacts, agent-based model, multi-agent-based simulation, calibration, preferences, hunting, forestry.

1 Introduction

Quantifying cumulative environmental impacts (cumulative effects) as part of environmental impact assessment has been a challenge due to the inherent complexity of the systems involved. Cumulative impacts can result from individually minor but collectively significant actions [11], where impacts of resource developments combine with those of others, with unintended outcomes occurring over time and distance [10]. We propose that cumulative effects are examples of emergent properties in complex adaptive systems (CAS), being systems where patterns at higher levels

G. Di Tosto and H. Van Dyke Parunak (Eds.): MABS 2009, LNAI 5683, pp. 1–13, 2010.

emerge from localized interactions and selection processes acting at lower levels [26]. Interactions between forestry and hunting provide a well-studied example of cumulative effects in natural resource management, with many examples in conservation biology literature where creation of roads and other access routes has an indirect consequence on wildlife by providing access for hunters. This paper explores the question of how decommissioning of forestry roads affects the sustainability of game populations. We argue a CAS perspective can inform policy decisions in a field frequented with stories of unintended consequences of management interventions. The specific contributions of the paper are a) quantification of emergent properties in natural resource management systems b) evaluation of different road decommissioning policies and the effect on game population sustainability c) calibration of agent behaviours from numerous empirical studies.

The objective of cumulative effects analysis is to scientifically assess impacts of past, present and proposed human activities in a manner that can be incorporated into planning approaches [31]. Modelling tools which allow for quantitative analyses of CAS include agent-based modelling (ABM), cellular automata (CA), network theory (NT), and systems dynamics modelling (SD). This study applies elements of ABM, CA, and NT, and notes the value of using SD, for example in [36] and [6]. Agent-based modelling was selected due to the ability to represent heterogeneous decision making of agents, being relevant to research questions of aggregate outcomes of spatial resource impacts.

The spatially-explicit ABM described here includes hunting and forestry 'agents', who perform behaviours within a simulated spatial environment. Decision making functions of hunter agents are calibrated from published stated and revealed preference measurement studies of hunting *Alces alces* (moose) in the boreal forest of Canada, namely [5] [8] [14] [22]. Immersing these calibrated agents within a spatial landscape which represents game populations, forests and roads, and simulating the system over time, yields different spatial configurations of extirpations (local extinctions). The goal of the study were to a) Model the spatial configurations of extirpations in response to road decommissioning at 2, 5, and 10 years. b) empirically calibrate agent behaviours to improve defensibility of spatial decision making and demonstrate how this can be done using existing results from econometrically-based preference measurement studies c) contribute to methods of quantification of cumulative impacts in natural resource systems.

Simulations reveal different spatial configurations of wildlife populations based on hunting pressure applied by the agent population over time. Behaviour of agents is influenced by access provided (or taken away) by forestry roads and their decommissioning. Different patterns are created by parameterising the hunter agent utility function from different secondary literature. In some cases the hunter agents apply an even spread of hunting pressure that does not push local game populations to extirpation. In other cases, with the same number of agents, game populations are uniformly extirpated simply due to a relatively small difference in preferences.

Emergent properties of the system are revealed during simulations, including parameter configurations that generate a self-emerging persistent spatial pattern of growing and dispersing concentric circles of game populations, termed a 'hunting pulsar'. Here we define emergent properties according to [17] and [3] as "stable macroscopic patterns arising from local interaction of agents". The emergent hunting pulsar can be considered a theoretical example of a self-regulating, persistent, and sustainable system of renewable resource use, which provides the hunter agent population with a steady stream of utility while not causing local extirpations of wildlife populations.

The following section further describes the resource issue of forestry and hunting. Section 3 describes the model design, calibration and operation, and Section 4 describes model results and provides discussion.

2 Forestry and Hunting Cumulative Effects

From an economic perspective, cumulative effects can be viewed as an open access problem where the actions of several agents jointly affect a public good because of incomplete property rights [40]. Legislation exists in many countries to include cumulative effects in environmental impact assessment (EIA). Australia requires cumulative impacts assessment on matters of national environmental significance [16], and the Canadian Environmental Assessment Act [10] requires EIA to account for cumulative effects, noting:

"there is no one approach or methodology for all assessments of cumulative environmental effects. Different circumstances, such as location of project and type of potential environmental effects will dictate appropriate methodologies. Modelling, expert systems and geographic information systems are being increasingly used. However, where information is lacking, qualitative approaches and best professional judgment are used."

The history of cumulative effects assessment in the United States dates to NEPA [11], and [37] reports the history of cumulative effects in legal challenges to resource developments, finding Federal agencies have a very poor track record in litigation, losing a large percentage of the cases. This is due to 1) lack of time and resources to effectively analyze multitude of individual impacts, and 2) the lack of sufficient data or methods to analyze some of the impact questions that will arise in such an analysis [37]. We argue that complex systems modelling, in this case ABM, can be used to quantitatively model cumulative effects, and contributes to the methodologies available for cumulative impact assessments under EIA. We use the example of forestry and hunting to show how cumulative effects can be thought of as emergent properties in complex systems, modeled, and their dynamics quantitatively analyzed.

Interactions between forestry and hunting are well documented, with studies finding hunting pressure being related to accessibility of a hunting site. Industries which create access within forested areas may indirectly affect wildlife populations as hunters use a variety of so called 'linear features' to gain access to hunting sites. In the case of the boreal forest of Canada, access is gained to hunting sites via vehicle travel on public roads, industrial roads, pipelines, forestry haul routes, and by ATV along seismic lines, forestry cut blocks, and on trails [36]. Linear features also cause habitat loss and fragmentation, and wildlife species dependent on intact forest structures may suffer population declines, reductions in range, or even extirpation [18]. For the species *Alces alces* (moose) a large number of studies in Canada's forests have recorded the effect of increased access on hunting pressure and the effect on moose populations. Multiple studies have observed an increase in hunting pressure following the creation of forestry roads or other linear features, which provides hunters easier access to what was previously a more remote site, and higher harvest rates result in population declines [15][29][33][13][20][38][21].

Multiple users accessing the landscape for different reasons presents a difficult management situation, and experience has shown that cumulative impacts of multiple land uses often outstrip the management ability and management intentions of any one agency [9]. One policy response is to manage linear features though revegetation and road decommissioning, effectively closing a site once its industrial purpose is served. From the perspective of the industry which created the linear disturbance, decommissioning is a reversal to prior environmental condition. However, for hunters, decommissioning a road alters the relative accessibility of their combined set of possible hunting sites. How do decision makers respond to a changing choice set, and what aggregate impacts will be realized when these responses interact?

Numerous studies on hunter decision making have been conduced, providing a pool of human decision making models based on individual preferences, for example [5][28][30][1][8][14][20][22]. In each of these studies, preferences related to attributes of the hunting experience are measured from a community of hunters. The next section describes how results from these studies were used to calibrate the decision making functions of agents.

3 Multi-agent System of Forestry / Hunting Interactions

In the discipline of ecological economics, ABMs have are well accepted in the suite of complex systems modelling tools. Issues remain over calibration and validation, consistent communications of models in the literature, and the ability to model and interpret emergent properties. The application of ABM to ecological economics is reviewed in [23], indentifying the above issues as challenges to the field. Novel ABMs have been applied to natural resource management and land use change, such as [4], which models cropping and forestry in subsistence farming communities, [35], examining resilience of irrigated cropping and fishing systems under different governance arrangements. A review of land use change models using consistent communication framework is presented in [32], and urban water management is modeled in [19]. Fuelwood harvest and giant panda habitat conservation is modeled in [2], and [27] examine the role of social networks and information on resource exploitation.

In this paper, the combined effects of forestry and hunting are modeled using a spatially explicit multi-agent system, constructed using Net Logo 4.0.4. The model code is available online (http://www.openabm.org/model-archive/huntingforestry). The model includes mobile hunter agents which reside in a 'city', and a cellular automata spatial landscape of forests, game populations and an evolving network of roads. During each time step representing 1 year, forestry roads are generated and decommissioned (discussed later), and hunter agents select and attend hunting sites.

Hunting agents maintain an internal utility function, based on a set of preference parameters for travel cost (negative marginal utility), game availability (positive marginal utility), and encounters with other hunters (negative marginal utility). Hunter agents i evaluate the expected utility, U_{ij} that would be gained by attending a given location j. Each location, represented in our model as a spatial cell, contains a vector of attributes X_j^k for the attributes k of travel cost, game availability, and hunter congestion. The utility function is a parameterized linear equation which utilizes taste weights, or preference parameters, β_i^k which represent the marginal utility derived by hunter i, from attribute k, at hunting site j.

$$U_{ij} = \sum_{k=1}^{K} \beta_i^k X_j^k \tag{1}$$

Preference parameters β_i^k are initialized for the agent population with a random-normal distribution $\beta_i^k \sim N(\beta^k, \sigma_\beta)$ where σ_β is the standard deviation as a percentage of the mean β^k, as defined by the model user. The σ_β value introduces agent heterogeneity through assignment of individual preference parameters. The resulting initialized population of hunting agents have unique preference structures. This technique uses results from existing studies based on surveys and econometric analysis of respondent data. Other techniques for empirically calibrating ABMs are presented in [23] and [25], such as using experimental economics, with an example in [24].

In this example, parameters β^k and (when available) σ_β for the utility function are drawn from a number of studies which examine preferences of hunters. Simulation runs were performed with parameter weightings reported for urban recreational hunters in Ontario [5] and Alberta [8], rural Alberta hunters [22], Alberta First Nations hunters [14], and Alberta Metis hunters [14].

Studies listed above use a variant of an econometric regression model to estimate the utility gained from a hunting experience based on a series of attributes of the site, such as abundance of game species, the travel cost to attend the site, and so forth. Each attribute contributes to, or detracts from, the utility derived by attending the hunting site. A challenge in calibrating agent decision making functions using secondary literature is whether reported utility functions are comparable. In one study 'access by water' may significantly influence preferences, yet is absent from other studies. The measurement of distance is continuous in some studies, and broken into discrete classes in other studies. Some measure moose population by animals / km^2, and some by number of sightings per day. Furthermore, each study offers a snapshot of preference in time and space, and within a certain context of very diverse geography, and cultural backgrounds. As a result, comparing one study to another, and deriving complete and comparable utility functions is not possible without broad assumptions. To address this problem, the authors opted for a simplification of parameters to what was common across all studies; travel cost, moose population, and hunter congestion. The marginal utility weightings measured in each study and used as model parameters, sometimes requiring interpretation from the original study.

The cells of the spatial landscape contain variables corresponding to parameters in the agent utility function as outlined in Equation 1. Agents calculate this utility function for a limited number randomly selected landscape locations, set by the model user [default 50 known cells] and select the one which returns the highest utility calculation. Utility is a function of travel cost, game population size and hunter congestion.

Congestion is the sum number of hunters in its 8 neighboring cells, representing the spatial interaction of agents in proximity to one another. Moose population for cells is calculated as N_{jt} [number animals / km^2], at time t is recorded for each cell j. The population increases through a growth function representing reproduction and mortality incurred by hunting, and is a logistic growth function.

$$N_t = N_{(t-1)} + r\left(\frac{1 - N_{(t-1)}}{K}\right)N_{(t-1)} - H_t \qquad (2)$$

Where r is the intrinsic population growth rate [0.2] which also accounts for natural predation and mortality, and K is the population carrying capacity [4.4 a/km^2], and H_t is the number of moose harvested in time t, as a function of hunting pressure, being the number of hunters present on the cell, multiplied by hunting success rate [0.3 based on Alberta hunting data 1997-2000]. If the moose population is reduced to 0, it will not recover and is considered a local extirpation. A further variable is included which allows adjacent cells to repopulate extirpated sites. For moose, discussions with government biologists confirm this generally does not occur and local extirpations persist. Thus the variable controlling this effect is disabled for our study, but offers interesting future research dealing with migratory animals or umbrella species with large ranges.

The system as described to this point involves mobile hunting agents which select a hunting site from a spatial landscape of cells. The cells contain a moose population which increases through reproduction and decreases hunting pressure, and cells also contain a measure of hunter congestion as a result of aggregate hunter site selection. Figure 1 shows outcomes for the simplified case where the 'city' is located at the centre of the map, and hunters select sites from surrounding cells. In this case with no forestry roads, distance and thus travel cost are uniform (travelling 1 cell incurs 1 unit of travel cost in all directions from the city). Each of the five circular patterns de-picted is the resultant outcome of parameterising the utility function based on the studies previously discussed. The simulation is run for 250 iterations of 80 hunters, in a 80 x 80 grid. The darkest cells contain 4.4 moose per km^2 (carrying capacity), and white cells have suffered extirpations from hunting.

During the model building process and testing performance of different utility functions, settings were explored which reproduced emergent properties as dynamic

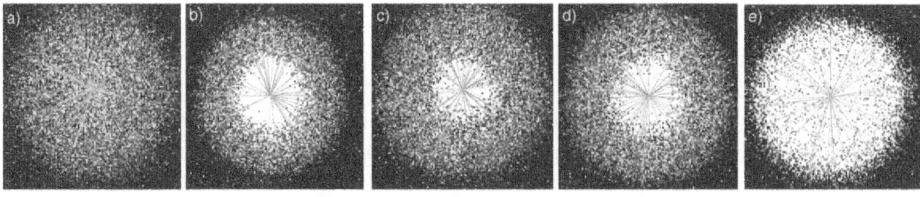

Fig. 1. Spatial configuration of game population in cells around a central origin, using param-eterized hunter agent utility function from preference measurement studies a) and b) [14], c) [5], d) [8], and e) [22]. Darker cells reach carrying capacity and white cells have been extir-pated through hunting.

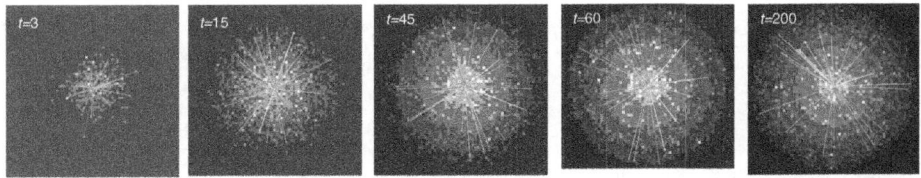

Fig. 2. Emergent property as persistent growing and dispersing concentric circles. Tradeoffs between these distance and density of game result in the 'pulsar' pattern.

and persistent spatial patterns over time. Figure 2 depicts a time series of a specific parameter configuration where aggregate hunter utility and moose population growth 'resonate' resulting in the emergence of a series of concentric circles which emanate from the central hunter city. The circles broaden and disperse, replaced by another expanding circle, ad infinitum, creating a persistent 'hunting pulsar'. This complex pattern emerges simply from the preference of hunters to travel relatively shorter distances (which reduces moose populations close to the city), and the preference for larger moose populations, and thus willing to travel further afield and trade off distance for quarry. The aggregate effect is to advance a frontier of hunting pressure until moose populations in cells closer to the city recover sufficiently to draw agents back. The heterogeneity of agent preferences allows the slow dispersal of the frontier. The example has interesting insights to notions of sustainability in linked human-environment systems given the parameter settings that generate this ideal sustainable system depend on natural processes such as animal population growth rates, but also and individual preference tradeoffs and the result of aggregate decision making.

Given our research questions addressing cumulative effects of hunting and access, we now include a road network which reproduces a choice situation analogous to that which hunters in the real world face when forestry road access is created and removed. We represent the accessibility of a site by a travel cost function, derived from [39] and [7], which apportions cost weights to travel through forest (by ATV), via forestry roads (4WD), and highways (2WD).

$$TC_j = \alpha^{DF} * DF_j + \alpha^{DR} * DR_j + \alpha^{DH} * DH_j \tag{3}$$

Where the α cost parameters are set via the model interface [default 1.2, 1.4, 2.4 respectively], and relate to the distance through the forest to the nearest road node DF_j, the distance along forestry roads to the highway DR_j, and the distance from the highway intersection to the city DH_j. By this fashion a travel cost landscape is calculated, as depicted in Figure 3, where darker cells are more costly to access. In this way space is altered according to travel cost to access a site, and a travel cost surface is generated which changes according to road development over time.

The purpose of the road network is to produce a changing set of access alternatives to hunter agents. Static road networks can be loaded from GIS data, however questions of cumulative effects are dynamic, hence the need to offer agents a changing set of alternatives from which to choose. A dynamic road system could be hard-coded based on historical trends, drawn from forestry company management plans and

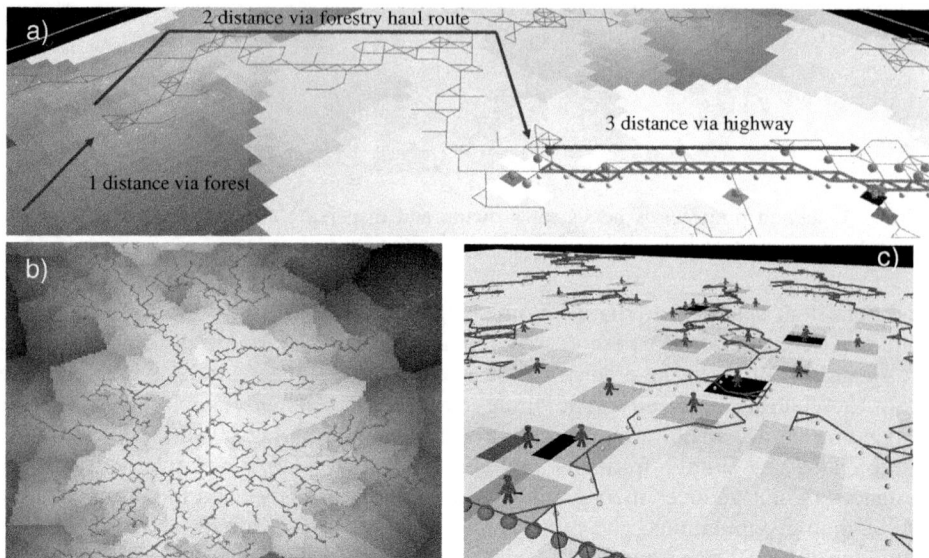

Fig. 3. Travel cost surface generated from evolving road network. Darker cells in a) and b) have higher travel cost of hunters accessing the cell, via forest, along forestry haul routes, and along highways. Hunters attend a cell c) with associated congestion metric in the cell neighborhood.

instituted as a time series, or functions can be modeled to simulate the process endogenously. To better explore the CAS nature of the resource issue, road development is modeled as an endogenously evolving network of connected nodes.

Road nodes, visible in Figure 3 c) are added to forested cells which are selected to be harvested. Selection is based on three conditions, 1) the cell's forest age must be greater than minimum harvestable age, 2) the cell must have at leased χ number (again set by model user) of neighboring cells which already have a road node, and 3) maximum allowable cut has not been reached.

Varying χ via the model interface results in different spatial configurations of forest age, as seen in Figure 4. Forest mosaics and patch patterns emerge from the local rule of interaction, simply through the number of 8-direction neighborhood cells with existing roads. The ability of a local rule of interaction to generate a landscape-scale forest mosaic has promising research contributions to different timber harvest strategies used, but is a topic for further research.

Forestry roads evolve through a selection process, and haul routes emerge and persist based on continued use, but unused road fragments are decommissioned as they age. When a cell is selected for forestry harvest, a road node with a 'decommissioning age' is created and identifies a 'parent road node' on a neighboring cell. Through time, the generation of a network of nodes develops in parent-child network, linking all nodes, inevitably back to the highway. On a newly created road node, a 'route finder' agent is created, which moves along the links from each child node to its parent, traversing a route to the highway nodes. Along its route, it updates the age of

Fig. 4. Spatial patterns resultant from parameter settings for the number of neighboring cells with existing roads required to create new roads. Darker cells contain older forest stands, and forestry road networks develop based on an endogenous selection algorithm, generating different forest age mosaics.

each node to 0. The age of each road node is incremented each time step, and if a route finder has not tra5versed the node within the decommission age (set via interface), the road node and its upward links are deleted, representing decommissioning of the road. The linked road fragment which is deleted may be only a small segment of one or a few cells in length, or may be a linked branch which extended for a considerable distance. Various spatial patterns can be created by changing the parameter χ, (number of neighboring road nodes needed to construct a new road node), as is depicted in Figure 4, all of which have road decommissioning of 5 years.

4 Results and Discussion

Combining the road, moose, and hunting agents, simulations examine the effect of decommissioning roads at variable ages of 2, 5 and 10 years. As depicted in Figure 5 a), earlier decommissioning of roads (2 years) has the effect creating extended, long tendril-like haul routes emanating from the central highway. This provides a small number of thoroughfares which attract agents. At 5 year decommissioning b) a greater number of persistent haul routes increase the options for travelling further afield, and again hunters are attracted leaving a visible imprint on game populations along these

a) Decommission - 2 years   b) Decommission - 5 years   c) Decommission - 10 years

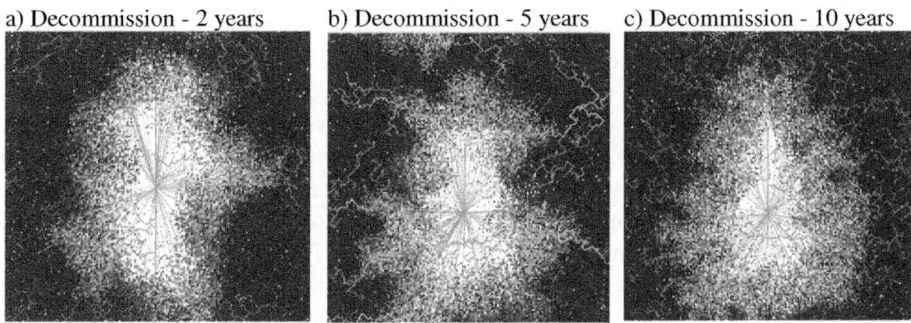

Fig. 5. Spatial pattern of game populations (darker cells contain more game, white cells are local extinctions) resulting from decommissioning roads at 2, 5, and 10 years, with central origin of hunter agents.

routes. Finally in Figure 5 c), when roads are decommissioned at 10 years, the tendril-like road system is more spread out, offering a more homogenous travel cost surface, with the presence of more roads having the effect to spread out hunting pressure across a wider area, and not follow a specific haul route as in the a) and b) example.

Early decommissioning of roads has a concentrating effect, and hunting pressure is focused on the fewer relatively accessible areas. The total number of extirpated cells is higher with earlier decommissioning, which is contrary to the notion that road clo-sures are good for game population numbers. This may be true for any given site, but at a landscape level our simulations describe a case where aggregately the reverse is true. Early decommissioning of roads has the effect of focusing hunting pressure on the fewer more accessible sites, resulting in more extirpations.

Future research will apply the model with spatial data on game populations and human settlement in order to see if trends observed in the simulation are consistent with real-world trends. For statistical robustness multiple runs would need to be con-ducted, and mean values with confidence intervals compared from one scenario to the next. This step is suitable for when further empirical data on a region's history is available, but for now we suffice with presenting the case upon an abstract landscape.

In conclusion, quantifying cumulative effects requires explicit representation of feedbacks and interactions within the linked human and environment system. With a perspective of modelling such phenomena as emergent properties, the goal of the study was to examine spatial configurations and patterns resulting from a) parameter-ising hunter agent utility functions from different stated and revealed preference stud-ies, b) test the effect of road decommissioning at 3, 5, and 10 years.

Noticeably different spatial configurations are created by parameterising the hunter agent utility function from different secondary literature. In some cases the hunter agents apply an even spread of hunting pressure that does not push local game popu-lations to extirpation. In other cases with the same number of agents, the landscape is uniformly extirpated, simply due to a small difference in preferences.

With respect to road decommissioning, modelling revealed a situation where early decommissioning of roads increased the total number of extirpated sites, because hunting pressure was focused onto the relatively fewer accessible cells. However, this finding is dependant on the assumption that moose do not re-populate extirpated sites.

Interesting emergent properties were observed through the modelling process, including a self-emerging persistent spatial pattern of growing and dispersing concen-tric circles, as a 'hunting pulsar', and indeed formed the function of a emergent self-regulating, persistent, and sustainable system, providing the hunter agent popula-tion with a steady stream of utility while not causing local extirpations of game popu-lations. Different forest mosaics were generated by altering a local neighborhood parameter for the construction of road building. It is noted that these interesting find-ings were generated with only five simple equations, 1) cell moose population growth 2) hunter agent utility calculation 3) cell travel cost calculation 4) cell eligibility for forestry harvest 5) aging, resetting the age of roads being used, and decommissioning of unused roads. NetLogo primitives (e.g. *move neighbors*, *distance*) are used as well. The models allows testing different empirical calibrations of agents, as was done here with five preference studies.

Further research steps involve addition of spatial metrics for comparison of simulation results across multiple runs, given the stochasticity of the model. Empirical validation activities for ABM are discussed in [23], and [34], and could include validation against historical moose population and hunting license data. For a very controlled case study, we might infer the preferences of the hunting population based on the pattern of extirpated sites in a real-world landscape. Where multiple parameter settings in the model are able to explain macro-patterns, laboratory experiments, surveys, and / or semi-structures interviews could be used to further refine the combinations which explain the real-world hunting population. Other relevant natural resource management issues which could benefit from these techniques are access created by illegal logging, poaching in parks and reserves, spatial positioning of reserves and wetlands for migrating animals, and interactions between mining and hunting of migratory animals. The study presented here contributes to a) quantification of cumulative effects as emergent properties, b) evaluation of road decommissioning policies and the effect on game populations, and c) techniques to calibrate agent behaviours from secondary empirical studies.

References

1. Adamowicz, W., Boxall, P., Williams, M., Louviere, J., Swait, J.: Perceptions versus objective measures of environmental quality in combined revealed and stated preference models of environmental valuation. J. Environmental Economics and Management 32, 65–84 (1997)
2. An, L., Linderman, M., Qi, J., Shortridge, A., Liu, J.: Exploring complexity in a human-environment system: An agent-based spatial model for multidisciplinary and multiscale integration. Ann. Ass. Amer. Geog. 95, 54–79 (2005)
3. Axelrod, R.: Advancing the Art of Simulation in the Social Sciences. Comp. 3, 193–99 (1997)
4. Bithell, M., Brasington, J.: Coupling agent-based models of subsistence farming with individual-based forest models and dynamic models of water distribution. Env. Mod. & Soft. 24, 173–190 (2009)
5. Bottan, B.: Exploring the Human Dimension of Thunder Bay Moose Hunters with Focus of Choice Behavior and Environmental Preferences. Lakehead Univ., Thunder Bay (1999)
6. Boumans, R., Costanza, R., Farley, J., Wilson, M., Porttela, R., Rotmans, J., Villa, F., Grasso, M.: Modeling the dynamics of the integrated earth system and the value of global ecosystem services using the GUMBO model. Ecological Economics 41, 529–560 (2002)
7. Boxall, P., McFarlane, B., Gartrell, M.: An aggregate travel cost approach to valuing forest recreation at managed sites. The Forestry Chronicle 72, 615–621 (1996)
8. Boxall, P., MacNab, B.: Exploring preference of wildlife recreationists for features of boreal forest management: a choice experiment approach. Can. J. Forest Res. 30, 1931–1941 (2000)
9. Burton, P., Messier, C., Adamowicz, V., Kuuluvainen, T.: Sustainable management of Canada's boreal forests: Progress and prospects. Ecoscience 131(3) (2006)
10. Canadian Environmental Assessment Agency. Reference Guide: Addressing Cumulative Environmental Effects (2004),
    http://www.ceaa.gc.ca/013/0001/0008/guide1_e.htm
11. Council on Environmental Quality CEQ: Considering Cumulative Effects Under the National Environmental Policy Act. Washington, D.C. (1997)

12. Coling, L., Walsh, R.: Influence de la Coupe Forestiere sur la Chasse a l'Original en Abitibi. Ministere des Forets du Quebec, Report (1991)
13. Courtois, R., Beaumont, A.: The influence of accessibility on moose hunting in Northwestern Quebec. Alces. 35, 41–50 (1999)
14. Dosman, D., Haener, M., Adamowicz, W., Marois, J., Boxall, P.: Assessing impacts of environmental change on Aboriginal People: An economic examination of subsistence resource use and value. Department of Rural Economy, University of Alberta (2002)
15. Eason, G., Thomas, E., Jerrard, R., Oswald, K.: Moose hunting closure in a recently logged area. Alces 17, 111–125 (1981)
16. EPBC Environment Protection and Biodiversity Conservation Act, Australia
17. Epstein, J., Axtell, R.: Growing Artificial Societies: Social Science from the Bottom Up. Brookings Institutions Press, Washington; MIT Press, Cambridge (1996)
18. Fleming, W.: Bird responses to pipeline right-of-ways. University of Alberta (2001)
19. Galán, J., López-Paredes, A., del Olmo, R.: An agent-based model for domestic water management in Valladolid metropolitan area. Water Resour. Res. 45 (2009)
20. Girard, F., Joyal, R.: L'impact des coupes a blanc mecanisees sur l'original dans le Nord-Ouest du Quebec. Alces 20, 3–25 (1984)
21. Gunn, J., Sein, R.: Effects of forestry roads on reproductive habitat and exploitation of lake trout (Salvelinus namaycush). Can. J. Fisheries and Aquatic Sciences 57, 97–104 (2000)
22. Haener, M., Dosman, D., Adamowicz, W., Boxall, P.: Can stated preference methods be used to value attributes of subsistence hunting by Aboriginal Peoples? A case study in Northern Saskatchewan. Am. J. Agricultural Economics 83, 1334–1340 (2001)
23. Heckbert, S., Baynes, T., Reeson, A.: Agent-based modeling in ecological economics. Ecological Economics Reviews, NYAS (2010)
24. Heckbert, S.: Experimental economics and agent-based models. In: Proceedings: MODSIM 2009, 18th World IMACS Congress (2009)
25. Heckbert, S., Bishop, I.: Empirical geosimulation: calibration of spatially explicit agent-based models. Advanced Geosimulation Models. Bentham (in Review)
26. Levin, S.: Ecosystems and the Biosphere as Complex Adaptive Systems. Ecosystems 1, 431–436 (1998)
27. Little, R., McDonald, D.: Simulations of agents in social networks harvesting a resource. Ecological Modelling 20, 379–386 (2007)
28. McLeod, K.: Incorporating Perceptions of Site Quality in a Discrete Choice Analysis. Thesis, Dept. of Rural Economy, University of Alberta (1995)
29. McMillan, B.: Effects of hunting closures and timber harvest on local moose densities and hunting opportunities in Northwestern Ontario: a case study. Ontario Ministry of Natural Resources, Technical Report 85 (1995)
30. Morton, K., Adamowicz, W., Boxall, P.: Economic effects of environmental quality change on recreational hunting in northwestern Saskatchewan: A contingent behaviour analysis. Canadian Journal of Forest Research 25, 912–920 (1995)
31. Nitschke, C.: The cumulative effects of resource development on biodiversity and ecological integrity in the Peace-Moberly region of Northeast British Columbia, Canada. Biodiversity Conservation 17, 1715–1740 (2008)
32. Parker, D., Brown, D., Polhill, G., Manson, S., Deadman, P.: Illustrating a new 'conceptual design pattern' for agent-based models and land use via five case studies: The Mr. Potatohead framework. In: Iglesias, C.H. (ed.) Agent-based Modelleling in Natural Resource Management, Universidad de Valladolid (2008)
33. Rempel, R., Elkie, P., Rodgers, A., Gluck, M.: Timber-management and natural disturbance effects on moose habitat: Landscape evaluation. J. Wildlife Manag., 517–524 (1997)

34. Robinson, D., Brown, D., Parker, D., Schreinemachers, P., Janssen, M., Huigen, M., Wittmer, H., Gotts, N., Promburom, P., Irwin, E., Berger, T., Gatzweiler, F., Barnaud, C.: Comparison of empirical methods for building agent-based models in land use science. Journal of Land Use Science 2(1), 31–55 (2007)
35. Schlüter, M., Pahl-Wostl, C.: Mechanisms of resilience in common-pool resource management systems: an agent-based model of water use. Ecol. & Soc. 12(4) (2007)
36. Schneider, R., Stelfox, J., Boutin, S., Wasel, S.: Management of Cumulative Impacts of Land-uses in the Western Canadian Sedimentary Basin: A Modeling Approach. Conservation Ecology 7(1) (2003)
37. Smith, M.: Cumulative Impact Assessment under the National Environmental Policy Act: An Analysis of Recent Case Law. Environmental Practice 8(4), 228–240 (2006)
38. Tombulak, S., Frissel, C.: Review of ecological effects of roads on terrestrial and aquatic communities. Conservation Biology 14, 18–30 (2000)
39. Ward, A., Loomis, J.: The travel cost demand model as environmental policy assessment tool: a Review of Literature. Western Journal of Agricultural Economics (1986)
40. Weber, M., Adamowicz, W.: Tradable land use rights for cumulative environmental effects management. Canadian Public Policy 28, 581–595 (2002)

Micro-scale Simulation of the Macro Urban Form: Opportunities for Exploring Urban Change and Adaptation

Tim Baynes and Scott Heckbert

CSIRO Climate Adaptation Flagship
P.O. Box 310, North Ryde
NSW 1670, Australia
Tim.Baynes@csiro.au

Abstract. Agent based models (ABM) and cellular automata (CA) micro-scale modeling have found abundant application in the area of urban land use and transport planning. These platforms enable a rich spatial representation of residential behavior. We present an urban ABM that deliberately emphasizes a sparse set of rules that influence agents' settlement decisions which interact with detailed spatial data on the geography and climate of a city region. Preliminary results are compared with historical data (1851 to 2001) of the urban growth of the City of Melbourne, the major urbanized area of the State of Victoria, Australia. We discuss potential extensions to the model and its value as an exploratory device for different transport and climate change scenarios.

Keywords: urban growth, agent-based modeling, social laboratory, data driven simulation.

1 Introduction

The urban system can be viewed from the perspective of a complex adaptive system, comprised of many acting and interacting elements with feedbacks in between, which inevitably determine the overall spatial form of the city within its landscape. The urban system contains human processes, such as settlement location decisions of millions of individual residents, and environmental processes such as hydrology and the geological form of the landscape. Understanding urban systems from this perspective requires the ability to explore the frequent non-linear and emergent phenomena that occur in space and time. The use of complex systems science modeling techniques offers a potentially appropriate toolbox, notably agent-based modeling and cellular automata.

To explore the dynamics of urban form, a spatially-explicit ABM was developed and applied to the city of Melbourne, Australia. The purpose of the model is to act as a computational 'social laboratory' in the spirit of pioneers studying urban form [1] who viewed the urban form as a pattern derived from "social ecology". Park [2] discussed the city as "a laboratory or clinic in which human nature and social processes may be conveniently and profitably studied". Our computational social laboratory is a

G. Di Tosto and H. Van Dyke Parunak (Eds.): MABS 2009, LNAI 5683, pp. 14–24, 2010.

simulated spatial landscape in which modeled representations of human behavior can be studied. We use this laboratory to explore how the evolution of urban form changes under different conditions, such as with various decision making algorithms for settlement choices by agents, or measuring a given agent population's response to changing environmental conditions such as a more variable climate under climate change scenarios.

This study aims to develop, or 'grow' the urban form of Melbourne initially with only a few simple functions describing agent behavior. We hypothesize that placing agents with these simple behaviors within a spatially explicit landscape representing the Melbourne geography will be sufficient to re-create the development pattern seen over time. Following simulation, this hypothesis is open to review and further sophistication may well be added to the model to achieve a closer reproduction of residential land use change. However, the intention is to keep the model as simple as possible and to document the outcome of any additional complexity in the model's specifications. The main reason for this dedication to simplicity is twofold: to allow greater tractability in understanding simulation results and to develop the potential for the model to be used in participatory research. We explicitly acknowledge the modeling exercise is actively biased towards the goal of re-creating a historical trend, which raises important validation issues.

2 ABM and CA in Urban Modeling

The history of using CA and ABM in urban systems modeling has shown that the use of spatial relationships through neighborhood interactions drives many dynamics of the urban system. CA of urban form are based on interaction rules that correlate to the micro-dynamics of cities and they can reproduce patterns of the same statistical character and fractal dimension as cities [3]. ABMs of urban form often represent heterogeneous and mobile agents. ABMs may also act in conjunction with CA or a cellular space as in Portugali [4]. Perhaps most distinctively, with agents we can represent qualitative choices and also adaptation: agents can react to and alter their environment in a recursive manner.

One of the first instances of the direct application of CA to represent urban development was Tobler [5] who proposed a cell-space model for Detroit. Later, Couclelis used ideas of local interactions in her study of growth in Los Angeles [6] but it wasn't until the early 1990s that a synergy of readily available computing power and widely communicated concepts of chaos, fractals and complexity produced investigations like those of White and Engelen [7] who used CA to model emergent density patterns and non-linearities based on urban development in Cincinatti, Milwaukee, Houston and Atlanta. Langlois and Phipps [8] also demonstrated emergent segregation of different land use types. CA operate strictly with reference to a neighborhood, and / or action-at-a-distance forces such as the gravitational analogues of social physics and they emphasize spatial change as a complement to the temporal process priorities of systems dynamics.

Most applications to real cities employ a mix of other modeling principles. Batty and Longley [9] incorporated the action-at-a-distance concepts with the micro-dynamics of cell interaction and similar hybridization can be found in models such as UrbanSim [10]. See also Wilson's [11] book on urban and regional spatial modeling.

ABMs and multi agent systems (MAS) have been used for urban research on issues of residential housing markets [12], segregation in residential dynamics [13] and intra-neighborhood behavior [14]. We concur with Batten and Perez [15] who define such systems as comprising of i) a passive environment that bounds agents' behavior and can be modified by agents and by spatial relationships, and ii) a set of autonomous and heterogeneous agents that interact with the environment, objects and other agents through well-defined relationships (e.g. like/dislike).

The model described here is similar in spirit to Clarke and Gaydos [16], where we have loose-coupled the model to GIS data in order to grow the city from its initial settlement. However, we use mobile agents with spatial references rather than CA, which is argued to be appropriate according to principles of object oriented programming of encapsulating causality within well defined classes. Spatial patterns of residential settlement are a function of human decision making upon a passive landscape, rather than a function of the landscape itself. This important separation of human – landscape causality potentially offers opportunities for validation beyond what can be captured in CA which compresses human elements into a landscape statistic. By employing agents with a utility function, our approach has commonalities with Li and Muller [12] though we are (currently) not looking at residential dynamics in such detail and are not starting with an existing city.

3 Melbourne and Its Physical Growth

As the subject of our model, it is worthwhile to give a short history of Melbourne: the major urban centre of the State of Victoria, Australia. The form and function of Melbourne has changed substantially since it was established in 1835 but, as with most cities, Melbourne was sited around fertile lands that provided food, energy and the

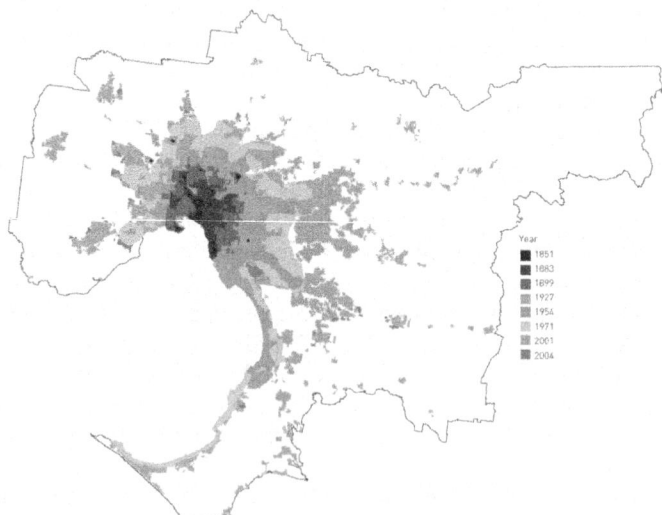

Fig. 1. Historical land development around Melbourne as defined by the boundary of Melbourne Statistical Division (from [17])

basis of a formative economy. Unlike many cities, Melbourne has been well planned as early urban designers established definite regulations on details such as the width of main thoroughfares and plot sizes. Initially, with a small population, this permitted people from a wide range of socio-economic backgrounds to afford high quality low density housing. This egalitarian tradition has produced a broad skirt of low density housing punctuated by several local centers but anchored by transport routes to a central core (see **Fig 1**).

Early metropolitan planning strategies (circa 1950s) allowed for unbounded geographical expansion and between 1971 and 2005 Melbourne's population grew by 44% extending the residential outer fringe, particularly to the west and south east. During this time the areas closest to the CBD experienced some slight depopulation though there has been a recent trend towards rejuvenation [17]. For comparison, in 1954, 70% of Melbournians lived *within* 10km of the city. In 2001, 84% lived further than 10km from the city (measured from the GPO).

4 Model

To explore the dynamics of urban form, a spatially explicit agent-based model was constructed. The model is described here in terms of it's a) human elements of resident agents, and b) spatially explicit landscape of distances, and features such as rivers and rainfall. The model is constructed using Net Logo 4.0.4.

4.1 Residential Agents

Population data for Melbourne from 1851 to 2001 were sourced from the Australian Bureau of Statistics historical censuses [18, 19]. The geographical definition of Melbourne used for the demographic information is consistent with the boundary of Melbourne Statistical Division shown as the outer-most boundary in **Fig 1**. These data were loaded into the model, with 1 agent initiated per 2,500 population increase (set via user interface). Note that each cell is approximately 60 hectares in area and, if filled with 2500 people, we can consider this cell "developed" i.e. with a residential density of about 42 persons per hectare which is at the upper end of the observed density for 70% of the city of Melbourne [17].

4.2 Landscape

The landscape is a spatial grid of 48 000 cells representing a 27 790km^2 rectangle of land that includes Melbourne Statistical Division. A cell is designated the CBD, from which agents are initialized and each cell contains a number of variables, such as rainfall, distances to other spatial elements, whether agents are present at the cell, population density considering agents on neighboring cells, etc…

GIS data layers were obtained for rainfall and rivers. Average rainfall data for all rainfall stations was sourced from the Rainman StreamFlow Version 4.3+ Database [20] and the locations of rivers and water courses were derived from Geoscience Australia's Global Map Australia, River Layer (1:1million scale, 2001). All geographical data used the same GDA94 projection.

An environmental amenity function is created to represent the suite of environmental services (water, productive soil) from which resident agent derive utility.

$$E_j = \alpha^R R_j + \alpha^{DR} DR_j + \alpha^{DW} DC_j .$$ (1)

Where R_j is rainfall [average mm/yr], DR_j is the distance to nearest river [km] and DC_j is the distance to the coastline. The weighting parameters α are set via the model interface, where the environmental amenity function is parameterized by the user. Initial conditions are shown in **Fig 2** for environmental amenity.

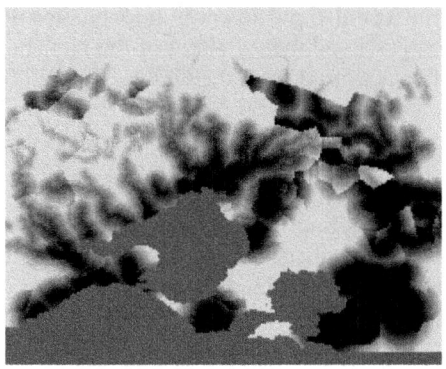

Fig. 2. The environmental amenity landscape based on the proximity to rivers, coastline and areas of higher rainfall, with darker areas providing greater environmental amenities

Agents are initialized in a pre-defined location of the Melbourne CBD, and perform a residential search function based on a weighted utility function, and a set of known grid cell from which to select from. The agents perform the decision once, and thus we are not modeling an iterated re-location decision. When selecting a cell, agents evaluate a limited set of all available cells, the size set by the model user. For known cells, agents evaluate the utility of residing in that cell based on a weighted utility function.

$$U_{ij} = \beta_i^E * E_j + \beta_i^{TC} * TC_j - (PD - S)^2 .$$ (2)

Where TC refers to "travel cost" measured by the distance of the agent from the CBD and PD is the population density measured as the number of agents per cell. β^E β^{TC} and S values are set by the model user interface, and are initialized to the agent population with a random normal distribution based on a standard deviation set by the model user, in order to introduce heterogeneity in preference to agents. Heckbert and Smaigl [21] describe a prior example of applying an agent utility function to residential decision making, as well as rationale for using a utility function, its function form, and derivation of such functions from econometric regressions of surveys and empirical data. A further example of modeling located decision making is outlined in Heckbert et al. [22], which uses a composite of preferences and environmental conditions.

The proposed utility function used in our model of urban form is comprised of 3 sets of terms, relating to utility derived from environmental amenities, the distance required to travel to the CBD, and population density of the cell and its neighboring cells. The environmental amenity and travel cost are linear relationships requiring a simple preference weighting parameter. The population density term is an inverse parabola, meaning that agents do not like too few neighbors, are happier with neighbors around value of S (set by model user), and again do not like overcrowding at densities above S.

5   Preliminary Results

The simulations conducted thus far have focused on establishing the rudimentary attributes of agents, and a loose-coupling with GIS data layers for climate, geography and demography. As such, it is readily conceded that many of the following results could have been achieved with some version of a sorting or allocation algorithm and without the need for agent-based modeling at all. However, as we discuss as the end of this paper, our intention is to add sophistication to our agents' behavior but in such a controlled way as to be able to recognize the effect of each new layer of sophistication. Given this guiding principle for the project in general, it is still instructive to observe the following early results of simulations where the complexity of agents has initially been kept deliberately low.

In sequence we present indicative results from simulations of the spatial growth of residential area using agents that select a cell to live based on: i) travel cost only, ii) tolerances of population density only, iii) population density, travel cost and environmental amenity together.

5.1   Travel Cost Only

Fig 3 displays results of a simulation where there is a physical limit of how many agents can fit on a cell and agents are solely interested in minimizing their travel time to the CBD. Agents simply fill up cells closer to the CBD to the allowed limit and new entrants are forced to locate further out in a roughly radial pattern (the apparent heterogeneity is really is an artifact of each agent having imperfect information about where to settle first).

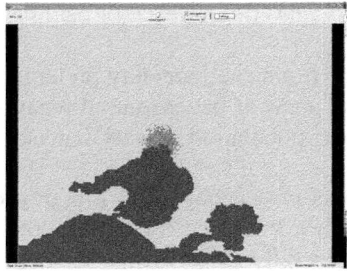

Fig. 3. Distribution of agents based on location choices that minimize travel cost

a) S = 0.5   **b)** S = 1.5

c) S = 4.5   **d)** S = 7.5

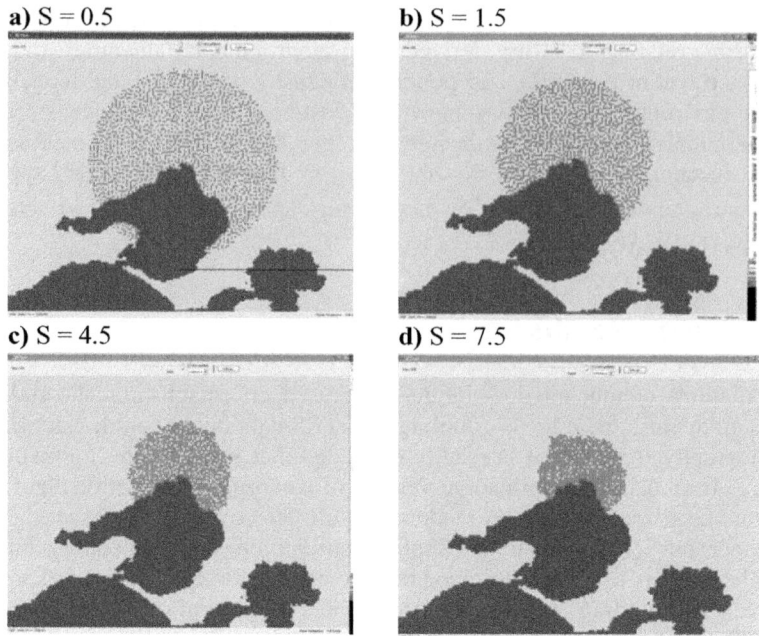

Fig. 4. Settlement of agents assuming a homogenous landscape, no travel penalty and varying tolerances for population density, S (a higher S represents a higher tolerance)

5.2 Population Density Only

When the preference for travel cost minimization is eliminated altogether and a measure of tolerance for population density is introduced (S), we can again see a radial symmetry in the pattern of growth. Increasing the tolerance, S produces simulated distributions of agents that are more compact – see **Fig 4** (a, b, c, d).

5.3 Population Density, Environmental Amenity and Travel Cost

Now we endow the agents with a utility function that includes a tolerance for population density, an awareness of the travel cost to Melbourne's CBD and a preference to locate closer to environmental amenity. Three very different settlement patterns result when we choose a range of values (high -low) for parameters that affect these utilities - refer to **Fig 5** (a, b, c).

In **Fig 5** (a) the higher environmental amenity preference influences agents to stick close to the coast, rivers and areas of better rainfall regardless of distance to the CBD and with a low tolerance for population density, agents are spread widely over the study area.

A simulation of higher travel cost penalty and a high preference for environmental amenity in combination with a tolerance for higher population densities produces a settlement pattern that is generally closer to the CBD though still attracted to river valleys and coasts (see **Fig 5** (b)). **Fig 5** (c) shows a settlement pattern when the

a)

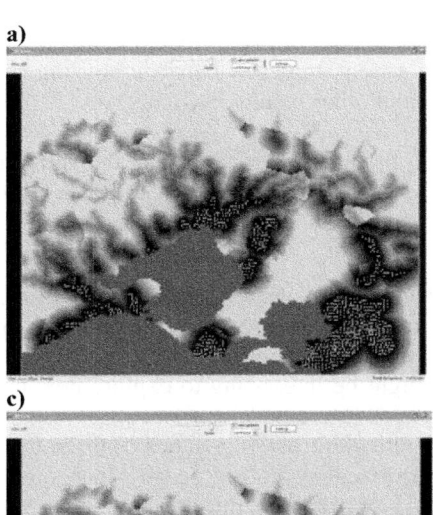

b)

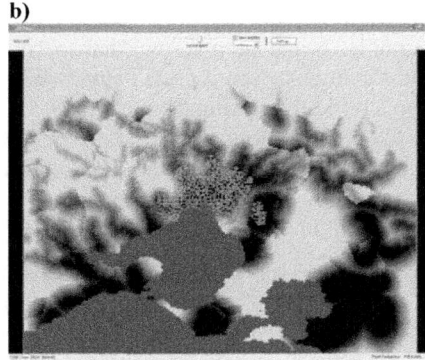

c)

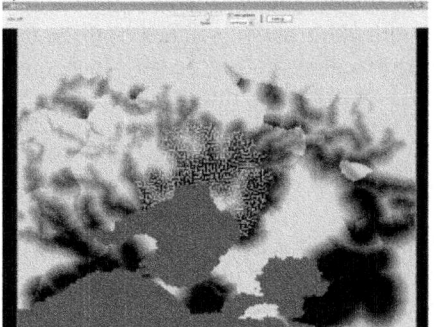

a) High preference for environmental amenity, low S, and no travel costs assumed

b) High travel cost penalty and a high preference for environmental amenity and also a high S.

c) Lower travel cost penalty, lower preference for environmental amenity and a low S value.

Fig. 5. Location of agents after 200 iterations based on a utility function that includes: population density, travel cost and environmental amenity. Background shows the environmental amenity landscape.

landscape of environmental amenity is less relevant, travel costs are low but higher population densities are not tolerated. The result has much in common with that shown in **Fig 4** (b).

6 Discussion

ABM and CA have been used previously to explore scenarios of urban land use change. Often these are simulations concerning an existing city with the intent of exploring possible future scenarios. We have endeavored here to simulate the development of a city from its first settlement to the present day under the boundary conditions of what we know about that city's demographic trajectory and its basic climate and geography. A similar approach has been used to simulate the growth of San Francisco and Washington/Baltimore [16] but here we employ mobile agents and a complicated CA landscape while attempting to keep the sophistication of residential agents to a minimum.

At this stage it would be premature to draws conclusions from the preliminary results but there is some encouragement to be gained from an initial comparison between the simulated form of Melbourne and the actual urban footprint shown in

Fig 1. In the next stage we can be guided by the history of prior modeling efforts. For example, it has been shown that there is only a weak trade-off between housing cost and travel cost (see a useful summary of this and other results by Benenson [13] and also a review by Timmermans [23]).

Many extensions are possible for the model though we re-iterate that the aim is to deliberately restrain the model from having greater sophistication in order to reproduce more detail. What follows are 6 examples of planned or possible modifications each with their attendant research questions:

1. Transport networks could be added and made aware of time-varying agent mobility to represent Melbourne's population before and after the wide uptake of the automobile. This would suggest a comparison with the historical development of road system and it might be interesting to explore how pre-automobile settlement patterns influenced future development.

2. Heterogeneity of residential agents: cities are heterogeneous both in form, with particular suburbs being characterized by higher density than others, and by social-ethnic groups which self-organize into communities with specific and reinforced attributes (for example, family size). This affects geographical distributions of people and land use. Data on traits like age structure of the population, income category or ethnicity can be obtained from census data.

3. Inheritance: agents may be provided with characteristics inherited by their parents (wealth, preferences, density tolerances). It might be presumed that such inheritance would produce convergent heterogeneity in the simulated results but mobility, mixing and the ability of agents to live anywhere in the city could be a counter-acting homogenizing force. By investigating this balance perhaps we may see how a metropolitan character emerges. For example, the real-life preference for Melbournians to live in detached housing has generated a spread out city. Is this effectively the result of inherited preferences?

4. Represent the history of planning for Melbourne: just as we have used the trajectory of population to bound the number of possible agents at any one time, we can use the historical development plans for Melbourne to guide where residential development has or has not been encouraged. For example, where large public spaces or catchment areas have been quarantined from residential development.

5. Co-evolution of agents and the city: each generation of agents could have their parameters updated to have greater tolerance of travel costs or population densities based on macro-properties of the city in their lifetime. This would provide a feedback between the settlement actions of the agents and the urban form that those actions help create.

6. Planners and developers as separate agents in the model enabling a possible future participatory function. Adding new species of agents permits complex interactions and relationships that ABM are uniquely suited to. This may seem contrary to our stated desire for tractability in calculations but the intention would be able to facilitate participatory input from planners, residents and developers.

Subject to these potential refinements, the model could be valuable as an exploratory device for different transport and climate change scenarios. Over the next 30-50 years, significant change is expected in the area around Melbourne both in rainfall, stream flow and sea-level and in the supply of fossil fuel for transport. To be able to represent these effects and simulate the concurrent reaction and adaptation strategies of city residents is a useful exercise in scenario analysis, particularly the outcome of different adaptations simulated in agents.

One criticism of micro-simulation is that it can overlook the broader social and economic causes for change. A counter argument might be that the collective and emergent actions of a city's residents, developers, decision makers and other actors actually *are* some of the broader social and economic causes of change. Neither of these arguments is comprehensive as, for example, imported technological innovations might widely influence mobility in society and the economy but that technology would both alter and depend upon socio-economic networks.

Even proponents of urban CA and ABM have said that they may be more useful as pedagogical devices [24] and that prediction, and therefore validation, are difficult. This has not deterred Clarke and Gaydos [16] who used statistical measures to validate a CA model loose-coupled to GIS data. Beyond the preliminary results stage we anticipate using statistical measures such as the Lee-Sallee shape index used in [16] to validate historical simulations and the model is also useful as a social laboratory. To be useful in this latter respect the model needs to be tractable so that users can learn from experiments. While the model might ultimately be capable of representing rich scenarios, as far as possible, we want to restrict the model from having too much sophistication and be careful to document each new attribute.

7 Conclusions

We are attempting to reproduce the urban form of Melbourne using agents that make settlement choices based on a sparse set of rules loosely coupled with detailed GIS data. Land use patterns are otherwise endogenously generated and preliminary results from the model are presented. The model is able to be extended to include more sophisticated agent attributes, more heterogeneity and evolutionary characteristics but part of this research effort is deliberately minimize the sophistication of the model to permit tractable understanding of the outputs. The model may also facilitate participatory input and has potential for the simulation of urban adaption to anticipated changes in climate and transport fuel supply.

References

1. Park, R.E., Burgess, E.W., McKenzie, R.D.: The City. University of Chicago Press, Chicago (1929) (reprinted 1969)
2. Park, R.E.: The City as a Social Laboratory. In: Smith, T.V., White, L.D. (eds.) Chicago: An Experiment in Social Science Research, pp. 1–19. University of Chicago Press, Chicago (1929)
3. Batty, M.: Cities and Complexity: understanding cities with cellular automata, agent based models, and fractals. MIT Press, London (2005)
4. Portugali, J.: Self-Organisation and the City. Springer, Berlin (1999)
5. Tobler, W.R.: A computer movie simulating population growth in the Detroit region. Economic Geography 42, 234–240 (1970)

6. Couclelis, H.: Macrostructure and microbehaviour in metropolitan area. Environment and Planning B 16, 141–154 (1989)
7. White, R.W., Engelen, G.: Cellular automata and fractal urban form: a cellular automata modelling approach to the evolution of urban land use patterns. Environment and Planning A 25, 1175–1193 (1993)
8. Langlois, A., Phipps, M.: Cellular Automata, Parallelism and Urban Simulation - Final Report on the Activities of the SUAC Project. Department of Geography, University of Ottawa, Ottawa, Canada (1995)
9. Batty, M., Longley, P.A.: Fractal Cities: A Geometry of Form and Function. Academic Press, San Diego (1994)
10. Waddell, P.: UrbanSim: Modelling urban development for land use, transportation and environmental planning. Journal of the American Planning Association 68, 297–314 (2002)
11. Wilson, A.G.: Complex Spatial Systems: The Modelling Foundations of Urban and Regional Analysis. Pearson Education, Harlow (2000)
12. Li, Y., Muller, B.: Residential location and the biophysical environment: exurban development agents in a heterogeneous landscape. Environment and Planning B 34, 279–295 (2007)
13. Benenson, I.: Agent-Based Modeling: From Individual Residential Choice to Urban Residential Dynamics. In: Goodchild, M.F., Janelle, G. (eds.) Spatially Integrated Social Science: Examples in Best Practice, ch. 4, pp. 67–95. Oxford University Press, London (2004)
14. Daniell, K.A., Kingsborough, A.B., Malovka, D.J., Sommerville, H.C., Foley, B.A., Maier, H.R.: Sustainability Assessment of Housing Developments: A New Methodology. In: Batten, D.F., Perez, P. (eds.) Complex Science for a Complex World: Exploring Human Ecosystems with Agents, pp. 113–146. ANU E Press, Canberra (2006)
15. Batten, D.F., Perez, P. (eds.): Complex Science for a Complex World: Exploring Human Ecosystems with Agents. ANU E Press, Canberra (2006)
16. Clarke, K.C., Gaydos, L.J.: Loose-coupling a cellular automaton model and GIS: long-term urban growth prediction for San Francisco and Washington/Baltimore. Geographical Information Science 12, 699–714 (1998)
17. DPCD: Melbourne Atlas 2006, vol. 2009. State Government of Victoria, Department of Planning and Community Development (2007)
18. ABS: Table 1 of Australian Historical Population Statistics, ABS Catalogue Number 3105.0.65.001, vol. 2008. Australian Bureau of Statistics (2003)
19. ABS: Table 18 of Australian Historical Population Statistics, ABS Catalogue Number 3105.0.65.001, vol. 2008. Australian Bureau of Statistics (2003)
20. Clewett, J.F., Clarkson, N.M., George, D.A., Ooi, D.A., Owens, D.T., Partridge, I.J., Simpson, G.B.: Rainman StreamFlow Version 4.3+. State of Queensland Department of Primary Industries (2003)
21. Heckbert, S., Smajgl, A.: Analyzing urban systems using agent-based modelling. In: Zerger, A., Argent, R. (eds.) MODSIM 2005: International Congress on Modelling and Simulation, Melbourne, pp. 134–140 (2005)
22. Heckbert, S., Adamowicz, W., Boxall, P., Hanneman, D.: Cumulative effects and emergent properties of multiple-use natural resources. In: Di Tosto, G., Van Dyke Parunak, H. (eds.) MABS 2009. LNCS (LNAI), vol. 5683, pp. 1–13. Springer, Heidelberg (2010)
23. Timmermans, H.: Modelling Land Use and Transportation Dynamics: Methodological Issues, State of the Art, and Applications in Developing Countries. Discussion Paper Series, vol. 2006-06, vol. 2009. Hiroshima International Center for Environmental Cooperation, HICEC (2006)
24. Couclelis, H.: Where has the future gone? Rethinking the role of integrated land-use models in spatial planning. Environment and Planning A 37, 1353–1371 (2005)

An Agent-Based Framework for Assessing the Cost of Committal Search in Supply Networks

Rodolfo García-Flores*, Rene Weiskircher,
Nectarios Kontoleon, and Simon Dunstall

CSIRO Mathematical and Information Sciences,
Private Bag 33 Clayton South VIC 3168,
Australia
Rodolfo.Garcia-Flores@csiro.au, Nectarios.Kontoleon@dsto.defence.gov.au,
Rene.Weiskircher@csiro.au, Simon.Dunstall@csiro.au
http://www.cmis.csiro.au/asn/

Abstract. The common assumption of unbounded rationality overlooks the facts that decision makers hold beliefs that influence their choices, and that agreement search between agents with conflicting interests is in itself a costly process. As a consequence, the actual cost of negotiation is seldom considered in optimisation literature. The aim of this paper is to contribute to the development of decision methods that distinguish between the costs of intra-agent (deliberative) and inter-agent (committal) searches of information by using a behaviour model produced by optimising agents' profit subject to the Cobb-Douglas production function. We propose and test a computational model of rent-seeking, haggling agents for explicitly assessing the cost of committal search. Simulation experiments show that the strategic value of good initial price estimates is higher when these estimates are very close to the actual equilibrium prices, and that agreements may be reached quicker by more selfish agents.

Keywords: Market simulation, negotiation, intentionality, distributed decision making, optimisation.

1 Introduction

Economists traditionally assume that individuals act with unbounded rationality, a circumstance that does not hold in many real situations. Interest in studying the consequences of this assumption dates back to the work of Simon [1], [2] on the effect of organisations in human rationality. As the effort to improve efficiency shifts from companies to supply networks, there is a renewed concern for understanding the effects of limited rationality in this new context; unbounded rationality may deprive us of valuable insights of the negotiation process.

Two important features overlooked when assuming unbounded rationality are: 1) actual decision makers hold beliefs about their environment, partners and

---

* Corresponding author.

G. Di Tosto and H. Van Dyke Parunak (Eds.): MABS 2009, LNAI 5683, pp. 25–36, 2010.
© Springer-Verlag Berlin Heidelberg 2010

competitors that influence their choices and are constantly updated by new experiences, and 2) information gathering and processing is costly, and these costs should also be considered. The information available from the surroundings may depend on the decision maker's relative position in the system, but this information greatly affects agreement and solution search costs.

To better manage the supply networks of an information economy, it is important to distinguish between the effort that goes into improving the network components' own business decisions, and the investment made to gather market information and influence their partners. Sandholm [3] identifies two separate search processes associated with economic negotiation. Intra-agent *deliberative* search involves an agent locally generating and evaluating alternative strategies, while inter-agent *committal* search is the process by which agents make binding agreements with each other. Because both processes are simultaneous and closely intertwined, the quality and completeness of available information from an agent's surroundings significantly affects the value of locally optimized solutions for a given agent.

The purpose of this paper is to contribute to the development of decision methods that distinguish between the costs of committal and deliberative searches. We present an agent framework that incorporates a general model of behaviour based on a production function. The framework enables modelling of economically-motivated agents that strive to maximise their income by haggling while embedded in a supply network, but their performance is affected by a partial view of the world. We claim that differentiating between deliberative and committal search will eventually enhance the analyses of negotiation processes by associating costs with beliefs and uncertainties. The main features of the system presented are

- The agent model proposed allows inaccurate but perfectible beliefs of the surroundings, in this case, the prices and quantities of the demand and supply required by the agents' neighbours.
- The problem statement does not assume a central optimiser or facilitator, but rather that individual components endeavour to maximise their own profit by haggling using their own model of the world, unknown to other members of the system.
- The approach integrates formal optimisation methods to quantify the cost of beliefs or uncertainties, which makes it better suited to formal analysis than pure computer science-based approaches.

The agents operate by using a model of behaviour produced by optimising their individual profit subject to the Cobb-Douglas (CD) production function, a model that makes the agents "selfish" (or rent-seeking). This function was chosen for its simplicity. We performed an agent-based simulation of a simple supply network where agents are initialised with varying degrees of rent-seeking behaviour. Agents obtain a strategic advantage by initially proposing good initial price estimates, although the estimates of buying and selling prices do not have a big effect on each other. Results also show that the estimates of elasticity have a minor effect on the cost of search. Most importantly, the simulation shows that an agent's intentions may greatly affect the outcomes of its partners.

The remainder of the paper is structured as follows. Section 2 is a non-exhaustive survey of relevant literature about negotiation. Section 3 describes in detail the agents' model of behaviour, which represents the deliberative search. Section 4 demonstrates that the model reflects the behaviour of real markets, while section 5 introduces negotiation and intentionality into the model, which comprise the committal search process. Sections 4 and 5 present representative results. Finally, Section 6 rounds the discussion and raises issues for future research.

2   Related Work

The problem of negotiation is recurrent, and appears in social sciences, management, operations research, game theory and computer science literature. We focus our review on work related to optimisation and computational economics. For instance, [4] investigate the optimisation of flows in a network of arbitrary topology where agents try to maximise their profit by trading commodities, and solution obtained with an integer linear program is compared to an agent-based simulation.

Agent-based computational economics (ACE) is a very relevant research effort [5,6]. In ACE, the approach is bottom-up, with the modeller constructing an economy with an initial population of agents. These agents include both economic agents (for example buyers, sellers, dealers, etc.) and agents representing various other social and environmental phenomena (government, land, weather, etc.). After specifying the initial conditions, the economy evolves over time without further intervention from the modeller. All events that subsequently occur must arise from the historical time-line of agent-agent interactions, with no extraneous coordination devices. ACE-related resources can be found in [7] or [8].

The research aims of [9] and [10] are the closest to our own. In [9], the authors weigh the trade-off between the costs of "exploring" and "exploiting" by analysing a system made up of one producer and a set of consumers. The present work differs from [9] in that there is no central producer gathering information, and merchants explicitly acquire knowledge from the environment through an active negotiation process with their peers. Similarly, [10] state that optimal decision making requires costly cognitive operations which are generally disregarded by economists and game theorists, and propose a framework where these operations are resource-constrained. While [10] deal with uncertainty by using probability theory and the theoretical framework of game theory's multi-armed bandit problem, we use a deterministic setting with emphasis in local optimisation, so we ensure that agents make the best decision to the best of their knowledge.

This brief overview shows that the main contributions of our proposal lie in 1) separating the costs of committal and deliberative search. 2) Proposing a computational framework where the information available to the decision makers is updated as the negotiation progresses, as agents acquire a more accurate view of the surrounding world. 3) Introducing an agent's individual beliefs and intentions as parameters into a model of decision making.

3   An Agent's Model of Behaviour

The following is loosely based on the model presented by [11] and [12]. The CD production function provides the basis for the individual agents' model of behaviour. Production functions are widely used to represent the relationship of a firm's output to inputs, and they can also be applied to utility. The form used in this paper is

$$O = AK^\alpha I^\beta \ , \tag{1}$$

where O is the agent's output, A is a positive constant related to technology, K represents the capital costs, I is the input of raw materials used to produce O, and α and β are positive scale factors. If $\alpha + \beta$ is lower than, equal to, or greater than one, the production function is said to have decreasing, constant or increasing returns to scale, respectively. The rest of the discussion assumes decreasing returns to scale to ensure that the profit optimisation problem yields a maximum.

3.1   Merchants

The total cost incurred by a merchant is

$$C = k + w_k K + pI \ , \tag{2}$$

where k represents the fixed costs, w_k is the rental rate of capital, and p is the buying price of raw materials per unit. If all the agent's income is produced by sales S, we have

$$S = qO \ , \tag{3}$$

where q is the unit selling price of finished product. The total profit P for an individual agent can then be written as

$$P = S - C = qO - k - w_k K - pI \ . \tag{4}$$

Given a required output, we want to minimise the costs incurred subject to the production function (1), that is,

$$\min \quad k + w_k K + pI \ ,$$

subject to

$$O = AK^\alpha I^\beta \ . \tag{5}$$

The solution by Lagrangean multipliers to this problem produces

$$O = A \left(\frac{p\alpha}{\beta w_k} \right)^\alpha I^{\alpha+\beta} \text{ and} \tag{6}$$

$$K = \frac{p\alpha I}{\beta w_k} \ . \tag{7}$$

The second derivative of Equation (6) shows that, for decreasing returns of scale, the solution of the optimisation problem (5) corresponds to a minimum.

Elasticities. The *price elasticity of demand* is defined as the percentage change in demand per a one-percentage point change in price, that is,

$$\varepsilon_p = \left(\frac{\Delta I}{I} \times 100\% \right) \div \left(\frac{\Delta p}{p} \times 100\% \right) = \left| \frac{d \ln I}{d \ln p} \right| = \frac{p}{I} \frac{dI}{dp} \tag{8}$$

Which, according to the model described, is

$$\varepsilon_p = \frac{\alpha - 1}{1 - \alpha - \beta} \tag{9}$$

The value of ε_p is negative because an increase in price is associated with a decrease in quantity bought. Similarly, the *income elasticity of demand*, ε_q is defined as the percentage change in demand per one percent change in income.

$$\varepsilon_q = \frac{q}{I} \frac{dI}{dq} = \frac{1}{1 - \alpha - \beta} , \tag{10}$$

and it is positive since an increase in income should be reflected in an increase in consumption.

Supply and demand curves. To produce believable market behaviour, the problem statement presented above should produce a supply function that increases when selling price increases, and a demand function that decreases when the buying price increases. The steps to produce these functions are as follows:

1. Solve Equation (6) for I and substitute it in (5) together with Equation (6) to obtain an expression of optimal profit as a function of input,

$$P = qO - (\alpha + \beta) \left(\frac{p^\beta w_k^\alpha}{A\alpha^\alpha \beta^\beta} \right)^{\frac{1}{\alpha + \beta}} O^{\frac{1}{\alpha + \beta}} - k . \tag{11}$$

2. Take dP/dO and equate it to a parameter $\rho > 0$. Because the agents have a limited budget, the profit of the agent is maximised by minimising ρ.
3. By solving the expression described in the previous step, the demand curve is obtained:

$$O(q) = (q - \rho)^{\frac{\alpha + \beta}{1 - \alpha - \beta}} \left(\frac{A\alpha^\alpha \beta^\beta}{p_t^\beta w_k^\alpha} \right)^{\frac{1}{1 - \alpha - \beta}}$$

$$= (q - \rho)^{\varepsilon_q} \left(\frac{A\alpha^\alpha \beta^\beta}{w_k^\alpha} \right)^{\varepsilon_q} p_t^{\varepsilon_p} \tag{12}$$

4. The supply curve is derived in a similar manner:

$$I(p) = \beta(q_t - \rho)^{\frac{1}{1 - \alpha - \beta}} \left(\frac{A\alpha^\alpha \beta^\beta}{w_k^\alpha} \right)^{\frac{1}{1 - \alpha - \beta}} p^{\frac{\alpha - 1}{1 - \alpha - \beta}}$$

$$= \beta(q_t - \rho)^{\varepsilon_q - 1} \left(\frac{A\alpha^\alpha \beta^\beta}{w_k^\alpha} \right)^{\varepsilon_q} p^{1 + \varepsilon_p} . \tag{13}$$

3.2   Sources and Sinks

Sources and sinks (represented by s and t, respectively) are functions that represent external supply and demand respectively, and which are a simplified version of the CD function. These are stated in Equation (14) for sources and in Equation (15) for sinks,

$$I = aq^b \tag{14}$$

and

$$O = cp^d \ , \tag{15}$$

where I represents the input of some product, O represents the output of some product, p is the selling price, q is the buying price and a, b, c and d are positive scale factors. These equations can be interpreted as stating that external product input and output are a function of their buying and selling prices respectively.

3.3   Sensors

Sensors are conceived as passive entities whose only purpose is to serve as an analytical aide. Essentially, sensor r_{ij} will listen to agent i's proposal to j and vice versa, and hold relevant information about the negotiation process. Sensors are capable of tracking the evolution of the negotiation respect to the final outcome.

4   Market Simulation

A simplified, deterministic supply network with three echelons of three agents each was set up to test the model's behaviour, analogously to that presented in [11]. Turn-based was preferred to event-driven simulation to ensure all agents played the same number of turns; the parameters used are shown in Table 1. The simulation ran for 25 time steps to observe the market's behaviour using INRIA's Scilab 4.1.1. The model captures the differences in productivity reflected in the α and β parameters, as shown in Figure 1. First, it must be observed that the market simulations eventually converge to equilibrium, which is the Pareto optimal value. Second, differences in performance for the same agent working under different scale factors are evident. Third, the changes in the scale factors affect the elasticities, which define how the agents react to prices in supply and demand and produces oscillations. As β increases, the elasticities increase and the agent's reaction to changes in prices proposed by other echelons is more pronounced. Similar changes in response when varying technology parameters and fixed costs can also be noticed.

Table 1. Sample parameter values

Parameter	A	α	β	k	w_k
Value	3.6958	0.417	0.186	200	13

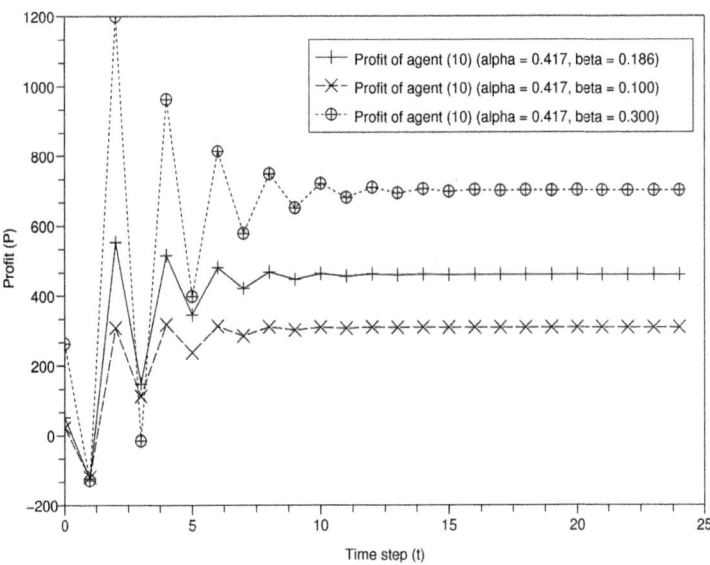

Fig. 1. Effect of productivity over an agent's profit

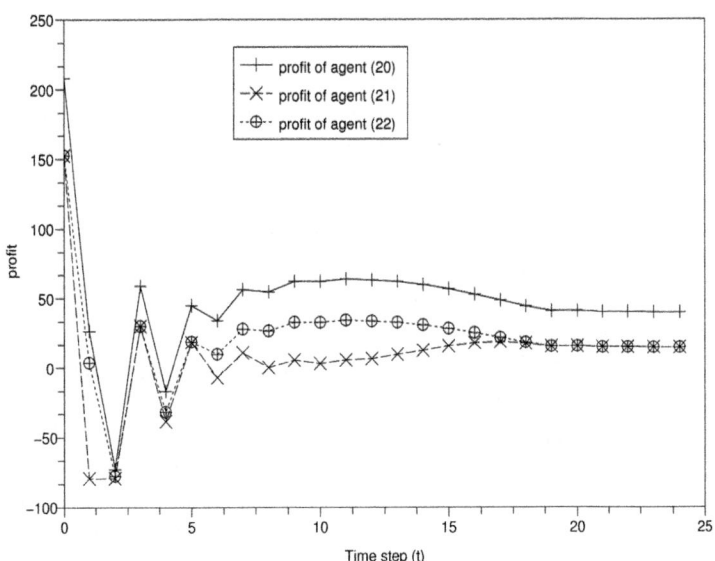

Fig. 2. Effect of limited budget over an agent's profit

Figure 2 shows the evolution of a market where the first agent of echelon 2 starts with a limited budget and eventually catches up. This agent is unable to afford the purchase of all the necessary input to satisfy the required demand, so the other two agents in the echelon increase their profit at the expense of the agent whose budget is limited. In this particular experiment, agent $(2, 0)$ starts with an advantage. Eventually, the disadvantaged agent $(2, 1)$ catches up with agent $(2, 2)$, although agent $(2, 0)$ maintains its initial advantage.

5   The Cost of Search for Agreements

Having checked that the model produces the expected behaviour, we proceed assessing the costs of negotiation. The purpose of negotiation between n_1 and n_2 is to define a *contract*, which is defined by the pair (*unit price at which the goods will be traded, quantity of traded goods*). These variables represent, for agent n_1, input and buying price (p_1, I_1), whereas for n_2 these are the output and selling price (q_2, O_2). For a given contract, the agents will try to achieve the optimal profit by using the model described above. Because the agents optimise with the (probably inaccurate) information available, proposing a tentative deal on one end will constrain the price and quantity proposed on the other end of the agent. The experimental network is shown in Figure 4. The market algorithm proceeds as follows:

1. Define a set P of proposing agents and a set CP of counter-proposing agents, $CP = P'$ (the complement of P). For the experiments, $P = \{s, n_2, n_3, t\}$, where s is the source, t is the sink and n_j are merchant nodes.
2. If this is the first proposal conveyed (i.e., haggle $= 0$), the set of acting agents V is equal to P; else V becomes V'.
3. Agents in the set V optimise and send proposals of the form (*unit price, quantity*) to suppliers and customers.
4. Suppliers and customers of the set of acting agents, all of which belong to V', update their internal variables.
5. Sensors store proposals of V and calculate disagreement. Use this information to update the efficient frontier.
6. Go back to 2 (i.e., start next haggle) until all disagreements are lower than a given threshold.

A haggle in this algorithm is represented as the execution of steps 2 to 6 by subset P or CP. The strategy used by the agents to propose in step 3 assumes that the received contract proposal lies in the proposer's supply (or demand) curve, so the receiver can "re-build" this curve and use it, in combination with the receiver's own updated demand (or supply) curve, to determine a new proposal. Partial knowledge of the environment is reflected in the elasticity parameter used to re-build the opponent's model of behaviour.

Intentionality has been incorporated into the model by introducing parameters Δp and Δq that displace the supply and demand curves, as shown in Figure 3. These parameters represent the unwillingness of the agent to pay more for the same amount of raw materials (if dealing with suppliers), or to sell out more raw material for a lower price (if dealing with customers).

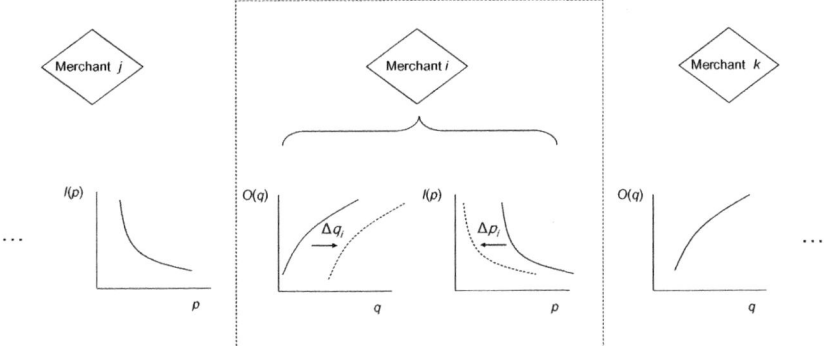

Fig. 3. Displacement of supply and demand curves in a greedy agent

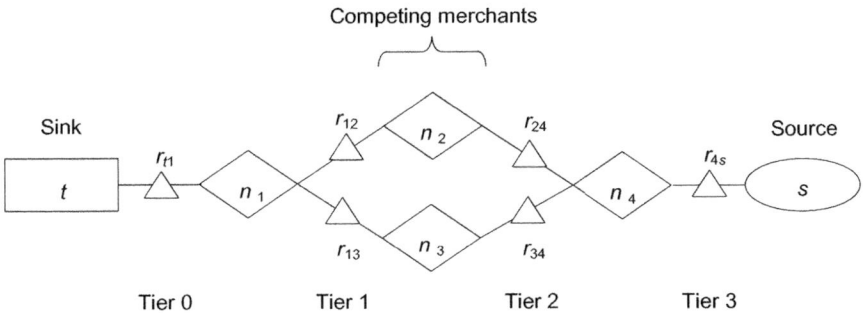

Fig. 4. Arrangement for testing the negotiation scheme

Simulation setup. Suppose that there are two agents in parallel, competing to fulfill the orders of the agents directly in contact with source and sink (Figure 4). In the first turn, agents n_2, n_3, source and sink send their proposals simultaneously, and in the second turn agents n_1 and n_4 reply with their counter-proposals. The process is repeated until one of the competing agents reaches an agreement with n_1 and n_4. For this setting, it will be assumed that n_2 and n_3 are under pressure to reach an agreement in a small number of haggles. It may be argued that n_1 and n_4 could afford to wait for both negotiation processes to finish before deciding which deal to choose on the basis of price. However, bounded rationality is assumed and we will consider that n_1 and n_4 prefer a quick deal to a good price, and the winner is the agent that completes the negotiation first. The parameter values for all nodes in this scenario are the same as for n_2 in Table 1 on page 30. It was assumed that n_1, n_2 and n_4 in Figure 4 started the negotiation rounds with (*price, quantity*) proposals that corresponded to the actual optimal solution, whereas n_3 had to explore the contract search space. In this way, a comparison between a disadvantaged agent (n_3) and one with perfect knowledge (n_2) can be made. The optimal solution can easily be found analytically, but it is not presented here because of limits on space.

Results. Costs in terms of number of iterations and profits were obtained. Each iteration represents a haggle between agents. The number of iterations required to reach an optimal solution does not decrease even if an agent's initial proposal is very close to the actual equilibrium price. Hence, the number of haggles required to reach the optimum is not very sensitive to the agents' initial estimate of price. To illustrate, it was found that an agreement could be reached in 18 iterations when the initial proposed price was \$0.50 from the optimum solution, compared to 27 when the initial proposal was \$5.00 away from the equilibrium price. It was also found that number of haggles does depend of initial estimates of buying or selling prices, but not on their combinations.

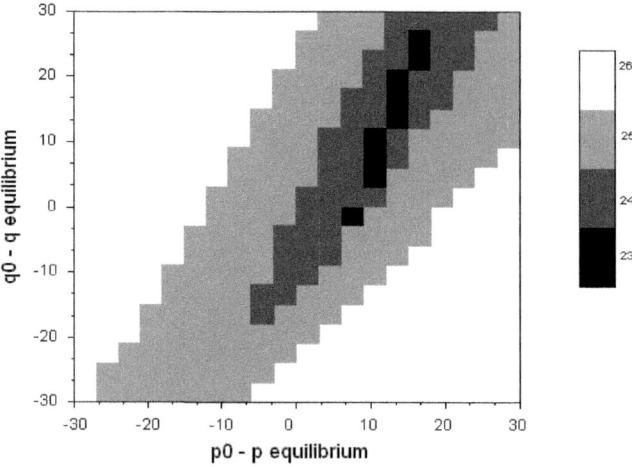

Fig. 5. Cost of intentionality on suppliers ($\Delta p_3 = 15$) in terms of number of iterations

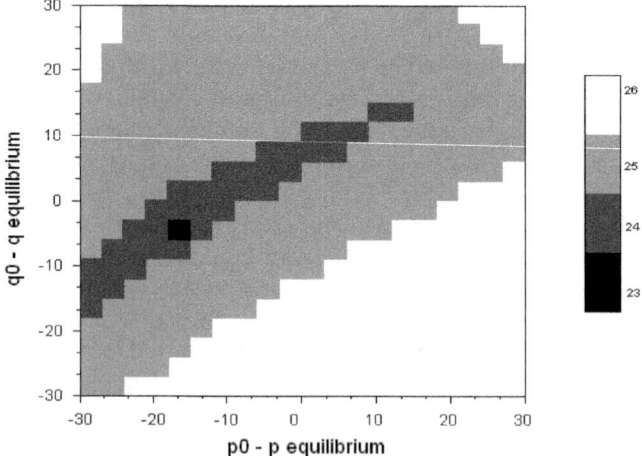

Fig. 6. Cost of intentionality on customers ($\Delta q_3 = 15$) in terms of number of iterations

Agents' intentions are accounted for by parameters Δp_i and Δq_i, which determine the intentions of i to its suppliers and customers, respectively. The effect of these parameters is shown in Figures 5 and 6. Runs were made varying the difference in initial price guess from the equilibrium price from $-30 to $+30 in intervals of three dollars.

Figure 5 shows that, for an agent willing to cheat its suppliers, the time needed to finish the negotiation decreases by providing an inflated estimate of price; this is represented by the darker areas in the first quadrant. Because the difference is higher for q than for p in the black area, this is the case particularly when proposing to customers. This means that negotiation that starts with an over-estimate of the selling price does terminate in less haggles than a negotiation that starts with a proposal with the same over-estimate of buying price. In contrast, Figure 6 indicates that an agent that deceives its customers finishes the negotiation earlier by underestimating prices. Because the difference for p is higher than for q at the black spot, this happens especially when proposing to suppliers.

Other results from this particular simulation setting show that the costs added by intentionality is transferred to the side of the supplier, no matter if the greedy agent is really concerned with abusing its suppliers or its customers. This is a feature of real supply chains, where the retailers can force the chain components upstream to provide products at lower prices at their own expense.

6   Conclusions and Directions for Research

We have presented a framework that incorporates a general model of behaviour of rent-seeking, negotiating agents. Agents' behaviour is based on the optimisation of individual profits subject to a production function. Within this framework, it is possible to compare the performance of an agent that starts the negotiation proposing the best possible contract vs an agent who starts haggling with partial information. Since each agent optimises its profit locally, the difference in performance can be interpreted as the cost of committal information gathering. Thus, costs of committal and deliberative searches can be distinguished.

The results presented are concerned mainly with the implications of computational limitations of agents with partial information, an aspect that has not been explored sufficiently. Experimental results show that the strategic value of good initial price estimates is higher when these estimates are very close to the actual equilibrium prices, and that the estimates of buying and selling prices do not have a big effect on each other. Most importantly, the simulation shows that an agent's intentions may affect the outcome. This result will be important when extending the model to more complex networks.

So far, the work has focused on testing the agents' capability to capture real market behaviour and testing basic ways to measure the cost of committal search. However, the computational framework presented in this paper can be extended to consider issues like learning algorithms, strategy, behaviour in more complex networks and uncertainty propagation down the network.

References

1. Simon, H.: A behavioral model of rational choice. Quarterly Journal of Economics 69, 99–118 (1955)
2. Simon, H.: Rational choice and the structure of the environment. Psychological Review 63, 129–138 (1956)
3. Sandholm, T.W.: Distributed Rational Decision Making. In: Multiagent Systems: A Modern Approach to Distributed Artificial Intelligence, pp. 201–258. MIT Press, Cambridge (1999)
4. Weiskircher, R., Kontoleon, N., Garcia-Flores, R., Dunstall, S.: Using agents for solving a multi-commodity-flow problem. European Journal of Operational Research 194(3), 888–900 (2009)
5. Tesfatsion, L.: Agent-based computational economics: Growing economies from the bottom up. Artificial Life 8, 55–82 (2002)
6. Tesfatsion, L.: Economic agents and markets as emergent phenomena. Proceedings of the National Academy of Sciences of the United States of America 99, 7191–7192 (2002)
7. McBride, M.: Computational labs, department of economics university of miami (2007), http://mcbridme.sba.muohio.edu/ace/labs/
8. Tesfatsion, L.: Agent-based computational economics webpage, iowa state university (2007), http://mcbridme.sba.muohio.edu/ace/labs/
9. Brooks, C., Gazzale, R., Das, R., Kephart, J., Mackie-Mason, J., Durfee, E.: Model selection in an information economy: Choosing what to learn. Computational Intelligence 8, 566–582 (2002)
10. Gabaix, X., Laibson, D., Moloche, G., Weinberg, S.: Costly information acquisition: Experimental analysis of a boundedly rational model. The American Economic Review 96, 1043–1068 (2006)
11. Kaihara, T.: Supply chain management with market economics. International Journal of Production Economics 73, 5–14 (2001)
12. Kaihara, T.: Multi-agent based supply chain modelling with dynamic environment. International Journal of Production Economics 85, 263–269 (2003)

Does Cognitive Capacity Matter When Learning Using Genetic Programming in Double Auction Markets?

Shu-Heng Chen[1], Chung-Ching Tai[2], and Shu G. Wang[1]

[1] AI-ECON Research Center, Department of Economics, National Chengchi
University, Taiwan
chchen@nccu.edu.tw, nccut104@nccu.edu.tw
[2] Department of Economics, Tunghai University, Taiwan
chungching.tai@thu.edu.tw

Abstract. The relationship between human subjects' cognitive capacity and their economic performances has been noticed in recent years due to the evidence found in a series of cognitive economic experiments. However, there are few agent-based models aiming to characterize such relationship. This paper attempts to bridge this gap and serve as an agent-based model with a focus on agents' cognitive capacity. To capture the heterogeneity of human cognitive capacity, this paper employs genetic programming as the algorithm of the learning agents, and then uses population size as a proxy parameter of individual cognitive capacity. By modeling agents in this way, we demonstrate a nearly positive relationship between cognitive abilities and economic performance.

1 Introduction

Information and cognitive capacity are the two sources of bounded rationality of human decision makers. While economists, either theorists or experimentalists, have mainly emphasized the importance of information, the significance of cognitive capacity has been lost but started to regain its position in economic experiments in recent years. We term experimental studies which discuss the implications of the heterogeneous cognitive capacity of human decision makers as *cognitive economic experiments* to highlight their emphasis on *human decision makers'* cognitive capability.

Some of the earliest experimental ideas concerning cognitive capacity came from Herbert Simon, who was the initiator of bounded rationality and was awarded the Nobel Memorial Prize in Economics. In problems such as the "concept formation" experiment and the arithmetic problem, Simon pointed out that the problem was strenuous or even difficult to solve, not because human subjects did not know how to solve the problem, but mainly because such tasks could easily overload human subjects' "working memory capacity" and influence their performance when decision supports such as paper and pencil were lacking [1].

More concrete evidence comes from the economic laboratories. Devetag and Warglien (2003) found a significant and positive correlation between subjects'

G. Di Tosto and H. Van Dyke Parunak (Eds.): MABS 2009, LNAI 5683, pp. 37–48, 2010.

short-term memory scores and conformity to standard game-theoretic prescriptions in the games [2]. Devetag and Warglien (2008) pointed out that subjects construct representations of games of different relational complexity and will play the games according to these representations. It is shown that both the differences in the ability to correctly represent the games and the heterogeneity of the depth of iterated thinking in games appear to be correlated with short term-memory capacity [3]. These cognitive economic experiments, together with other emerging ones such as Segal and Hershberger (1999), Casari, Ham, and Kagel (2007), and Jones (2008), demonstrate the economic significance of human decision makers' cognitive capacity at both the individual level and the aggregate level [4][5][6].

While more and more evidence is discovered by experimental economists in various game and market settings, most agent-based economic models, as a complementary research tool to human experiments, do not take cognitive capacity and its heterogeneity into account in a corresponding way[1]. This creates a discrepancy between human experiments and agent simulations in economic research, whereas there is a tendency to integrate these two fields to advance our understanding of economic systems.

This paper aims to make an effort to eliminate this gap. To achieve this goal, an operable method to characterize the cognitive capacity of autonomous agents should be proposed. In this paper, Genetic Programming (GP) is employed as the agents' learning algorithms in double auction markets. GP is employed to model agents because it can develop efficient strategies autonomously based on relatively little background knowledge. Furthermore, the parameter of population size will be regarded as the proxy variable for traders' cognitive ability. In so doing, we have a chance to advance our understanding of the hypothetical link between cognitive capacity and economic performance, similar to Simon's ideas of "Studying human intelligence by creating artificial intelligence." [1]. A series of simulations will be reported, and the results will be compared with what we have known about cognitive capacity from psychological studies.

The remainder of this paper is organized as follows: Research questions will be elaborated in Section 2. Section 3 depicts the experimental design, including the market mechanism, trading strategies, and experiment settings. The results, evaluations, and analysis of the experiments are presented in Section 4. Section 5 provides the conclusion.

---

[1] There are indeed agent-based systems where agents are endowed with different degrees of "cognitive capacity". For example, Takashina and Watanabe (1996) model the entropy of the sensor output of agents in a quasi-ecosystem [7], and Savit, Manuca, and Riolo (1999) model the length of memory of decision makers in a minority game [8]. However, a real challenge is how to characterize the cognitive capacity of autonomous agents, whose strategies can change and adapt to the environment. As far as we know, [9] is the only study that explicitly models the cognitive capacity of autonomous agents in economic models.

2   Cognitive Capacity, Learning, and Economic Performance in Double Auction Markets

In this paper, we choose the double auction (DA) market as the environment in which to study cognitively heterogeneous agents. An important reason why the DA market is chosen is that the DA market has been intensively studied both in experimental economics and in agent-based computational economics. Therefore, the DA market can serve as a good starting point to narrow the gap between these two fields.

The double auction market experiment is probably the oldest and the most intensively conducted experiment in experimental economics. However, most conventional studies are concerned with only the aggregate outcomes. Rust, Miller, and Palmer (1993, 1994) are the only few exceptions, and study the DA market from the individual perspective [10] [11].

Rust, Miller, and Palmer (1993, 1994) conducted double auction tournaments with software trading strategies in the Sante Fe Institute. They raised 30 trading algorithms and categorized them according to whether they were simple or complex, adaptive or nonadaptive, predictive or nonpredictive, stochastic or nonstochastic, and optimizing or nonoptimizing. The result is rather surprising: the winning strategy is simple, nonstochastic, nonpredictive, nonoptimizing, and most importantly nonadaptive. In spite of this, other strategies possessing the same characteristics may have performed poorly. Based on their findings, does it really mean that decisions in double auction markets do not require much cognitive capacity? To answer this question, we can test the relationship between agents' cognitive capacities and their performances.

Cognitive capacity is a general concept used in psychology to describe human's cognitive flexibility, verbal learning capacity, learning strategies, intellectual ability, etc [12]. Although cognitive capacity is a very general concept and can be measured from different aspects with different tests, concrete concepts such as intelligence quotient(IQ) and working memory capacity are considered highly representative of this notion.

Two additional questions are also worthy of investigation. First, in a series of human-agent competition studies, researchers found that human subjects did learn, but most people were defeated by software trading programs, and only few of them performed comparably to software agents [13] [14] [15]. This leaves us a question: How much cognitive capacity should a learning agent have to defeat other well-designed software trading strategies?

Second, as the psychological literature points out, high intelligence does not always contribute to high performance–the significance of intelligence in performance is more salient when the problems are more complex. In addition, it appears that intelligence exhibits a decreasing marginal contribution in terms of performances[2]. Can our model generate phenomena consistent with these observations?

---

[2] [16] demonstrates that the correlation between intelligence and performance increases when the tasks are made more complex. As to the decreasing marginal value of intelligence, please see [17] and [18].

Finally, an important issue here concerns which aspect of cognitive capacity to consider while cognitive capacity can be expressed or measured in different ways. Although *intelligence quotient* may be an intuitive candidate, it is not easy to model since intelligence is multi-dimensional and is used to describe many related abilities. In this regard, we model agents' cognitive capacity via the concept of *working memory capacity*. Working memory is the mental resources used in our decision-making processes and is highly related to *general intelligence* [19]. In this paper, GP agents' cognitive capacity is measured in terms of the number of strategies in their population–a counterpart of the working memory capacity of human traders[3].

In the next section, we will introduce an agent-based double auction market where GP's population size is treated as the proxy variable for cognitive capacity (working memory). By doing so, we can try to answer the questions mentioned above.

3   Experimental Design

Experiments in this paper were conducted on the AIE-DA (Artificial Intelligence in Economics - Double Auction) platform which is an agent-based discrete double auction simulator with built-in software agents.

3.1   Market Mechanism

AIE-DA is inspired by the Santa Fe double auction tournament held in 1990, and in this study we have adopted the same token generation process as in Rust et al.'s design [11]. Our experimental markets consist of four buyers and four sellers. Each of the traders can be assigned a specific strategy–either a designed trading strategy or a GP agent.

During the transactions, traders' identities are fixed so that they cannot switch between buyers and sellers. Each trader has four units of commodities to buy or to sell, and can submit only once for one unit of commodity at each step in a trading day. Every simulation lasts 7,000 trading days, and each trading day consists of 25 trading steps. AIE-DA is a discrete double auction market and adopts AURORA trading rules such that at most one pair of traders is allowed to make a transaction at each trading step. The transaction price is set to be the average of the winning buyer's bid and the winning seller's ask.

At the beginning of each simulation, each trader will be randomly assigned a trading strategy or as a GP agent. Traders' tokens (reservation prices) are also randomly generated with random seed 6453. Therefore, each simulation starts with a new combination of traders and a new demand and supply schedule[4].

---

[3] Such kind of analogy has been applied to autonomous agents modeled by Genetic Algorithms, see [9] for a concrete example.

[4] Considering the vast number of combinations and permutations of traders, we did not try out all possible trader combinations. Instead, 300 random match-ups were created for each series of experiment.

3.2 Trading Strategies

In order to test the capability of GP agents, we developed several trading strategies from the double auction literature as GP agents' competitors. They are: **Kaplan, Ringuette**, and **Skeleton** modified from Rust et al.'s tournament [11]; **ZIC** from Gode and Sunder [20]; **ZIP** from Cliff and Bruten [21]; **Markup** from Zhan and Friedman [22]; **Gjerstad-Dickhaut (GD)** from Gjerstad and Dickhaut [23]; **BGAN** from Friedman [24]; **Easley-Ledyard (EL)** from Easley and Ledyard [25]; and the **Empirical** strategy which was inspired by Chan et al. [26], and works in the same way as Friedman's BGAN but develops its belief by constructing histograms from opponents' past shouted prices[5].

Although most of the strategies were created for the purpose of studying price formation processes, we still sent them to the "battlefield" because they can represent, to a certain degree, various types of trading strategies which can be observed in financial market studies.

3.3 GP Agents

In this paper, GP is employed as the learning algorithm of the autonomous agents, whose goal is to maximize their profits for each trading day. Each GP trader is endowed with a very fundamental terminal set, which consists of the average, maximum, and minimum prices/bids/asks as well as some public information concerning the time. The function set used to develop strategies is also quite simple, which means that GP traders have to build up their strategies from scratch[6].

Each GP trader has a number of strategies in his/her mind. In this paper, we regard the population size of each GP trader's strategies as the proxy parameter of his/her cognitive capacity. The reason why population size can be a proper parameter of cognitive capacity is straightforward: since we tackle the issue of cognitive capacity via the concept of working memory, the largest number of *chunks* stored in each agent's mind becomes a natural measurement of the agent's cognitive capacity. A chunk is a unit of information, which may be as simple as a digit or as complex as a formal concept stored in a human's short-term memory [27]. Similarly, the strategies of a GP agent can be represented by parse trees which may comprise a single terminal element or a tree with many levels. As a result, we can analogize a strategy tree of a GP agent as a chunk stored in a human's short-term memory[7].

---

[5] Named by or after their original designers, these strategies were modified to accommodate our discrete double auction mechanism in various ways. They were modified according to their original design concepts as well as we possibly could. As a result, they might not be 100% the same as they originally were.

[6] The elements of the function set are plus, minus, multiplication, division, abs, log, exp, sin, cos, max, min, if-then-else, if-bigger-than-else, and bigger.

[7] To put it in another way, working memory capacity matters to human decision makers because they will operate different numbers of chunks in their minds–even if they have the same source of information and knowledge. Similarly, every GP trader has the same terminal and function set, but what really matters is how many operable concepts each agent develops out of these primitives.

GP agents in this study adopt only standard crossover and mutation operations, by which is meant that no election [28], automatically defined functions
(ADFs) or other mechanisms are implemented. At the beginning of every trading
day, each GP trader randomly picks a strategy from his/her population of strategies and uses it throughout the day. The performance of each selected strategy
is recorded, and if a specific strategy is selected more than once, a weighted
average will be taken to emphasize later experiences.

GP traders' strategies are updated–with selection, crossover, and mutation–
every N days, where N is called the "select number." To avoid the flaw that
a strategy is deserted simply because it was not selected, we set N as twice
the size of the population so that theoretically each strategy has the chance of
being selected twice. Tournament selection is implemented and the size of the
tournament is 5, however big the size of the population is. We also preserve the
elite for the next generation, and the size of the elite is 1. The mutation rate is
5%, in which 90% of this operation is tree mutation.

In order to examine the validity of using population sizes as GP traders'
cognitive capacity, a series of experiments were conducted, in which GP traders'
population sizes were set at 5, 20, 30, 40, 50, 60, 70, 80, 90, and 100, respectively.
Such   a   sampling   enables   us   to   scrutinize   the   issues   posted   in
Section 2.

4   Results and Discussion

In this section, we evaluate the traders' performances with an efficiency point of
view. Profitability is measured in terms of *individual efficiencies*[8].

4.1   Learning Capabilities of GP Agents

In investigating the GP traders' learning capability, we simply compare GP
agents with designed strategies collected from the literature. We are interested
in the following questions: (1) Can GP traders defeat other strategies? (2) How
many resources are required for GP traders to defeat other strategies?

GP traders with population sizes of 5, 50, and 100 are sampled to answer
these questions[9]. Figure 1 is the result of this experiment. Here we represent GP
traders of population sizes 5, 50, and 100 with P5, P50, and P100 respectively.

---

[8] In order to compare the performance across simulations, we adopted the notion of
individual efficiency. Individual efficiency is calculated as the ratio of one's actual
profits to one's theoretical surplus. For example, if a buyer has only one token whose
value is 10, and the theoretical equilibrium price is 6 (acquired in the intersection of
the demand and supply curves), then its theoretical surplus will be 4. If this trader
makes a transaction and actually earns 3, the individual efficiency of this trader will
be $3/4 = 75\%$.

[9] The corresponding N (select number) were set at 10, 100, and 200, respectively.
Briefly put, N is the evaluation cycle for each GP generation.

Profits earned by these traders (both GP agents and designed strategies) are computed as the mean of the average profits in a specific generation across different simulations[10]. We have the following observations from Figure 1:

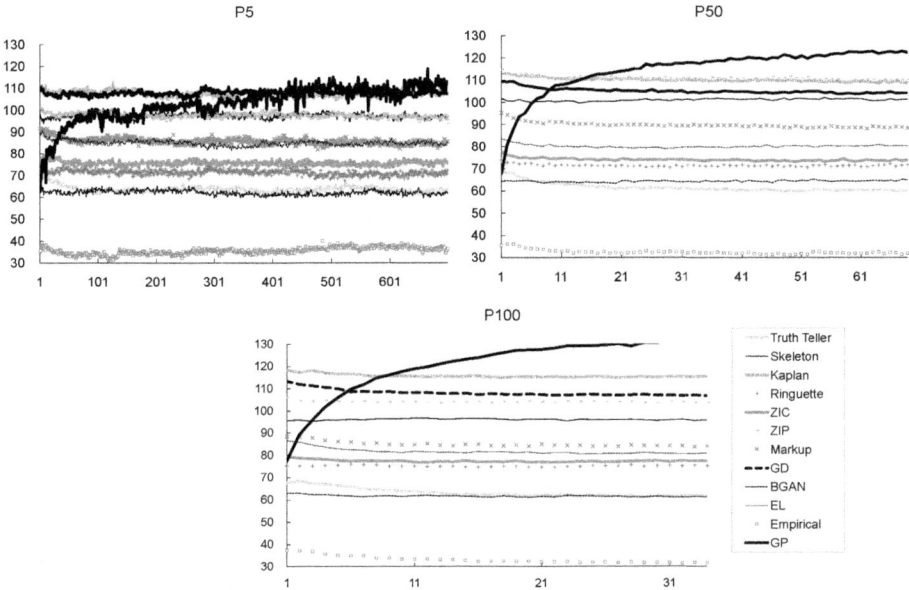

Fig. 1. Comparison of GP Traders with Designed Strategies. The horizontal axis denotes the generation, and the vertical axis denotes their performance in terms of individual efficiency (in percentages).

First, no matter how big the population is, GP traders can gradually improve and defeat other strategies. Second, GP traders can still improve themselves even under the extreme condition of a population of only 5^{11}. In the case of P5, the average complexity almost equals 1 at the end of the experiments, meaning that GP traders could still gain superior advantages by constantly updating their strategy pools composed of very simple heuristics[12]. In contrast with P5, in the case of a bigger population, GP develops more complex strategies as time goes

---

[10] For example, "P100's profit in generation 10 is 106.56" indicates that the mean of the average profits in generation 10 across the 198 simulations where P100 traders took part equals 106.56. Here the average profit in generation 10 of a specific simulation is the mean of individual efficiencies achieved by a P100 GP trader during the 200 trading days in the 10th generation.

[11] The fact that the tournament size is also 5 means that strategies in the population might converge very quickly.

[12] In this paper, we measure GP agents' strategy complexity in terms of node complexity–the average number of terminal and function nodes of GP trees.

by. But even so, the average complexity of P100 is only around four[13]. Finally, what is worth noticing is that GP might need a period of time to evolve. The bigger the population, the fewer generations are needed to defeat other strategies. In any case, it takes hundreds to more than a thousand days to achieve good performances for GP traders.

The result of this experiment shows that learning GP traders can outperform other (adaptive) strategies, even if those strategies may have a more sophisticated design.

4.2   Cognitive Capacity and the Learning Speed

Psychologists tell us that the intelligence of human beings involves the ability to "learn quickly and learn from experiences" [29]. Figure 2 delineates GP traders' learning dynamics with a more complete sampling. Roughly speaking, we can see that the bigger the population size, the less time GP traders need to perform well. In other words, GP traders with higher cognitive capacity tend to learn faster and consequently gain more wealth.

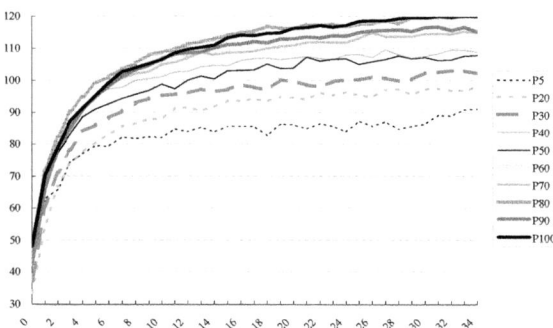

Fig. 2. GP traders' performances at different levels of cognitive capacity. The horizontal axis denotes the generation; the vertical axis denotes the individual efficiency (in percentages).

However, we may also notice that this relationship is not as monotone as we might have thought. It seems that there are three groups of learning dynamics in this figure. From P5 to P30, there exists a manifest positive relationship between "cognitive capacity" and performance. P40 and P50 forms the second group: they are not very distinguishable, but both of them are better than traders with lower "cognitive capacity". The most inexplainable part is P60 to P100. Although this group apparently outperforms traders with lower "cognitive capacity", the

---

[13] The best strategy of P100 traders in the 34th generation is a selling strategy–
Max(PMinBid, PAvg, PAvgAsk, LT), a simple rule which adjusts to the market situations by choosing whichever is bigger among several types of market and private information.

inner-group relationship between "cognitive capacity" and performance is quite obscure.

For a better understanding of this phenomenon, a series of nonparametric statistical tests were performed on these simulation results. The outcomes of these tests are presented in part A of Table 1. Pairwise Wilcoxon Rank Sum Tests show that when the "cognitive capacity" levels are low, small differences in cognitive capacity may result in significant differences in final performances. On the contrary, among those who have high cognitive capacity, differences in cognitive capacity do not seem to cause any significant discrepancy in performances.

Table 1. Wilcoxon Rank Sum Tests for GP traders' performances on individual efficiencies. " * " symbolizes significant results under the 10% significance level; " ** " symbolizes significant results under the 5% significance level.

		P5	P20	P30	P40	P50	P60	P70	P80	P90	P100
	P5	X									
	P20	0.099*	X								
	P30	0.010**	0.328	X							
A	P40	0.002**	0.103	0.488	X						
	P50	0.000**	0.009**	0.129	0.506	X					
	P60	0.000**	0.000**	0.003**	0.034**	0.130	X				
	P70	0.000**	0.000**	0.015**	0.121	0.355	0.536	X			
	P80	0.000**	0.000**	0.003**	0.036**	0.131	1.000	0.558	X		
	P90	0.000**	0.000**	0.011**	0.079*	0.250	0.723	0.778	0.663	X	
	P100	0.000**	0.000**	0.000**	0.002**	0.009**	0.284	0.093*	0.326	0.150	X
	P5	X									
	P20	0.571	X								
	P30	0.589	0.288	X							
	P40	0.170	0.060*	0.442	X						
B	P50	0.090*	0.020**	0.236	0.834	X					
	P60	0.004**	0.001**	0.019**	0.159	0.207	X				
	P70	0.066*	0.015**	0.191	0.671	0.848	0.280	X			
	P80	0.016**	0.003**	0.062*	0.333	0.422	0.656	0.577	X		
	P90	0.043**	0.010**	0.144	0.552	0.714	0.384	0.845	0.658	X	
	P100	0.001**	0.000**	0.008**	0.062*	0.091*	0.736	0.150	0.444	0.201	X

4.3 Can Diligence Make Up for Cognitive Capacity?

One interesting question about cognitive capacity and learning is that if we let those with lower cognitive capacity learn longer in financial markets, are they able to discover better strategies so that they can have as competent performances as those with high cognitive capacity?

To test this, we simply let GP traders with lower cognitive capacity evolve longer. Table 2 is the learning time for different types of GP traders. For example, traders with a population size of 5 have only 1/20 of the cognitive capacity of those whose population size is 100. Therefore, we let traders with a population of 5 evolve 20 times longer than traders with a population of 100.

Part B of Table 1 demonstrates the results of this experiment. We can observe that if the difference in cognitive capacity is not so large, it is possible to make up for the deficiency in endowed ability by hard work. However, diligence can only partially offset such a deficiency when the difference in cognitive capacity is large.

Taking GP traders with a population of 5 as an example, they can catch up with traders with a population of 40 if they work eight times longer. Nevertheless, when facing traders with a population of 100, they cannot reduce the gap even by working twenty times longer. This result seems to deny the hypothesis that traders with low cognitive capacity can fairly achieve appreciable performances just as smarter ones in double auction markets.

Table 2. Learning Span of GP traders

Cognitive Capacity	Generations	Cognitive Capacity	Generations
5	699	60	57
20	174	70	49
30	115	80	42
40	86	90	37
50	69	100	34

5   Conclusion

The purpose of this paper is to raise the issue of heterogeneity in individual cognitive capacity since most agent-based economic or financial models do not deal with it. In this paper, we propose a method to model individual cognitive capacity for autonomous agents in double auction markets. The autonomous agents are modeled with Genetic Programming, and their cognitive capacity is characterized by the population size of their strategies. A series of experiments were conducted to answer the questions raised by the experimental double auction literature. In general, there is a positive relationship between cognitive capacity and learning performance, and a decreasing marginal contribution of extra cognitive capacity. This exemplifies the significance of cognitive capacity in double auction markets. The results also show that the differences in agents' cognitive capacity cannot easily be compensated with extra efforts when the differences are large enough.

The results of this study also bring about issues such as the multi-dimensional properties of cognitive capacity, the classification of strategies developed by agents with different cognitive capacity, or the testing of cognitively heterogeneous agents in various environments to find the limiting behavior, etc. Such questions have already been studied in experiments with human agents, but are still new in agent-based economic simulations with autonomous agents. This suggests a closer collaboration between experimental economics and agent-based computational economics, and it is reasonable that psychological and even neural findings should also be consulted more properly in designing autonomous agents.

Acknowledgements

The authors are grateful to four anonymous referees for very helpful suggestions. The research support in the form of Taiwan NSC grant no. NSC 95-2415-H-004-002-MY3 is also gratefully acknowledged by the authors.

References

1. Simon, H.: The Sciences of the Artificial. MIT Press, Cambridge (1996)
2. Devetag, G., Warglien, M.: Games and phone numbers: Do short-term memory bounds affect strategic behavior? Journal of Economic Psychology 24, 189–202 (2003)
3. Devetag, G., Warglien, M.: Playing the wrong game: An experimental analysis of relational complexity and strategic misrepresentation. Games and Economic Behavior 62, 364–382 (2008)
4. Segal, N., Hershberger, S.: Cooperation and competition between twins: Findings from a prisoner's dilemma game. Evolution and Human Behavior 20, 29–51 (1999)
5. Casari, M., Ham, J., Kagel, J.: Selection bias, demographic effects, and ability effects in common value auction experiments. American Economic Review 97(4), 1278–1304 (2007)
6. Jones, G.: Are smarter groups more cooperative? Evidence from prisoner's dilemma experiments, 1959–2003. Journal of Economic Behavior and Organization (forthcoming)
7. Takashina, T., Watanabe, S.: The locality of information gathering in multiagent systems. In: Proceedings of Second International Conference on Multi-Agent Systems (ICMAS 1996), p. 461 (1996), http://homepage.mac.com/t_takashina/paper-dir/ICMAS96_takashina.pdf
8. Savit, R., Manuca, R., Riolo, R.: Adaptive competition, market efficiency, and phase transitions. Physical Review Letters 82(10), 2203–2206 (1999)
9. Casari, M.: Can genetic algorithms explain experimental anomalies? An application to common property resources. Computational Economics 24, 257–275 (2004)
10. Rust, J., Miller, J., Palmer, R.: Behavior of trading automata in a computerized double auction market. In: Friedman, D., Rust, J. (eds.) Double Auction Markets: Theory, Institutions, and Laboratory Evidence. Addison Wesley, Redwood City (1993)
11. Rust, J., Miller, J.H., Palmer, R.: Characterizing effective trading strategies: Insights from a computerized double auction tournament. Journal of Economic Dynamics and Control 18, 61–96 (1994)
12. Boender, Z.J., Ultee, J., Hovius, S.E.R.: Cognitive capacity: No association with recovery of sensibility by Semmes Weinstein test score after peripheral nerve injury of the forearm. Journal of Plastic, Reconstructive and Aesthetic Surgery (forthcoming)
13. Das, R., Hanson, J.E., Kephart, J.O., Tesauro, G.: Agent-human interactions in the continuous double auction. In: Proceedings of the 17th International Joint Conference on Artificial Intelligence (IJCAI). Morgan-Kaufmann, San Francisco (2001)
14. Taniguchi, K., Nakajima, Y., Hashimoto, F.: A report of U-Mart experiments by human agents. In: Shiratori, R., Arai, K., Kato, F. (eds.) Gaming, Simulations, and Society: Research Scope and Perspective, pp. 49–57. Springer, Heidelberg (2004)
15. Grossklags, J., Schmidt, C.: Software agents and market (in)efficiency–A human trader experiment. IEEE Transactions on System, Man, and Cybernetics: Part C, Special Issue on Game-theoretic Analysis & Simulation of Negotiation Agents, IEEE SMC 36, 56–67 (2006)
16. Christal, R.E., Tirre, W., Kyllonen, P.: Two for the money: Speed and level scores from a computerized vocabulary test. In: Lee, G., Ulrich, T. (eds.) Proceedings, Psychology in the Department of Defense. Ninth Annual Symposium (USAFA TR 8-2). U.S. Air Force Academy, Colorado Springs (1984)

17. Detterman, D.K., Daniel, M.H.: Correlations of mental tests with each other and with cognitive variables are highest for low-IQ groups. Intelligence 13, 349–359 (1989)
18. Hunt, E.: The role of intelligence in modern society. American Scientist, 356–368 (July/August 1995)
19. Conway, A., Kane, M., Engle, R.: Working memory capacity and its relation to general intelligence. Trends in Cognitive Sciences 7(12), 547–552 (2003)
20. Gode, D., Sunder, S.: Allocative efficiency of markets with zero-intelligence traders: Market as a partial substitute for individual rationality. Journal of Political Economy 101, 119–137 (1993)
21. Cliff, D., Bruten, J.: Zero is not enough: On the lower limit of agent intelligence for continuous double auction markets. Tech. Rep. no. HPL-97-141, Hewlett-Packard Laboratories (1997), http://citeseer.ist.psu.edu/cliff97zero.html
22. Zhan, W., Friedman, D.: Markups in double auction markets. Journal of Economic Dynamics and Control 31, 2984–3005 (2007)
23. Gjerstad, S., Dickhaut, J.: Price formation in double auctions. Games and Economic Behavior 22, 1–29 (1998)
24. Friedman, D.: A simple testable model of double auction markets. Journal of Economic Behavior and Organization 15, 47–70 (1991)
25. Easley, D., Ledyard, J.: Theories of price formation and exchange in double oral auction. In: Friedman, D., Rust, J. (eds.) The Double Auction Market-Institutions, Theories, and Evidence. Addison-Wesley, Reading (1993)
26. Chan, N.T., LeBaron, B., Lo, A.W., Poggio, T.: Agent-based models of financial markets: A comparison with experimental markets. MIT Artificial Markets Project, Paper No. 124 (September 1999),
   http://citeseer.ist.psu.edu/chan99agentbased.html
27. Miller, G.: The magical number seven, plus or minus two: Some limits on our capacity for processing information. Psychological Review 63, 81–97 (1956)
28. Arifovic, J.: Genetic algorithm and the cobweb model. Journal of Economic Dynamics and Control 18, 3–28 (1994)
29. Gottfredson, L.S.: Mainstream science on intelligence: An editorial with 52 signatories, history, and bibliography. Intelligence 24(1), 13–23 (1997)

A Multi-Agent System for Adaptive Production Networks

Samir Hamichi[1,2], David Brée[1], Zahia Guessoum[2], and Diana Mangalagiu[3,4]

[1] Institute for Scientific Interchange Foundation, Italy
[2] Laboratoire d'Informatique de Paris 6, University of Paris 6, France
[3] Reims Management School, France
[4] Institute for Science, Innovation and Society, University of Oxford, UK

Abstract. The dynamics of production networks is a complex and still poorly understood phenomenon. This complexity arises from the large number of heterogeneous actors involved and from the spatial distribution and interdependence of these actors. We investigate the geographical distribution of firms and the emergence industrial clusters. We use a multi-agent simulation approach, considering each production firm as an agent. We use adaptive agents taking into account investment decisions according to their business efficiency. In a constant return to scale economy, firms adapt their prices in order to be competitive and get larger market share. They adapt their business-to-business relations both to reduce costs of inputs and to ensure orders are satisfied. The agent proactivity, based on very simple decision mechanisms at a micro level, leads to the emergence of meta-stable business clusters and supply chains at the macro level of the global production system.

Keywords: Multi-Agent Simulation, Production Networks, Firm Dynamics.

1 Introduction

The production networks of firms linked by supply-customer relationships embedded in a geographical space are among the phenomena not yet well understood by practitioners and scientists. Such networks are highly non-linear and exhibit complex behavior through the interplay of their structure, environment and function, this complexity making it difficult to manage, control or predict their behavior. Production networks and supply chains have received considerable attention from researchers in various disciplines over the past two decades. Agent-based modeling (ABM) and simulation are regarded as one of the best candidates for addressing different aspects of these networks. Indeed, ABMs allow the study of complex systems, such as production networks, from a micro-macro evolutionary modeling perspective. They are able to take into account both the heterogeneity and autonomy of the agents, as well as their temporal-spatial dynamic relations and to exhibit the emergent evolutionary nature of collective phenomena.

G. Di Tosto and H. Van Dyke Parunak (Eds.): MABS 2009, LNAI 5683, pp. 49–60, 2010.

In this paper, we present a multi-agent system (MAS) studying the dynamics of production networks; the geographical distribution firms and the emergence of industrial districts through self-organization processes. The paper is organized as follows: after a brief literature review, we introduce the framework of our model and present its dynamics which depend on the pricing mechanisms we designed. Then, we present the implementation of the model and the results of our simulations. Finally, we draw our conclusions and future research directions.

2   Related Work

Most studies provide software frameworks with primitives that allow development of realistic supply chain models and use simulation techniques to analyze supply chains and evaluate effects of various supply chain strategies on demand. There are two main research streams concerned with modelling supply chains using ABMs. One focuses on managing such systems, the other on their natural evolution. Concerning the former, Turowski [13] and Ghiassi and Spera [6] developed agent-based techniques for coordinating activities of e-commerce and Internet-based supply chain systems for mass customization markets. Li and Fong [9] and Choy and Lee [4] proposed agent-based architectures to facilitate the formation and organization of virtual enterprises for order management. Bo and Zhiming [2] developed a MAS supply chain management tool to evaluate various scheduling developed algorithms for orders allocation to different suppliers. Sadeh et al. [10] developed and implemented a reconfigurable multilevel agent-based architecture for coordinated supply chain planning and scheduling, while Swaminathan et al. [12], Zeng and Sycara [17], and Valluri and Croson [14] adopted agent technology to develop frameworks to evaluate and improve the performance of supply chain structures.

Hereafter we review the contributions in supply chains and production networks, which are most relevant to the question we investigate: the emergence of industrial districts. We focus on studies of firm dynamics within production networks from the economic perspective. Their aim usually to repoduce some of the empirically derived stylized facts such as the distribution of size and geographical location of firms.

Battiston et al. [1] identified mechanisms which reproduce qualitatively the main stylized facts and the correlation between output, growth and bankruptcy rate across firms. They show that the aggregate variables of the network of firms as a whole can be traced back to the direct firm-firm interdependence.

Weisbuch and Battiston in [15] [16], using a very simple framework, investigated wealth concentration and production regionalization through self-organization. They show local production failures can result in avalanches of shortages and bankruptcies across the network and lead to separating economic regions into poorer and richer regions with scale free distribution of wealth.

Boero and Squazzoni [3] introduced an ABM studying the role that firm behavior plays on the generation of different industrial district interaction structures. They also investigated the role that external partnerships and supporting institutions play on the evolution of industrial district structure through improving effective connections with the external environment.

The studies mentioned above aim to improve our understanding of the reasons of geographical concentration of businesses. They show that the interaction of agents drives the dynamics of the whole economic system. However, most of these studies are based on assumptions which are not supported by fundamental economic features such as compititive price setting, market clearance and geographical constraints. They assume agent behavior as a black box automatically and naturally shaped by the properties of the social and spatial networks in which the agents are embedded.

The motivation of our work is to build a model that is sound from an economic point of view. So, for our approach, we start from the simple model proposed by Weisbuch and Battiston [16] and introduce more realistic mechanisms based on standard economic principles. As our interest is not limited to the issues discussed in this paper, we want to go farther in studying micro-macro vs. macro-micro feedback and self-organization in production chains on the one hand, allowing us to find the relevent parameters driving the emergence of organizations and on the other hand, and vertical vs. horizontal integration in supply chains. We investigate how the behavior at a micro-level (agent-level) determines the proximity relations at a macro-level. Our agents are adaptive taking investment decisions according to efficiency criteria. They adapt their prices in order to be competitive and get a larger market share. Also, they adapt their business relations (i.e. their suppliers) in order both to reduce costs of inputs, including transportation cost and geographical reach and also to get orders satisfied. The agent proactivity, based on very simple decision mechanisms at a micro level, leads to the emergence of meta-stable business clusters and supply chains at the macro level of the global production system.

3 Description of the Model

3.1 The Firm Model

Our model, based on the model of Weisbuch and Battiston [16] (the W&B model), consists of a network in which the nodes are production firms and the links are the business to business (B2B) relations between firms. In this section, we first introduce the model: the network structure, the characteristics of the firm and the dynamics of the economic system; then we present the agentification of the model describing the adaptive behavior of the firm.

The network. The production network consists of a regular grid with l layers of m nodes. The network is oriented from an input layer $l-1$ (natural resources) towards an output layer 0 (supermarkets) (see Fig 1). In each node of the grid we place a firm; firm $F_{k,i}$ is located at position i in a layer k. The network is initialized with $n = l * m$ firms. Each firm $F_{k,i}$ / $k \in [1, l-2]$ is linked to its customers in the layer $k-1$ and its suppliers in the layer $k+1$.

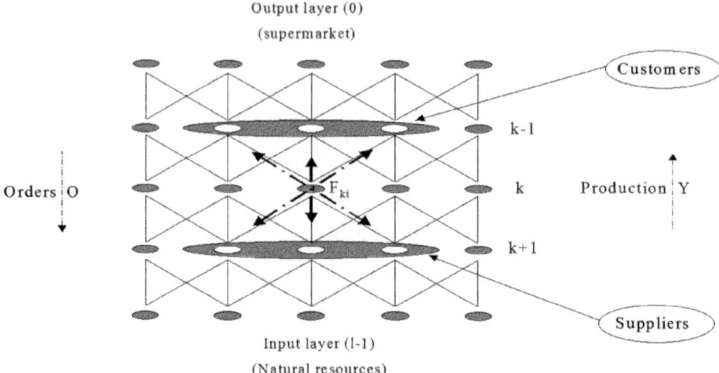

Output layer (0)
(supermarket)

Customers

k-1

Orders O   k   Production Y

k+1

Suppliers

Input layer (l-1)
(Natural resources)

Fig. 1. Network of firms

The firm. Each firm $F_{k,i}$ has capital invested in the means of production and has a production process converting Y^{in} units of input bought from firms in layer $k+1$ into Y^{out} units of output. To design adaptive process of the firm in terms of investment strategies and production adjustments, we define the capital of the firm as production capacity $A_{k,i}$ which depreciates in time at a certain rate and liquid assets $L_{k,i}$ which do not depreciate.

We also introduce pricing mechanisms. We base our model on the markup pricing mechanism where the price is calculated by adding a markup (margin) to the average unit cost of the production. For the final market (firms at the output layer), a market clearing mechanism sets the price to clear the market following principle of demand/supply.

The variables we use to describe a firm $F_{k,i}$ located in the position (k, i) in the network are:

- $K_{k,i}(t) = A_{k,i}(t) + L_{k,i}(t)$: Capital at time t ($A_{k,i}(t)$ and $L_{k,i}(t)$ are respectively production capacity and liquid assets;
- $S_{k,i}(t)$: suppliers list;
- $C_{k,i}(t)$: customers list;
- $O_{k,i}(t)$: orders to its suppliers;
  - $O_{k,i}^{k+1,j}(t)$: orders sent to the supplier $F_{k+1,j}$;
- $Y_{k,i}(t)$: production;
  - $Y_{k,i}^{k-1,j}(t)$: production delivered to the firm $F_{k-1,j}$;
- $c_{k,i}^u(t)$: cost of one unit of product;
- $p_{k,i}(t)$: sale price of one unit of product;
- $\Pi_{k,i}(t)$: profit;

The dynamics. The production process is based on B2B interactions and is executed within each time step t. One time step represents a full production process:

Each firm places orders. A firm receiving an order, calculates its needed inputs for production and then places orders to its suppliers. Note that in W&B model, customers and the suppliers of each firm were fixed and remain the same for all the simulation, while in our model, we have dynamic lists of suppliers and customers. Once orders propagate down to the input layer, each firm produces according to the received inputs and delivers. The firm can lose a fraction of its production, due to exogeneous event. After delivery, each firm calculates its profit and updates its assets and, if needed, it invests some of this in production capacity. Bellow, we describe the main processes executed by each firm in a time step.

1. **Orders at the output layer**
   For the orders $O_{0,i}(t)$ of the firm $F_{0,i}$, Weisbuch and Battiston use the following simplifying assumptions for the model, inspired from [5]. The orders are limited only by the production capacity of the firm and all output production is sold. Consequently, the firms in the output layer place orders for full production. In our model, we use the same assumption.

2. **Orders at the intermediate levels**
   The firm $F_{k,i}$ ($k = 1..l - 2$) calculates the quantity to be produced by summing all orders received from customers and comparing this to its production capacity. The planned production is then the minimum between production capacity and orders coming from downstream. Once the planned production quantity has been calculated, the firm orders the needed amount of products from its suppliers, i.e. divides and transfers these orders upstream in order to get products from layer ($k + 1$), allowing suppliers to plan and order at their turn.

3. **Orders at the input layer**
   Firms at the input layer $k = l - 1$ are not required to order any inputs. It is assumed that they have unlimited access to needed raw materials.

4. **Production**
   The production process starts from the input layer, each firm starting producing according to the inputs it receives.
   A firm's goal is to produce the amount ordered by its customers, but its actual production depends on events happening during the production process. With a probability P (taken from a uniform distribution), a random fraction ϵ of its production is lost.
   The production function, including exogenous and unplanned events, is:

$$Y_{k,i}(t) = \alpha.Y_{k,i}^{in}(t).(1 - \epsilon) \tag{1}$$

   where α is a transformation coefficient.
   The production efficiency ratio, Z, used by the firm to decide its investment according to its capacity utilization.

$$Z_{k,i}(t) = \frac{Y_{k,i}(t)}{q.A_{k,i}(t)} \tag{2}$$

   where q is a technological proportionality coefficient relating the quantity of product Y to the production capacity A, combining the effect of capital and labor. q is taken to 1 without loss of generality.

5. **Profit and production capacity increase**
   Production delivery always results in payments. For each firm, profits are
   the difference between the value of the quantity of delivered products and
   production costs. Profits Π_{ki} are then:

$$\Pi_{ki}(t) = (p_{k,i}(t) - c^{u}_{k,i}(t)).Y_{k,i}(t) \tag{3}$$

where $p_{k,i}$ is the price of the product sold by the firm, $c^{u}_{k,i}$ is its average unit
cost of production.
All profits are intially placed in liquid assets. If needed, the firm adapts its
production capacity by increasing it. The investment process depends on
capacity utilization as follow:

$$
\begin{aligned}
&\text{if } (Z_{k,i}(t) = 1 \text{ and } \Pi_{k,i}(t) > 0) \text{ then} \\
&\qquad L_{k,i}(t+1) = L_{ki}(t) + \Pi_{k,i}(t) - \theta.A_{k,i}(t); \\
&\qquad A_{k,i}(t+1) = A_{k,i}(t).(1 - \lambda + \theta); \\
&\text{else} \qquad L_{k,i}(t+1) = L_{ki}(t) + \Pi_{k,i}(t); \\
&\qquad A_{k,i}(t+1) = A_{k,i}(t)(1 - \lambda); \\
&\text{endif};
\end{aligned}
$$

where θ is the investment rate and λ is the capital decay constant due to
interest rates and material degradation.

Class of the model. The dynamical system defined here belongs to a large class
of non linear systems called reaction-diffusion systems from chemical physics [11].
The reaction part here is the autocatalytic loop of production and capital growth
coupled with capital decay and death processes. The characteristics of the model
are: a dynamical behavior with spatio-temporal patterns, well characterized dynamical regimes separated in the parameter space by transitions or crossovers,
and scale free distributions since the dynamics is essentially multiplicative and
noisy.

3.2   The Agentification of the Model

The W&B Model, with its some strong assumptions regarding the regularity of
the network, the orders from the market, the non-existence of pricing mechanisms and investment strategies, is very far from reality. Indeed, the firms are
considered, to behave uniformly, while in real market, firms are very heterogeneous. Our approach is to start with this simple model characterized by well
known stylized facts and to use MAS paradigm in order to make a more realistic
and flexible model allowing us to further study issues production network and
supply chain important issues in Agent-based Computational Economics (ACE).

The Firm environment. A firm's environment is its market; from the upstream side the firm gets inputs and to the downstream side it sells products.
So, the firm interacts only with firms within its environment. Regarding the
output layer ($k = 0$) as a final market, the firms in this layer sell the production directly to the final consumers. As in W&B model, we assume that all the
production $Y_0(t) = \sum_{i=1..m} Y_{0,i}(t)$ will be sold (absorbed by the market). But

instead of a fixed unit cost and unit price as in W&B model, we designed a market pricing mechanism based on the principle assumed in the economic literature setting the price as function of demand and supply of the production. This mechanism is a market clearing mechanism which confronts the aggregate production $Y_0(t)$ to a demand curve and sets the market price $p^{\mathrm{m}}(t)$ for the firms in the market where the aggregate production is sold.

The agent (firm). We regard the firm as the main entity of our MAS. It interacts with other firms in it's environment following B2B rules.

In WB's Model, the firm has a fixed set of suppliers and customers with which it interacts. In our model, firms change suppliers over time depending on the their economic performance. The firm, by assessing its business exchange, adapts its relations with its partners: suppliers in its supply side and customers in its market (upstream / downstream). It reinforces the supply links with the profitable suppliers by continuing to order inputs from them and proceeds to substitute the less profitable ones by seeking new suppliers offering best prices. In the sourcing adaptation process, the firm has access to the price, the geographical distance and the production capacities of all the firms in its supply side that are within its geographical reach. It sorts them by unit cost including transportation cost.It takes then the decision to substitute the higher cost supplier by the firm which has the the minimum unit cost. So the the firm adapts its list as follow:

$$S_{k,i}(t+1) = S_{k,i}(t);$$

if $\left(\dfrac{(Y_{k,i}^{\mathrm{in}}(t))}{O_{k,i}^{\mathrm{out}}(t)}\right) < SatThresh)$ then

for $F_{k+1,j} \notin S_{k,i}(t)\ j \in [1..m]$
return j with $min(p_j + c^{\mathrm{T}}.d_{(i,j)})$;

for $F_{k+1,h} \in S_{k,i}(t)$
return h with $max(p_h + c^{\mathrm{T}}.d_{(i,h)})$;

if $(p_h + c^{\mathrm{T}}.d_{(i,h)} > p_j + c^{\mathrm{T}}.d_{(i,j)})$
$S_{k,i}(t+1) = S_{k,i}(t) - F_{k+1,h} + F_{k+1,j};$
endif;

endif;

where
p_j (resp. p_h) is the unit price of the firm $F_{k+1,j} \notin S_{k,i}$ (resp. $F_{k+1,h} \in S_{k,i}$)
c^{T} is the transportation cost of unit of production per unit of distance,
$d_{(i,j)}$ is the geographical distance between firm $F_{k,i}$ and firm $F_{k+1,j}$

The firm, as a supplier, has to have competitive prices in order to get more customers. Therfore, the firm adapts its fixed markup in its pricing policy.

To reach its goal, the firm has to take decisions according to strategies. This local adaptation leads to changes in the form of the organizational structure in which the firm is involved by gaining or loosing customers. Using these decision mechanisms at the firm level, we are interested in the effect of these decisions on the production regionalization and the economic performance of the whole system.

4   Simulation and Results

The results of simulations were obtained, using the multi-agent platform $DIMA$ [7], for a production network with 1250 nodes in five layers, run for 10000 time steps. The initial wealth is uniformly and randomly distributed among firms:

$$A_{k,i}(t = 0) \in [1.0, 1.1] \tag{4}$$

$$L_{k,i}(t = 0) = 0 \tag{5}$$

We have studied the impact of the transportation cost on the network structure and its stability. We have compared the economic performance of the system under different conditions.

The two different price mechanisms used in the model - market clearing mechanism for firms in output layer and markup mechanism for firms in other layers - lead to two different economic outcomes for the firms. First, the intermediate firms selling with markup pricing make a profit under competition between the firms of the same layer. In other words, if a given firm is less competitive through price than other firms, it will get fewer orders and in the worst case no orders at all from customers. Second, the firms at the output layer which order for full capacity, assuming that all what they produce will be sold, indeed sell all the production but at a market price which depends on the total amount of production.

4.1   Emergent Pattern

Across the network, we have studied different cases of geographical reach. First, we have considered that each customer could see and place an order with any supplier from its supply layer. In other cases, we have considered that each customer could see only a proportion of suppliers: closest half, closest third ,.... closest tenth. We call this proportion the geographical reach $GeoLimit$.

We observe, in all the cases we studied, that the firms self-organize into regions and spatial patterns emerge. By changing the rules at the micro level we could see different results at the macro level: the shape and the number of the patterns in the network.

The evolution of the network (a regular grid as shown in Fig. 1 with 5X250 firms) is shown in Fig. 2 and Fig. 3, corresponding to different time steps: 1000 and 10000 respectively . The number of regions we get at the end of each simulation depends on the $GeoLimit$ parameter. As shown in Fig. 3 with geographical reach $GeoLimit = 1/5$ and transportation cost $c^{\mathrm{T}} = 0.1$ and Fig. 4 with $GeoLimit = 1/5$ and $c^{\mathrm{T}} = 0$, the fewer suppliers a firm has access to, the higher the number of regions we get.

Fig. 2. The network after 1000 time steps, with transportation cost $c^T = 0.1$

Fig. 3. The network after 10000 time steps, with transportation cost $c^T = 0.1$

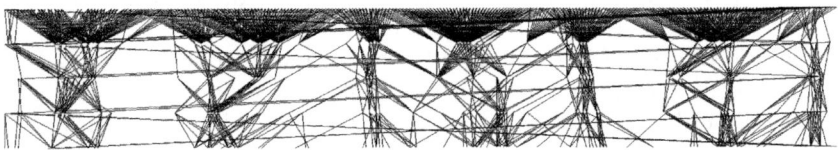

Fig. 4. The network after 10000 time steps, transportation cost $c^T = 0$

In case of full visibility, we end up with only one active region with all the active firms in the output layer connected to a very few firms in the supply layers. The markup pricing mechanism makes the market within each layer very competitive and a very few competitive firms get all the customers.

We notice that the transportation cost has a high impact on the regionalization. With zero transportation cost we end up with patterns which are not influenced by geographical distance while clustred (see Fig. 4), where, rich firms are not all clustered in the same region as in the case with high transportation costs (see figures 2, 3).

4.2 Aggregate Economic Performance

We analyzed the aggregate values of the global system : market price, aggregate production and total growth of the capital.

We show the aggregate production in time, which corresponds to the production sold by the firms at the output layer, and the market price corresponding to the aggregate production (see Fig. 5). For each variable, we display the case of transportation cost $c^T = 0$ with three different studies of geographical limit *GeoLimit* (displayed in the same plot).

Considering the aggregate growth $G(t)$ defined by Equation 6, we show in Fig. 6 the evolution of the growth in time (log log scale). We can clearly see

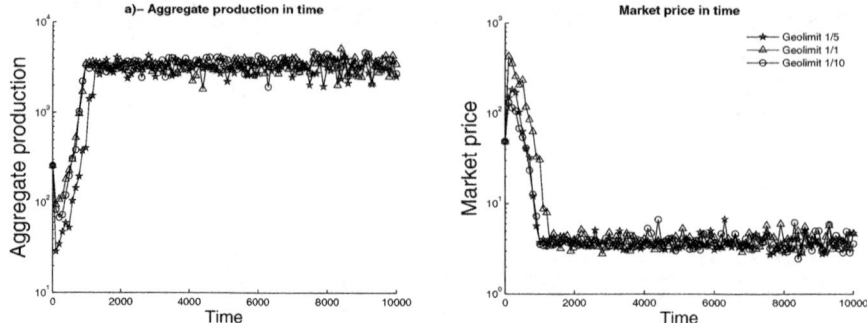

Fig. 5. Left: Aggregate production sold to the market - Right: Market price

how the market evolves from a early development stage (with the demand much higher than the offer) to a mature stage. As the production initially is not high enough to satisfy the demand, the market price is largely higher than average unit cost at the end of the production chain. Firms in the output layer take advantage of this situation, selling all their production with very high profit. This leads them to increase production capacity, investing part of liquid assets as previously described. Firms at the output layer share the market in proportion to their respective production capacity, while firms in intermediate layers sell production with a fixed margin. These two simplified behaviors are realistic. The profits of the firms in intermediate layers are influenced by their suppliers' prices and by the quantities of products ordered by their customers. The large firms, as they are able to set low prices, take the oligopoly of the market. Detailed simulation parameters and results are available in [8].

$$G(t) = \frac{\sum_{i,k} K_{k,i}(t+1) - \sum_{i,k} K_{k,i}(t)}{\sum_{k,i} K_{k,i}(t)} \qquad (6)$$

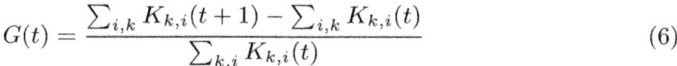

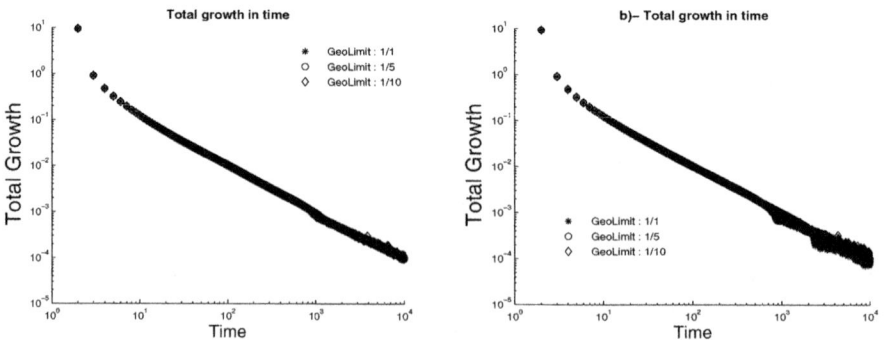

Fig. 6. Distribution of the wealth -a) $c^T = 0$; b) $c^T = 0.1$;

5   Conclusions and Perspectives

In this paper, a MAS is introduced and preliminary simulation results are discussed. Inspired by a very simple production network model [16], the MAS is designed in a way which allows us to alleviate shortcomings of the original framework and its strong assumptions. Our target is to get to a more realistic model starting from a simple one that includes standard economic principles. We have integrated price mechanisms into the model and reproduced stylized facts such as the regionalization of production and wealth with heterogeneous and adaptive agents. We have modeled and simulated the impact of the transportation cost and the geographical reach on the shape of the regionalization production and wealth patterns. The results of the simulations have shown that the individual firms, with local B2B interactions and decisions, form stable production systems based on the supply/demand and market growth mechanisms leading to the maturation of the market.

From these preliminary results, we plan to investigate, using MAS concepts such as stigmergy and self-organization mechanisms, various sourcing and investment policies as well as more global issues, such as the vertical vs. horizontal integration and collaboration in competition. This will allow us to further investigate industrial and business cluster dynamics and to confront our findings to empirical data.

References

1. Battiston, S., Delli Gatti, D., Gallegati, M., Greenwald, B., Stiglitz, J.E.: Credit chains and bankruptcy propagation in production networks. JEDC 31, 2061–2084 (2007)
2. Bo, X., Zhiming, W.: Modeling of supply chain: a multi-agent approach. In: American control conference, p. 11. Denver, CO, United States (2003)
3. Boero, R., Squazzoni, F.: Proximity relations, partnership structure and supporting institutions in an agent-based model of an industrial district prototype. The Electronic Journal of Evolutionary Modeling and Economic Dynamics (1028), 27 (2004)
4. Choy, K., Lee, W.: Multi-agent based virtual enterprise supply chain network for order management. In: Portland international conference on management of engineering and technology, PICMET (2002)
5. Delli Gatti, D., Di Corrado, G., Gaffeo, E., Giulioni, G., Gallegati, M., Palestrini, A.: A new approach to business fluctuations: heterogeneous interacting agents, scaling laws and financial fragility. JEBO 56(4), 489–512 (2005)
6. Ghiassi, M., Spera, C.: Defining the internet-based supply chain system for mass customized markets. Computers and Industrial Engineering 45(1), 17–41 (2003)
7. Guessoum, Z., Briot, J.: From active object to autonomous agents. IEEE Concurrency 7(3), 68–78 (1999)
8. Hamichi, S., Guessoum, Z., Mangalagiu, D.: A multi-agent system of adaptive production networks. Internal report, LIP6 (2008), http://www-poleia.lip6.fr/~guessoum/TR01.pdf

9. Li, T., Fong, Z.: A system architecture for agent based supply chain management platform. Canadian Conference on Electrical and Computer Engineering, CCECE 2(4-7), 713–716 (2003)

10. Sadeh, N., Hildum, D., Kjenstad, D., Tseng, A.: MASCOT: an agent-based architecture for coordinated mixed-initiative supply chain planning and scheduling. In: Workshop on agent-based decision support in managing the internet-enabled supply-chain, pp. 133–138 (1999)

11. Shnerb, N.M., Louzoun, Y., Bettelheim, E., Solomon, S.: The importance of being discrete: Life always wins on the surface. Proceedings of the National Academy of Sciences 97(19), 10322–10324 (2000)

12. Swaminathan, J., Smith, S., Sadeh, N.: Modelling supply chain dynamics: a multi-agent approach. Decision Science 29(3), 607–632 (1998)

13. Turowski, K.: Agent-based e-commerce in case of mass customization. International Journal of Production Economics 75(1-2), 69–81 (2002)

14. Valluri, A., Croson, D.C.: Agent learning in supplier selection models, decision support systems. Decision theory and game theory in agent design 39(2), 219–240 (2005)

15. Weisbuch, G.: Self-organized patterns in production networks. Complexus 387(2), 217–227 (2008)

16. Weisbuch, G., Battiston, S.: From production networks to geographical economics. JEBO 64, 448–469 (2007)

17. Zeng, D., Sycara, K.: Agent-facilitated real-time flexible supply chain structuring. In: Workshop on agent-based decision-support for managing the internet-enabled supply-chain, Seattle, WA, pp. 21–28 (1999)

A Multi-environment Multi-agent Simulation Framework for Self-organizing Systems

Maíra Athanázio de Cerqueira Gatti and Carlos José Pereira de Lucena

Departamento de Informática – PUC-Rio,
Rua Marques de São Vicente, 225, 4o andar RDC
Rio de Janeiro, RJ, Brazil
{mgatti,lucena}@inf.puc-rio.br

Abstract. This paper introduces a multi-environment simulation framework for building self-organizing multi-agent systems. From an engineering point of view, the multi-environments approach brings the necessary modularity and separation of concerns to build self-organizing multi-agent systems that address hierarchy, interoperability and multi-aspects problems and domains. Our framework provides higher abstractions and components to support the development of self-organizing systems with multiple environments, which can be situated or not. Furthermore, the framework provides a coordination component and self-organizing mechanisms to be instantiated and flexibility to evolve the framework with more complex ones.

Keywords: Multi-Environment, Multi-Agent Systems, Self-organization, Coordination, Framework.

1 Introduction

Depending on each agent type being developed, the environment types vary. The environment defines its own concepts and their logics and the agents must understand this in order to perceive them and to operate. The environment might be accessible, sensors give access to the complete state of the environment or inaccessible; deterministic, the next state can be determined based on the current state and the action, or nondeterministic, and so on.

Each application domain has its own view of what is an environment and what are the functionalities implemented by an environment. In current approaches, each time a different aspect of the application domain is identified this aspect is then appended to the environment in an ad hoc manner. As a result, the environment centralizes all the different aspects of the targeted application.

In particular, for a situated environment, an additional element characterizes this agent-environment relationship: the localization function is specifically provided by the situated environment. In a situated environment, one can define the location of an agent in terms of coordinates within the environment [4].

During the last years, there has been significant research in the field of self-organization in computer science. Several definitions [1-4] and mechanisms have been examined in order to understand how computing can model self-organizing systems and how self-organizing systems can empower computer science.

G. Di Tosto and H. Van Dyke Parunak (Eds.): MABS 2009, LNAI 5683, pp. 61–72, 2010.

In particular, self-organizing systems - where each component of a system acquires and maintains information about its environment and neighbors without external control and where the emergent system behavior may evolve or change over time [1-4], a self-organizing system has a structurally distributed environment; in other words, at any point in time, no centralized entity has complete knowledge of the state of the environment as a whole. Furthermore, a designer may decide to model environments using various underlying structures. For example, an environment can be modeled as a graph, a discrete grid, a continuous space or a combination of these. In addition, to achieve performance in a cluster or computer grid, or even because of the domain application, the environment can be distributed from a processing perspective if it is designed to be executed in a distributed network. So, the more choices for environment structures, the broader its application in the field of multi-agent simulation systems.

That said, we propose a multi-environment simulation framework for building self-organizing multi-agent systems, called MESOF. From an engineering point of view, the multi-environment approach brings the necessary modularity and separation of concerns to the building of self-organizing multi-agent systems that address hierarchy, interoperability and multi-aspect problems and domains. MESOF provides higher abstractions and components to support the development of self-organizing systems with multiple environments, which can be situated or not.

2 A Multi-environment Framework

The process of building such a self-organizing system with a multi-environment framework that merges several aspects is made clearer at both the design and implementation levels. So, the agents can exist in several and independent environments.

Each environment is concerned only with a specific aspect and can be developed independently from other environments. Existing environments do not need to be re-defined or modified. The environment has a dual role as a first-order abstraction: (i) it provides the surrounding conditions for agents to exist [30], which implies that the environment is an essential part of every self-organizing multi-agent system, and (ii) the environment provides an exploitable design abstraction to build multi-agent system applications.

At the conceptual meta-model of the multi-environment multi-agent simulation framework proposed in this work, we have the simulator engine that schedules the main environment. All the agents and sub-environments on the main environment are scheduled by the main environment and added to the simulator engine depending on their states. The environment state is dynamic and if one agent leaves the environment or moves, the environment state changes. Moreover, the environment provides the conditions under which agents exist and it mediates both the interaction among agents and their access to resources.

Moreover, the environment is locally observable to agents and if multiple environments exist, any agent can only exist as at most one instance in each and every environment. In self-organizing systems, the environment acts autonomously with adaptive behavior just like agents and interacts by means of reaction or through the propagation of events.

We classify the events as: (i) emission: signal an asynchronous interaction among agents and their environment. Broadcasting can be performed through emissions; (ii) trigger: signal a change of agent state as a consequence of a perceived event. For instance, an agent can raise a trigger event when perceiving an emission event that changed its state; (iii) movement: signal an agent movement across the environment; (iv) reaction: signal a synchronous interaction among agents, however without explicit receiver. It can be a neighbor of the agent or the environment; and (v) communication: signal a message exchange between agents with explicit receivers (one or more).

Each of these events may be raised by actions performed by agents or by the environment and updates their states. In self-organizing mechanisms [4], the way in which the agents interact is of paramount importance and most of the benefits involved in self-organization are actually due to the right way of interacting. When we talk about interaction and coordination we refer to any kind of mechanisms allowing some agents to orchestrate and influence each other's activities.

Among all the possible interaction mechanisms, MESOF supports uncoupled and anonymous ones. Uncoupled and anonymous interaction can be defined by the fact that the two interaction partners need neither to know each other in advance, nor to be connected at the same time in the network. Uncoupled and anonymous interaction has many advantages. It naturally suits open systems, where the number and the identities of components are not known at design time. It also suits dynamic scenarios in that components can also interact in the presence of network glitches and temporary failures. Moreover, it fosters robustness, in that components are not bound to interact with pre-specified partners but rather interact with whoever is available. Summarizing, uncoupled and anonymous interaction is suited in those dynamic scenarios where an unspecified number of possibly varying agents need to coordinate and self-organize their respective activities. Not surprisingly, this kind of interaction is ubiquitous in nature; cells, insects and animals adopt it to achieve a wide range of self-organizing behaviors [4].

Therefore, the taxonomy created of the events in our framework relies on what and how information is being communicated: explicit or implicit interaction, directly to the receiver, propagation though neighbors, and so on. Moreover, the agent may react in a different way according to the information type.

2.1 The Architecture

In this subsection we describe the architecture, hot spots and the coordination component of a basic and general multi-environment simulation framework for self-organizing systems implemented on top of MASON [5-7]. MASON is a fast, discrete-event multi-agent simulation library core in Java. It contains both a model library and an optional suite of visualization tools in 2D and 3D, which we extended to provide a continuous space and the coordination component regarding the environment approach. For the sake of brevity, we shall neglect a full description of MASON—the interested reader can refer to the official MASON documentation [7]—though some of its main aspects are presented throughout.

The entire core simulation engine provided by MASON was reused and is a frozen spot. MESOF (Fig. 1) provides higher abstractions and components to support the development of self-organizing systems with multiple environments.

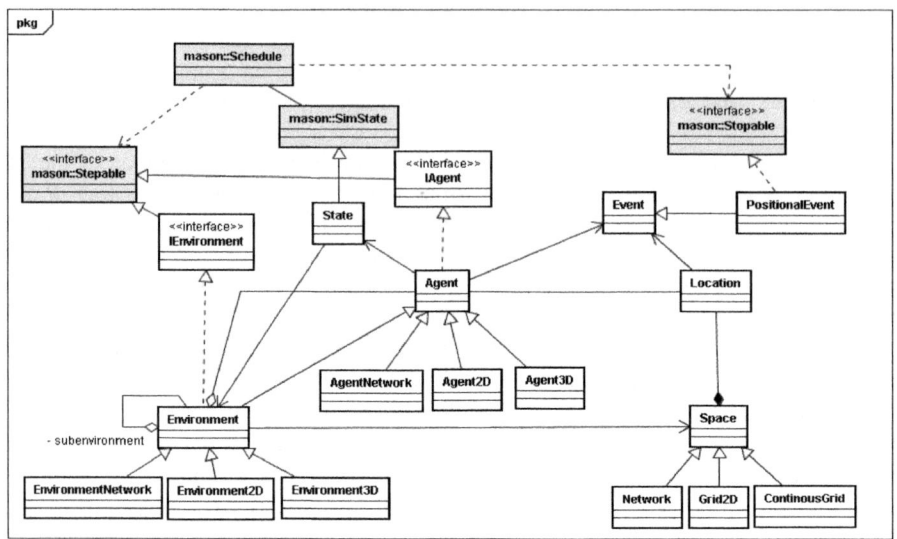

Fig. 1. The Architecture Class Diagram Overview

The first hot spot is the core architecture for a simulation without visualization. There is one interface for agents and one for environments. We provide two classes (*Agent* and *Environment*) that implement those interfaces and they provide a set of reusable behaviors that can be used for any application to be instantiated. There is a main environment, and the agents' interactions are encapsulated by the main environment and by sub-environments which have active behavior and can interact with other agents or other environments. In a discrete event simulation system, an entity is allowed to behave from time to time. These slices of time are called steps. So, a basic entity will usually implement the step method where it will perform its activities. The agent or environment has a set of events, i.e., the information provided for the self-organizing mechanism and implicit coordination, to handle on each time step of simulation. An agent can behave and execute actions on the environment where it resides or on itself.

The Environment manages the schedule of its sub-environment and agents when it is started by the simulator. And, for each time step, it manages the entrance of agents or environments and schedules each new entity. The entities being scheduled can be both executed in all modes provided by the MASON library, i.e., sequential types and parallel sequence.

The second hot spot is the core architecture of the situated multi-environment multi-agent simulation framework for a discrete 2D/ 3D and continuous 3D simulation. For instance, the framework provides the Agent2D and Environment2D classes for situated environment using a discrete 2D double point grid, which is represented by the class *Grid2D*. This class handles the addition, removal and search of agents and events in a double point location. The environment uses the grid to realize the several strategies for self-organizing mechanisms, such as the atomic ones Replication, Death, Diffusion, and Aggregation [4], or the combined ones as Gradient Fields and Pheromone Path [9], for instance, as it will be further explained in the Coordination Component (next section).

Regarding the 3D environment, the framework provides a 3D continuous space through the *ContinuousGrid* class, and the entities are represented by a triple (x, y, z) of floating-point numbers. All the agent-environment relationships and simulation schedule described for a non-situated environment is reused in these components.

2.1.1 The Coordination Component

Coordination is defined as the management of the communication between agents – coordination defines how agents interact. In self-organizing systems this interaction occurs through the environment (e.g. gradient fields, pheromones) [9], which is why the development of an environment for coordination is important. Another motivation for developing a coordination component that supports more than message passing is the emergence of highly decentralized and dynamic distributed systems. A middleware that supports an environment where agents can interact indirectly through intentional events, for example by leaving objects in an environment for other agents to see, is more scalable and convenient for the application developer [9].

For a non-situated environment, on which the environment manages the agents and events on a graph (for a peer-to-peer network, for instance) the coordination is achieved using a neighborhood in a graph (Figure 2a). Each event to be fired by an agent or by the environment will be located in a node and, if desired, propagated to the neighbors according to the rules specified.

Regarding a situated environment, the coordination is achieved using a neighborhood in 2D/ 3D and discrete/ continuous grid (Figure 2b and 2c). Moreover, there is a specific type of event, called Positional Event, which can be propagated instead of a regular event. The Positional Event has a time to live in the environment. Therefore, if an agent takes too many time steps to reach the source location of the event, it might have disappeared. This is useful for the Diffusion pattern, for instance, and for its combination with other patterns.

MESOF also provides a set of neighborhood lookups for each environment type such as: get agents at a node/ position, get agents within distance, get available nodes/positions within distance, get events at location, and so on. In addition, the environment uses the Template Method and Strategy design patterns [11]. They provide reusable classes and methods that can be implemented for the propagations rules that depend on the self-organizing mechanism increasing reuse. Also, we provide two self-organizing mechanisms in the framework that can be reused. They have already been refactored from the applications developed: the Diffusion and Evaporation mechanisms. We are still adding mechanisms to the framework, such as the Gradient Field, which is the combination of the Evaporation, Aggregation and Diffusion [9].

Another important concept of the framework that allows the coordination component to be flexible and fast is that the grids of the situated environments are sparse fields. Therefore, many objects can be located in the same position and different search strategies exist for each type of entity: sub-environment, agent, event or positional event.

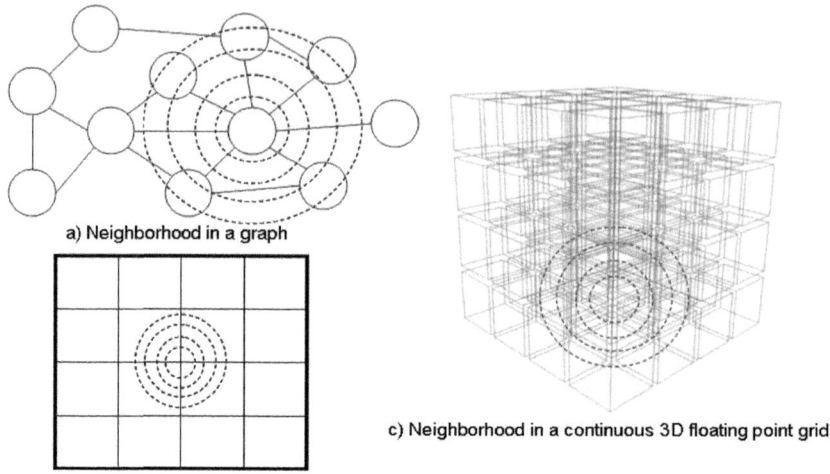

a) Neighborhood in a graph

b) Neighborhood in a discrete 2D double point grid

c) Neighborhood in a continuous 3D floating point grid

Fig. 2. *a)* Graph: each agent or sub-environment can be located in a node and perceives its neighbors; *b)* 2D double point grid: each agent or sub-environment can be located in a discrete 2D double point position in the grid; *c)* 3D continuous grid: each agent or sub-environment can be located in a 3D floating point grid

3 Framework Evaluation

The design of the multi-environment framework here proposed and its coordination component is the result of many iterative cycles of designing and refactoring. We have been developing self-organizing systems in different domain areas with the goal to develop a novel and suitable software engineering for these types of systems. Our main application areas are: distributed autonomic computing and biological systems.

Autonomic Application Networking. The autonomic application networking provides a platform that aids developing and deploying network applications by providing reusable software components. These components abstract low-level operating and networking details (e.g. I/O and concurrency), and provide network applications with a series of runtime services. We want to achieve two macro properties: scalability and adaptation.

Each application service and middleware platform is modeled as a biological entity, analogous to an individual ant in an ant colony. An application service is designed as an autonomous and distributed software *agent*, which implements a functional service and follows simple biological behaviors such as replication, death, migration and energy exchange. In this way, agents may implement a grid application or Internet data center application on a wired network.

A middleware platform is a *non-situated sub-environment*. It runs on a network host and operates agents (application services). Each platform implements a set of runtime services that agents use to perform their services and behaviors, and follows biological behaviors such as replication, death and energy exchange. Similar to biological entities, agents and platforms in our case study store and expend energy for living. Each agent gains energy in exchange for rendering its service to other agents or human users, and expends energy to use network and computing resources. Each platform gains energy in exchange for providing resources to agents, and continuously evaporates energy to the network environments. Agents expend more energy more often when receiving more energy from users. Platforms expend more energy more often when receiving more energy from agents. An abundance of stored energy indicates higher demand for the agent/platform; thus the agent/platform may be designed to favor replication in response to higher energy level. A scarcity of stored energy (an indication of lack of demand) may cause the death of the agent/platform.

The exchange energy behavior drives all other behaviors. The exchange energy behavior of the application service AS is *coordinated* with the exchange energy behavior of the platform P: whenever the AS stores or releases energy, P also perceives and stores or releases energy. And whenever one of them is in a higher demand, they fire an *emission type event* that will activate the respective replication behaviors, contributing to a positive feedback loop.

Automated Guided Vehicles. Regarding the well known Automated Guided Vehicles (AGV) case study, an AGV warehouse transportation system uses multiple computer guided vehicles AGVs, which move loads (e.g. packets, materials) in a warehouse. Each AGV can only carry out a limited set of local actions such as move, pick up load, and drop load. The goal is to efficiently transport incoming loads to their destination. The AGV problem is dynamic: many lay-outs, loads arrive at any moment, AGVs move constantly and fail, obstacles and congestion might appear, etc. AGV movement should result in feedback with each other and the environment.

Each station is a *non-situated environment*. Therefore, there are three different types of sub-environments in the main environment, which is a *situated 2D environment* and manages the factory layout where the stations are. The vehicles are *agents* that move from one station to another in the *main environment*.

The dispatching and routing requires a mechanism that enables aggregation and calculation of extra information while flowing through intermediate stations. The *gradient fields pattern* allows the pick up stations to generate gradients while they have loads to be delivered and the intermediate stations also propagate them with information about obstacles and congestions. And the agents follow the gradient.

For instance, at the implementation level, when a pickup station (PS) executes the *Pick Up Behavior* and is dispatching loads, it fires the *load_gradient emission event*, which is *propagated* in the environment. The PS station remains in the dispatching load state while a vehicle does not pick up the load. On the other hand, a vehicle is following the *load_gradient event* propagated by the environment. When it finds a different load gradient, it decides which one to follow according to distance and to avoid obstacles. Once the vehicle chooses one load, it follows the gradient through the intermediate stations until reaching the pick up station. When the vehicle is at the pick up station, it picks up the load to be routed to one drop off station and fires the *AGV_pick_up_load* reaction event. The PS station thus reacts to this event looking for more loads to dispatch. This feedback loop is executed while there are loads to be dispatched.

Stem Cells. In developmental biology, cellular differentiation is the process by which a less specialized cell becomes a more specialized cell type [12],[13],[14]. The stem cells can be specialized into several kinds of cells, such as heart cells, skin cells or nerve cells. We are interested in the case of a stem cell that differentiates into a mature neuron.

In the computational model, there are three kinds of cells: multi-potent cells are cells with a high power of differentiation that can give rise to several other cell types; neuron progenitor cells are cells able to self-differentiate into a neuron; and non-neuron progenitor cells are cells able to self-differentiate into any kind of cell but neuron's types.

The simulator presents the macro scale to the users by means of a visualization area (3D) [15] that represents the niche where the cells evolve in their life-cycles. In another scale, each phase of cell life-cycle has a 3D graphical representation (Figure 2), presenting the state of the main entities involved in the process. These graphical representations, besides presenting a phase of the life-cycle, show the capacity of differentiation of the cell by means of colors.

The niche is the *main environment* and manages and regulates a *3D continuous space*. Each protein and intracellular entity is a *3D agent*. Each cell is a *3D sub-environment* and contains the intracellular entities. One novel behavior in this computational model is how the cells perceive the environment, i.e., the neighbor's cells, proteins, etc. If the protein is in a specific radius scope, then the cells attract the protein to its surface and the protein is bound to the cell until the specific regulatory network inside the cell is activated. Once it is activated, the protein leaves the cell and becomes inactive. Only active proteins can be bound. The intracellular entities must perceive each other and, if the protein is inactive, i.e., not bound to any other substance or inactive or truncated, then it can bind. The rules for binding vary according to the physicochemical attraction reactions specified for each entity.

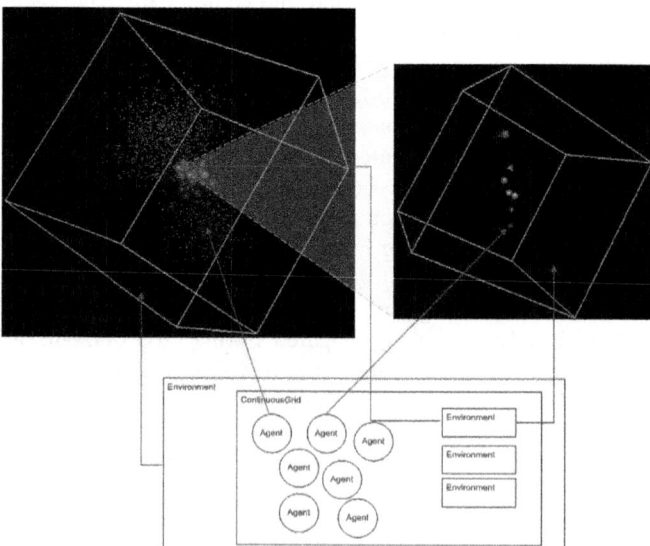

Fig. 3. The Stem Cell multi-environment case study. Each cell is a 3D situated sub-environment with entities (agents) running on it.

For instance, when *Cyclin D* – which is an intracellular entity – is inactive, if it perceives the *event synthesize_cyclin_D*, it executes the action *activate_cyclin_D* as a reaction. Then it changes its state to active, and fires an event *cyclin_D_synthesized* to the environment. Once the *CDK2* is active, it perceives the last event and changes its state to *BINDED TO CYCLIN*. The same happens to the Cyclin. Once bound, they enable the activation of the CDK-Cyclin complex behavior that regulates the cell cycle.

In order to model the 3D spatial self-organization [15] of the stem cells, we must find an empty space among its neighbors that minimizes the cell effort. Pushing the smallest amount of neighbor cells minimizes the cell effort. Thus, it can be accomplished by choosing the nearest empty space in its neighborhood followed by the pushing behavior. The problem was reduced to the 3D Nearest Neighbor problem [17], which is well studied in the field of Computational Geometry combined with the strategy similar to a Ray Tracing technique [16].

Framework Performance

Regarding the stem cell domain – which is the most complex case study - in order to achieve an increase in order, thousand of agents have to be running at the same time. A computer with the following features was used: Intel(R) Core (TM) 2 CPU T5200@ 1.60 GHz, 2GB of RAM. We executed the simulation in a 3D grid with dimensions 50×50×50 that allows visualizations of up to 100,000 cells and 500,000 extra cellular proteins. For the case for the cell visualization, we need less than 100 entities.

Our current solution does not take advantage of a parallel computation environment, although we are working on the problem [18],[19]. Even though the number of cells running together and the time of execution in the simulation for a single computer were satisfactory, we need to increase this number and to achieve this goal we are distributing the framework and application in a cluster architecture with eight QUAD CORE Q9300 processors.

4 Related Work

There are two categories for environment related work: those that emphasize the agent component and downplay the environment [20-21],[23-25], and those that consider the environment an important component of the system and decouple it from the agents. The former does not fully value an environment as a first order entity. For instance, in Jade [21], the agent environment is reduced to a mechanism for passing messages around to other agents, such as matchmakers and brokers. This is also the norm in the FIPA standard [22].

Several researchers have shown that coordination through an environment has interesting properties: Mamei et al. [26] provide an environment that allows agents to coordinate their movements in a mobile network; Parunak [27] describes several optimization algorithms for which an environment is needed; Brueckner [28] has developed an environment for the application of ant algorithms in manufacturing control; coordination of parallel processes (agents) through tuplespaces [29] can be seen as early (and ongoing) work to provide an environment wherein agents can interact.

A recent work [30], [31] evaluated five tools that acknowledge the importance of the environment in a multi-agent-based simulation system. These are NetLogo [32], MASON [5-7], Ascape [33-36], RePastS [37], and DIVAs [39].

5 Conclusions and Future Work

The design of the multi-environment framework here proposed and its coordination component is the result of many iterative cycles of designing and refactoring. As a result we think that the framework is both easy to learn and expressive at the same time. Regarding a situated environment, the coordination is achieved using a neighborhood in 2D/ 3D and a discrete/continuous grid. Another main contribution of the framework consists of providing reusable self-organizing mechanisms to be instantiated and the flexibility to evolve the framework with more complex ones. To date, the literature does not present any architectural self-organizing pattern reuse at implementation level.

There are also two features currently being developed in the framework: an autonomic experimental verification which uses online planners [40], and a transparent middleware for parallelization and distribution in a cluster using a virtual space [18-19]. The experimental autonomic verification method may autonomously analyze the emergent behavior and would be used to eventually refine the models as design feedback.

Acknowledgments. This work was supported by MCT/CNPq through the *"Grandes Desafios da Computação no Brasil: 2006-2016"* (Main Computational Challenges in Brazil: 2006-2016) Project (Proc. CNPq 550865/2007-1).

References

1. Di Marzo Serugendo, G., Gleizes, M.-P., Karageorgos, A.: Self-organization in multi-agent systems. The Knowledge Engineering Review 20(2), 165–189 (2005)
2. Visser, A., Pavlin, G., van Gosliga, S.P., Maris, M.: Self-organization of multi-agent systems. In: Proc. of the International workshop Military Applications of Agent Technology in ICT and Robotics, The Hague, the Netherlands (November 23-24, 2004)
3. Di Marzo Serugendo, G., Fitzgerald, J.S., Romanovsky, A., Guelfi, N.: Generic Framework for the Engineering of Self-Adaptive and Self-Organising Systems. CS-TR-1018 (2007)
4. Mamei, M., Menezes, R., Tolksdorf, R., Zambonelli, F.: Case studies for self-organization in computer science. J. Syst. Archit. 52(8), 443–460 (2006)
5. MASON George Mason University,
   http://cs.gmu.edu/_eclab/projects/mason/
6. MASON documentation,
   http://cs.gmu.edu/~eclab/projects/mason/docs/#docs
7. Luke, S., Cioffi-Revilla, C., Panait, L., Sullivan, K.: MASON A New Multi-Agent Simulation Toolkit, Department of Computer Science and Center for Social Complexity. In: Proceedings of SwarmFest, Michigan, USA (2004)

8. Gardelli, L., Viroli, M., Omicini, A.: Design Patterns for Self-Organizing Multiagent Systems. In: 2nd Int. Workshop on Eng. Emergence in Decentralised Autonomic Systems (EEDAS 2007), To be held at the 4th IEEE Int. Conf. on Autonomic Computing (ICAC 2007), Jacksonville, Florida, USA, June 11 (2007)
9. De Wolf, T.: Analysing and engineering self-organising emergent applications, Ph.D. Thesis, Department of Computer Science, K.U. Leuven, Leuven, Belgium, p. 183 (May 2007)
10. Weyns, D., Boucké, N., Holvoet, T.: A field-based versus a protocol-based approach for adaptive task assignment. AAMAS 17(2), 288–319 (2008)
11. Gamma, E., Helm, R., Johnson, R., Vlissides, J.: Design Patterns: Elements of Reusable Object-Oriented Software. Addison-Wesley, Reading (1995)
12. Loeffler, M., Grossmann, B.: J. Theor. Biol. 150(2), 175–191 (1991)
13. Loeffler, M., Roeder, I.: Cells Tissues Organs 171(1), 8–26 (2002)
14. Lord, B.I.: Stem cells, pp. 401–422. Cambridge Academic Press, London (1997)
15. Faustino, G.M., Gatti, M.A.C., Bispo, D., de Lucena, C.J.P.: A 3D Multi-Scale Agent-based Stem Cell Self-Organization. In: SEAS 2008 - Fourth Workshop on Software Engineering for Agent-Oriented Systems, Capinas. XXV SBES (2008)
16. Glassner, A.: An Introduction to Ray Tracing. Academic Press, London (1989)
17. Smid, M.: Closest-Point Problems in Computational Geometry. In: Sack, J.-R., Urrutia, J. (eds.) Handbook of Computational Geometry, ch. 20, pp. 877–935. North-Holland, Amsterdam (2000)
18. Motta, P., de Gatti, M.A.C., de Lucena, C.J.P.: Towards a Transparent Middle\ware for Self-Organizing Multi-Agent Systems on Clusters. In: The Third International Workshop on Massively Multi-Agent Systems: Models, Methods and Tools (MMAS 2009) at AAMAS 2009 (2009)
19. Valeriano, A., Motta, P., Gatti, M., Lucena, C.: Requisitos Funcionais para um Midleware Paralelo e Distribuído de Sistemas Multi-Agentes Auto-Organizáveis. Monografias em Ciência da Computação, DI, PUC-Rio (2009)
20. Giunchiglia, F., et al.: The tropos software methodology: Processes, models and diagrams. Technical Report Techincal Report No. 0111-20, ICT - IRST (2001)
21. Bellifemine, F., Poggi, A., Rimassa, G.: Jade, A FIPA-compliant Agent Framework. In: Proceedings of PAAM 1999, London, UK (1999)
22. FIPA: Foundation for intelligent physical agents, http://www.fipa.org/
23. DECAF, http://www.cis.udel.edu/~decaf/
24. Graham, J., Windley, V., McHugh, D., McGeary, F., Cleaver, D., Decker, K.: Tools for Developing and Monitoring Agents in Distributed Multi Agent Systems. In: Workshop on Agents in Industry at the Fourth International Conference on Autonomous Agents, Barcelona, Spain (June 2000)
25. JACK: Documentation, http://www.agentsoftware.com/products/jack/documentation_and_instructi/jack_documentation.html
26. Mamei, M., Zambonelli, F.: Self-maintained distributed tuples for field-based coordination in dynamic networks. In: The 19th Symposium on Applied Computing, SAC 2004 (2004)
27. Parunak, V.: Go to the Ant: Engineering principles from natural multi-agent systems. Annals of Operations Research 75, 69–101 (1997)
28. Brueckner, S.: Return from the Ant - Synthetic Ecosystems for Manufacturing Control. PhD thesis, Humboldt University Berlin (2000)
29. Omicini, A., Zambonelli, F., Klusch, M., Tolksdorf, R. (eds.): Coordination of Internet Agents: Models, Technologies, and Applications. Springer, Heidelberg (2001)

30. Arunachalam, S., Zalila-Wenkstern, R., Steiner, R.: Environment Mediated Multi-Agent Simulation Tools: A Comparison. In: Proc. of IEEE Workshop on Environment-Mediated Coordination in Self-Organizing and Self-Adaptive Systems, Venice, Italy, October 20-24 (2008)
31. Railsback, S.F., Lytinen, S.L., Jackson, S.K.: Agent based Simulation Platforms: Review and Development Recommendations. Simulation 82 (2006)
32. Wilensky, U.: NetLogo for Connected Learning and Computer-Based Modeling, Northwestern University. Evanston, IL,
    http://ccl.northwestern.edu/netlogo/Center
33. Ascape, http://ascape.sourceforge.net/index.html
34. Ascape documentation,
    http://ascape.sourceforge.net/index.html/#Documentation
35. Parker, M.T.: What is Ascape and Why Should You Care. Journal of Artificial Societies and Social Simulation 4(1) (January 2001)
36. Inchiosa, M.E., Parker, M.T.: Overcoming design and development challenges in agent-based modeling using ASCAPE. Proceedings of National Academy of Sciences (PNAS) of United States of America 99 (May 2002)
37. RePastS, http://repast.sourceforge.net/
38. North, M.J., Tatara, E., Collier, N.T., Ozik, J.: Visual Agent-based Model Development with Repast Simphony. In: Proc. of the Agent 2007 Conf. on Complex Interaction and Social Emergence, Argonne National Laboratory, Argonne, IL USA (November 2007)
39. Mili, R.Z., Steiner, R., Oladimeji, E.: DIVAs: Illustrating an Abstract Architecture for Agent-Environment Simulation Systems. Multi agent and Grid Systems, Special Issue on Agent-oriented Software Development Methodologies 2(4) (2006)
40. Soares, B.C.B.A., Gatti, M.A.C., Lucena, C.J.P.: Towards Verifying and Optimizing Self-Organizing Systems through an Autonomic Convergence Method. In: The Fourth Workshop on Software Engineering for Agent-Oriented Systems, Capinas, XXV SBES (2008)

Software Development Process Simulation: Multi Agent-Based Simulation versus System Dynamics

Redha Cherif and Paul Davidsson

School of Computing, Blekinge Institute of Technology, SE-372 25, Karlskrona, Sweden
and
School of Technology, Malmö University, SE-205 06, Malmö, Sweden
redha@telia.com, paul.davidsson@bth.se

Abstract. We present one of the first actual applications of Multi Agent-Based Simulation (MABS) to the field of software process simulation modelling (SPSM). Although there are some recent attempts to do this, we argue that these fail to take full advantage of the agency paradigm. Our model of the software development process integrates individual-level performance, cognition and artefact quality models in a common simulation framework. In addition, this framework allows the implementation of both MABS and System Dynamics (SD) simulators using the same basic models. As SD is the dominating approach within SPSM, we are able to make relevant and unique comparisons between it and MABS. This enabled us to uncover quite interesting properties of these approaches, e.g., that MABS reflects the problem domain more realistically than SD.

Keywords: MABS application, Software Development Process, System Dynamics.

1 Introduction

Software process simulation modelling (SPSM) is an approach to analysing, representing and monitoring a software development process phenomenon. It addresses a variety of such phenomena, from strategic software management to software project management training [13], including a number of different activities, e.g., requirements specification, programming, testing, and so on. Simulation is a means of experimentation, and so is SPSM. Such experimentation attempts to predict outcomes and improve our understanding of a given software development process. While controlled experiments are too costly and time consuming [15] SPSM carries the hope of providing researchers and software managers with "laboratory-like" conditions for experimenting with software processes. There are numerous techniques that can be used in SPSM. Kellner et al. [13] enumerate a number of these, such as: state-based process models, discrete event simulations and system dynamics (SD) [7]. The two former are discrete in nature while the latter is continuous.

A number of SD models have been quite successful in matching real life quantitative data [4]. Most notable are those of Abdel-Hamid [1], [2], Abdel-Hamid and Madnick [3], Madachy [14], Glickman and Kopcho [8]. However, SD models represent a centralistic activity-based view that does not capture the interactions at the individual level [19]. When an activity-based view is applied to SPSM the various characteristics

G. Di Tosto and H. Van Dyke Parunak (Eds.): MABS 2009, LNAI 5683, pp. 73–85, 2010.

of the developers, that are individual in nature, are represented by group averages, such as *average productivity, average assimilation delay* and *average transfer delay*, as in [1]. Models based on these views are in effect assuming homogeneity among the developers [19], leading to difficulties [16], which may result in the model not being able to account for or explain certain facts observed in real-life. For example, Burke reported in his study [4] that one of the real-life developer teams observed, turned out to be far more efficient than anticipated by his activity based model.

Since software development is a human-intensive activity, an interest for incorporating social considerations in to SPSM models has emerged [19]. Christie and Staley [6] were among the first to introduce social issues into such models. They attempted to study how the effectiveness of human interactions affected the quality and timeliness of a Joint Application Development requirement process. For this purpose, they used a discrete event-based approach to model the organisational process, while continuous simulation was used for their social model. Integrating the continuous and the discrete models proved challenging due to the inherent difference in paradigms [6]. Burke [4] followed up by integrating societal considerations in the modelling of a high-maturity software organisation at NASA. Here too, system dynamics was used. However, as it was noted above, equation based models such as system dynamics often embody assumptions of homogeneity yielding less accurate results than those excluding such assumptions. Parunak et al. [16] summarise this in a case study comparing agent-based modelling (ABM) to equation-based modelling (EBM). Their findings are that ABMs are "most appropriate" for modelling domains characterised by being highly distributed and dominated by discrete decisions, while EBMs are more appropriate for domains that can be modelled centrally "and in which the dynamics are dominated by physical laws rather than information processing". Finally, Wickenberg and Davidsson [19], build the case for applying multi agent-based simulation (MABS) to software development process simulation. They base their arguments on a review of the field and enlist most of the shortcomings, described above: activity-based views, homogeneity assumptions and the human-intensive (thus individual) nature of software processing. Despite all these arguments in favour of MABS, consolidated by the information processing dynamics [16] of SPSM, hardly any research can be found on integrating the two.

Of the few attempts, we can mention an article by Yilmaz and Phillips [21] who present an agent-based simulation model that they use to understand the effects of team behaviour on the effectiveness and efficiency of a software organisation pursuing an incremental software process, such as the Rational Unified Process (RUP). Their research relies on organisation theory to help construct the simulation framework. This framework is then used to compare and identify efficient team archetypes as well as examine the impact of turbulence, which they describe as requirement change and employee turnover, on the effectiveness of such archetypes. While the authors use agents to represent teams of developers, their focus is articulated at the team level, not the individual one as each team is represented by a single agent. Yet, although they view teams as autonomous entities, it is our opinion that they draw only limited advantage of the agency paradigm because they are forced to rely on group averages for representing e.g. developer performance, which as explained earlier introduces false assumptions of homogeneity.

In another study Smith and Capilupp [18] apply agent-based simulation modelling to the evolution of open source software (OSS) in order to study the relation between size, complexity and effort. They present a model in which complexity is considered a hindering factor to productivity, fitness to requirement and developer motivation. To validate their model they compared its results to four large OSS projects. Their model, so far, could not account for the evolution of size in an OSS project. The model they present however is rather simplistic as both developers and requirements are modelled as agents, implemented as patches on a grid (NetLogo). This grid introduces a spatial metaphor that we find inappropriate. For example, the authors use the notion of physical vicinity to model the "chances" of a given requirement to attract a developer "passing through cyberspace". Although they speak of cyberspace, vicinity actually implies physical space. One of the strengths of the agency paradigm is that it allows designing systems using metaphors close to the problem domain, especially in presence of distributed and autonomous individuals or systems. Therefore, using physical vicinity of a requirement or a task to a bypassing individual as a measure of the probability of the individual taking interest in that task is a metaphor that in our opinion does not map well to reality suggesting an inappropriate use of agents.

1.1 Aims and Objectives

The aim of this research is to establish the appropriateness of MABS to the field of SPSM by, among other means, comparing it to SD – a well-established SPSM methodology. To reach our goal, the following objectives need to be achieved:

1. Derivation of an SDP model that takes an individual-based view of the process,
2. Implementation of this SDP model as a common simulator framework providing a fair comparison ground for both MABS and SD simulators,
3. Quantitatively and qualitatively compare MABS to SD highlighting the advantages and weaknesses of each approach.

There appears to be ground for claiming that MABS is an appropriate alternative for SPSM, probably more appropriate than SD in simulating the software process from an individual-based view. However, we are not aware of any evidence of this, as there seems not to exist any serious attempts to apply MABS to SPSM, and even less so to compare it to SD (in an SPSM context).

In order to derive an individual-based view, we need to address these questions: How do we model the individual characteristics of a software developer? How do we model a software artefact (specification, doc., code, etc.)? How is the interaction between developers and artefacts modelled? When comparing MABS and SD we focus on: Do MABS and SD actually present any significant differences in projections? What are the advantages and disadvantages of MABS with regards to SD? What aspects of the software development process is MABS or SD more appropriate for?

1.2 Approach

Our research led us to investigate a number of questions related to modelling. Our answers to these are mainly based on our analysis of the literature. As described in the next section, this provided us with a performance and cognitive model, which we adapted and completed with an artefact quality model. In section 3 the integration of these models into a simulation framework is described as well as its verification and validation using a number of methods presented in [20]. Section 4 then presents how we studied the differences between MABS and SD using this platform. For this an extensive experiment was set-up with large series of simulations. The projections were then collected and statistical characteristics of the samples were derived establishing the significance of the findings. We conclude the paper with a discussion of the results and experiences achieved, together with some pointers to future work.

2   Modelling the Individual-Based View of the Software Process

In order to derive an individual-based view of the software development process we need to identify which individual characteristics of a developer are relevant. The ones we found most relevant were performance and knowledge.

2.1   The Effort Performance Model (EPM)

Rasch and Tosi [17] presented a quite convincing model of individual performance, that we term the Effort Performance Model (EPM). Despite it dating back to the early 90s, the scope of their study (230 useable answers) and the statistical rigour used for its validation lead us to consider it for our individual-based view. Their work is based on a conceptual framework that integrates expectancy theory and goal setting theory with research on individual characteristics. Figure 1 illustrates their model.

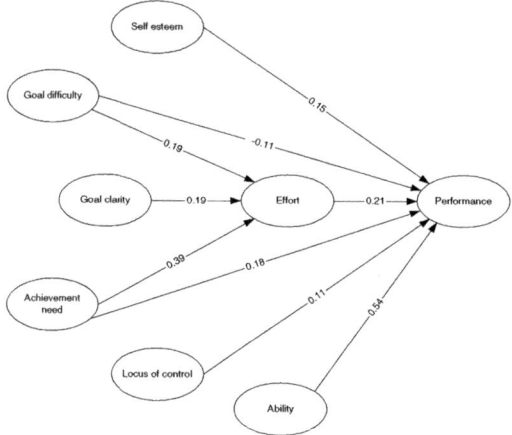

Fig. 1. The parameters affecting effort and performance as determined by Rasch and Tosi [17]

Yet EPM does not account for the experience cumulated by a developer during the execution of a task. Such gains are evident in projects that last sufficiently long and comprise a variety of challenges providing therefore opportunities to learn and improve.

2.2   The Knowledge Model (HKM)

Hanakwa et al. [9] initially presented a learning curve simulation model that relates fluctuation of a developer's knowledge of a task with the time spent working on it.

After that, a description of how to apply the model within an industrial setting was published [10], followed by an updated model [11], which considers the impact of prerequisite knowledge on knowledge gain. They quantify knowledge of a given task as the score an individual would achieve on a test evaluating her knowledge of that task. Their model consisted of three sub-models, of which only the knowledge model, which we term HKM, was relevant to our research.

According to HKM there is no knowledge gained for a developer in performing a task of which she has more knowledge than required. On the other hand, if the task requires somewhat more knowledge than available, then significant gains can be achieved but barely any if the task is too difficult i.e. current knowledge level is well below what is required. Equation (1) captures these facts (taken from [11]).

$$L_{ij}(\theta) = W_j \begin{cases} K_{ij}\, e^{-\,E_{ij}(\theta - b_{ij})} \\ b_{ij} \le \theta; 0 \\ b_{ij} > \theta; \end{cases} \tag{1}$$

Where:

$L_{ij}(\theta)$: Knowledge gained by developer i executing activity j requiring a level of knowledge θ.

K_{ij}: Maximum knowledge gain to developer i when executing task j

b_{ij}: Developer i's knowledge about activity j

E_{ij}: Developer i's downward rate of knowledge gain when executing activity j
    Required level of knowledge to execute activity j

θ

W_j Total size of activity j

At each time step t, the original knowledge level b_{ijt}, is increased by $L_{ij}(\theta)_t$:

$$b_{ijt + 1} = b_{ijt} + L_{ij}(\theta)_t \tag{2}$$

2.3 Artefact Quality Model (AQM)

Quality, as its name suggests, is hard to quantify. In our attempt, we first define a causal relation between knowledge, experience and quality of an artefact.

Knowledge provides a developer with the abstract and theoretical foundations for accomplishing a given task. Experience enhances these foundations with a practical perspective allowing one to gain awareness of the limits of certain theories or practices and the crucial importance of others. An artefact as such is the synthesis of several sub-activities carried out by probably more than one person.

The *size* of an artefact is simply the sum of all contributions. We denote c_{ij} the individual contribution of developer i on sub-activity j, such that:

$$c_{ij} = performance_{ij}\, duration_{ij} \tag{3}$$

The total size of the artefact is therefore:

$$s = \sum_{j=1}^{n} \sum_{i=1}^{d} c_{ij} \tag{4}$$

As noted earlier, we relate *quality* to ability. An artefact being a synthesis of maybe several activities, we can present an average quality q_j measure of an activity j based on the ability of its contributors in the following terms where s_j is the size of sub-activity j:

$$q_j = \sum_{i=1}^{d} ability_{ij}\, c_{ij}/s_j \tag{5}$$

Quality being a subjective matter, it is very probable that the quality of given aspects, herein modelled as activities, are more important than others depending on who's perspective is being considered. We therefore introduce a weighted sum measure of artefact quality q.

$$q = \left(\sum_{j=1}^{n} w_j\, q_j \right) \Big/ \sum_{j=1}^{n} w_j \tag{6}$$

Where w_j is a weight factor that attributes to activity j, of the artefact, the relative importance of its quality to the user (of the simulation).

2.4 Integrating the Models

Let us now explain how the EPM, HKM and AQM models are integrated. In the EPM model, *ability* is defined as a measure of native intellectual capacity and the quality of ones formal studies. Similarly HKM considers knowledge level b_{ij} to represent a measure of the knowledge of developer i for a given task j allowing us to assert:

$$Ability_{ij} = b_{ij} \tag{7}$$

The *difficulty* of a knowledge task represents its "intellectual challenge". In a sense difficulty is the difference between level of knowledge b_{ij} and the required level of knowledge θ_j for a given task j.

$$Difficulty_{ij} = \begin{cases} \theta_j - b_{ij} \\ b_{ij} < \theta_j; 0 \\ \text{otherwise} \end{cases} \tag{8}$$

A developer performs the activities of the current phase on artefacts produced in prior ones. The quality of the input artefact determines therefore the *clarity* of the task j at hand. In other words a task is only as clear as the quality of the specification/artefact defining it.

$$Clarity_j = quality(input\ artefact_j) \tag{9}$$

Having defined in (7) how ability and knowledge level of a given task are related we can rewrite our AQM equation for quality q_j of a sub activity j as:

$$q_j = \sum_{i=1}^{d} b_{ij}\, c_{ij}/s_j \qquad (10)$$

2.5 Developer/Artefact Interaction Model

The simulation framework allows the definition of each phase of a software development process in terms of its activities and the competence required for performing these. At runtime, the Manager agent orchestrates the allocation of these activities and the relevant component of the input artefact to each developer agent based on its competence or role such as architect, software engineer, tester etc. For a detailed description of the developer/artefact interaction model, please refer to [5].

3 Simulation Framework

For the purpose of comparing MABS to SD on equal grounds, we designed and implemented a common SPSM simulation framework that integrates and abstracts the above-described models (EPM, HKM and AQM). This framework allows flexible definition of the software development process (its phases, their activities and termination criterion), project participants (their role/s, individual and knowledge characteristics) and the input requirement specification (knowledge type, required knowledge level, scope estimate, and even an estimate of the quality of the scope estimation). The output of the simulator is a set of progress, knowledge gain and performance curves presented on a graphical interface. Below we briefly describe the MABS and SD simulators. For a detailed description please refer to [5].

3.1 The Multi Agent-Based Simulator

The Multi Agent-Based Simulator comprises the following agents:

Developer Agents: Each developer is modelled as a simple reactive agent employing situation action rules as its decision-making mechanism. Each agent embodies individual and knowledge characteristics (for every type of knowledge task defined in the system).

The Manager Agent: A project manager agent is used to prepare the work breakdown structure (WBS) of the requirement specification, in the initial phase. Thereafter, it converts the output artefact of a preceding phase into a set of activities to carry on in the current one. The manager is also in charge of allocating the correct type of activity to the right competence.

3.2 The System Dynamics Simulator

Similarly to the MABS simulator, the SD one runs atop the common simulator framework. The main difference resides in that individual characteristics of the developers are averaged out before being input as initial SD-level values to the SD model. Since developer characteristics are inherently individual we would like to model these as a property of each developer. Although it is possible to model as many participants as wanted, in SD, it is not possible to "instantiate" these as *models*, which means that the participants are "hard coded" into the main SD model and therefore neither their number nor their characteristics may change from one simulation to another without changing the SD model itself. Not to confuse this with an SD *variable* (level or auxiliary) that holds the number of participants, which may change dynamically. On this particular point, comparing SD to MABS resembles comparing a procedural programming language to an object-oriented one. Although it is in principle possible to "coerce" the former into the later, its underlying ideas belong to another paradigm.

3.3 Validation

Establishing the validity of a model is probably the most difficult aspect of simulation modelling, and in all likelihood full validity cannot be established. The validation methods available can only help improve confidence in a model –not guarantee it.

In our attempt, and after a number of adjustments suggested by our *face validity tests* [20] (for details see Appendix A of [5]) we became satisfied with the simulator's projections. Since our agents "sleep" and "wakeup" in a "soft" real-time fashion we needed to perform *internal validity* tests to ensure that the ensuing stochastic behaviour did not introduce significant variations into the projections. We run, therefore, a multitude of times the same simulation making adjustments until observed variances became insignificant. Given the fact that Hanakawa et al. [10] documented the outcome of three test cases (1-1, 1-2 and 1-3) and the fact that our simulator could project both duration and knowledge gains, we proceeded with so-called *Model-to-Model validation* [20] by comparing the outcomes of our simulator to the documented outcomes in Hanakawa et al [10]. Of the three cases, our simulator obtained very close results to two of them, cases 1-1 and 1-3. However, in case 1-2 a very large difference was observed. We analysed a number of related documents by Hanakawa et al. ([11], [9]) and our model to understand the reason of the discrepancy. Through this analysis we found a few shortcomings in these publications that are documented in [5]. Therefore no changes were made to accommodate case 1-2. Finally, we performed some basic *predictive validation*, i.e. testing the simulator's ability to correctly predict outcomes known to us [20]. We know, for example, that MABS and SD should not present any significant difference when simulating a single developer, as average and individual values should become equal. We therefore run 200 simulations in the range 10-60 hours and obtained no significance in difference not even at 5%. For more details please refer to [5].

Given the verification and validation steps we documented above, and the corrections and adjustments they inspired we are satisfied with the overall validity of the model so far. However, this is no guarantee that the model does not have any flaws, it only says that to the best of our efforts, *it seems as if* the model behaves in accordance with our understanding of the real-world problem.

4   Comparing MABS to SD

4.1 Experimental Comparison

First we wanted to investigate if any *statistically significant* difference in projections existed between MABS and SD. We performed a large experiment for multi-developer single-manager software projects. To ensure its statistical reliability we decided to run 1000 pairs of simulations. Each pair consisted of one SD run and one MABS run. For each simulation run, projections were systematically collected for the following variables: duration, performance, cost and quality. The project scope, i.e. the predicted effort described in the requirement specification, is the only input variable that changed for each simulation pair, in the range 100 to 1000 hours. Five developers, described in Table 1, were engaged in each of the simulations.

Table 1. Individual and knowledge characteristics of the five participants

Developer	Individual characteristics			Knowledge characteristics		
	Achievement needs (%)	Self-esteem (%)	Locus of Control (%)	bij(%)	Kij	Eij(%)
1	70	60	50	35	1	60
2	65	50	55	60	4	44.8
3	70	60	50	60	5	45
4	50	50	50	30	1	60
5	65	60	55	60	5	45

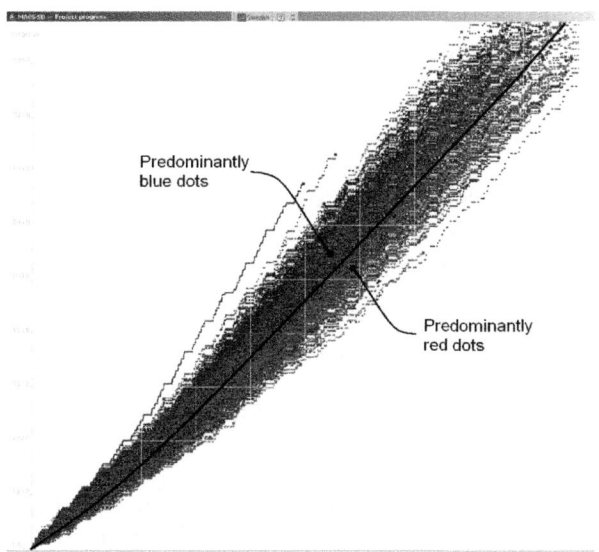

Fig. 2. The progress as a function of time passed for 1000 different MABS (in red) and SD (in blue) simulation runs. See [5] for original coloured document.

Figure 2 illustrates the output of the simulators for 1000 pairs of MABS and SD runs. The vertical axis represents the effort completed or size of artefact (in hours), while the horizontal axis represents the time spent (in hours). Red curves represent MABS simulations, while the blue ones represent SD simulations. It is worth mentioning that for each run, the SD simulation is executed first followed by MABS. Therefore, when a MABS point is plotted on an already existing SD point, that point will turn red, which explains the predominance of red. One can observe that blue

Table 2. Result of the statistical analysis of 1000 simulation pairs of MABS and SD runs with varying project scopes drawn at random in the range 100 to 1000 hours

Output variable	MABS		SD		Analysis	
	M	s	M	s	z value	p<=1%
Duration (Hours)	772.24	343.41	731.41	325.91	2.73	True
Performance (Effort/Hour,%)	72.98	8.66	77.04	6.26	-12.01	True
Cost (kSEK)	519.20	240.99	478.08	217.54	4.01	True
Quality (%)	59.82	5.35	61.49	6.82	-6.09	True

seems to dominate the upper left side, while red dominates the lower right. This suggests that SD is more optimistic in its predictions than MABS.

The following statistical analysis assumes that the output variables considered are normally distributed with regards to the input. Based on this assumption we designed our analysis around two samples: MABS and SD. For each we determined the statistical parameters: Mean (M), standard deviation (s) and then performed a z-analysis to see if any significant difference exists at $p<=1\%$ significance level. The results, as shown in Table 2, make it quite clear that the difference between the samples MABS and SD is significant for each variable.

With regards to *duration*, MABS projects larger values than SD. This suggests that either MABS overestimates or SD underestimates the duration of the project (or that one does it to a larger degree than the other). One probable explanation for this is that a project, with a quite small team, terminates only once the "slowest" developer is done, as is the case in real-life. Given the individual-based view of MABS, it easily reproduces this real-life phenomenon, while SD is unable to account for it, as it cannot represent such thing as slowest developer, having averaged all developers out. Therefore, we are inclined to believe that it is SD that underestimates the true duration, in this experiment. Consequently, for *performance* the opposite happens, i.e., suggesting that SD overestimates it. This is consistent with the previous explanation, as performance is inversely proportional to duration.

MABS forecasts a higher cost than does SD, in this experiment. Again we believe that it is SD that "faults", as it cannot account for the cost of the delay induced by the "slower" developers while MABS can.

As explained in the AQM model, we consider *quality* to be based on the knowledge level of the various contributors at the moment they contribute. This means that earlier contributions lower the quality of the artefact while later ones raise it. Given MABS more realistic approach in calculating the knowledge gain of each developer separately while SD is only approximating it for the entire team, we are more inclined to rely on the MABS projection for this variable too which is significantly lower than in SD.

4.2 Comparing Modelling Issues

During *model elicitation* for MABS purposes there are a wide variety of approaches to choose from. Quite formal methodologies, such as MAS-CommonKADS as applied in [12] can be used, yet when appropriate more informal ones can do the job. In the case of SD, however, the modeller is not as free. SD is so strongly built around the concepts of *levels* and *flows* that one starts to look almost exclusively at how these are exhibited by the system, maybe at the expense of other crucial model aspects. A system dynamic model in our opinion is not a declarative one, i.e., it does not just state relational facts (the what); it goes much further in expressing the proportions and equations governing these relations (the how). Therefore we feel that SD abstracts some modelling phase or activity. Thus, SD influences the domain problem formulation too much, forcing the modeller to view everything as levels and flows in a very early phase.

Another aspect of modelling is *model configuration and initialisation*. In our MABS case for example, we needed to define the development process and the initial values of the various knowledge and individual characteristics of the participants. For an SD simulation, besides the process definition, only group averages of the participants need be furnished. In practice, average values of such individual characteristics are more likely to be available than actual individual values, as required by MABS. Also, the collection such information is a tedious task as it involves individually interviewing or testing the persons to simulate. From this perspective SD is at an advantage.

5   Conclusions and Future Work

The main contribution of our work is having provided evidence of the appropriateness of MABS to SPSM as it is both feasible and lends itself quite neatly to the metaphors of the individual-based view.

Based on a literature review we identified, analysed and integrated an individual model of performance, a cognitive model and an artefact quality model resulting in an integrative model that made it possible to design a simulation framework for comparing MABS and SD on equal grounds. After verification and validation, which provided us with sufficient confidence in our final model, we can say that we now have an individual-based view of the software development process that accounts for what we believe to be the most important individual factors of a software developer, namely performance, experience and the quality of the artefacts to which she contributes.

Our experimental comparison of MABS and SD demonstrated MABS ability to account for realistic aspects of the SPSM problem domain that is not feasible for SD such as the actual delay incurred by a software project due to individuals with lower performance (and/or competence). In this experiment MABS was actually risk averse in comparison to SD, which averaged out low performers against high ones ignoring in its average-based projection the fact that a project is not done until the very last developer checks in its last artefact. From a modelling perspective we found that SD restricts the modeller during model elicitation unlike MABS that provides more opportunities. However, SD can do with averages unlike MABS that requires an individual-based data collection effort. Thus, the accuracy of MABS comes at an expense. Additionally we found that although MABS and SD belong to different paradigms they share common views on system complexity and emerging behaviours.

Future work should focus on empirically validating the integrated model, based on real-world case studies. Another possible extension of this work would be to include the interaction between software developers, as well as alleviating a number of shortcomings uncovered in the EPM and HKM models. EPM relies on Rotter's 15-item Internal-External (I-E) scale [22]. This scale has been challenged in a number of publications for excluding important nuances and for being susceptible to "desirability bias". While HKM's knowledge gain equation $L_{ij}(\theta)$ considers W_j to represent the size of the entire activity. i.e., the amount of work performed so far does not matter. b_{ij} is therefore the only variable that changes with time. A more intuitive use of the model would be to replace W_j by the amount of activity performed since the last update. This would reflect the experience of the developer with the task and provide a dynamic increment of the knowledge levels.

References

1. Abdel-Hamid, T.: The Dynamics of Software Development Project Management: An Integrative System Dynamics Perspective. PhD diss., MIT (1984)
2. Abdel-Hamid, T.: The Dynamics of Software Project Staffing: A System Dynamics Based Simulation Approach. IEEE Transactions on Software Engineering 15(2), 109–120 (1989)
3. Abdel-Hamid, T., Madnick, S.: Software Project Dynamics. Prentice Hall, Englewood Cliffs (1991)
4. Burke, S.: Radical Improvements Require Radical Actions: Simulating a High Maturity Software Organization. Technical Report, CMU/SEI-96-TR-024 ESC-TR-96-024, Carnegie Mellon University, Pittsburgh, Pennsylvania US (1997)
5. Cherif, M.R.: Software Process Simulation Modelling: A Multi-Agent Based Simulation. MSc Thesis, MCS-2008: 5, Blekinge Institute of Technology, Sweden (2008)
6. Christie, A.M., Staley, J.M.: Organizational and Social Simulation of a Software Requirements Development Process. In: Proceedings of the Software Process Simulation Modeling Workshop (ProSim 1999), Silver Falls, Oregon (1999)
7. Forrester, J.: System Dynamics and the Lessons of 35 Years. In: Greene, K.B.D. (ed.) Systems-Based Approach to Policymaking. Kluwer Academic Publishers, Dordrecht (1993)
8. Glickman, S., Kopcho, J.: Bellcore's Experiences Using Abdel-Hamid's Systems Dynamics Model. In: 1995 COCOMO Conference, Pittsburgh, PA, USA (1995)
9. Hanakawa, N., Morisaki, S., Matsumoto, K.: A Learning Curve Based Simulation Model for Software Development. In: Proceedings of the 20th International Conference on Software Engineering, Kyoto, Japan, pp. 350–359. IEEE Computer Society Press, Los Alamitos (1998)
10. Hanakawa, N., Matsumoto, K., Torii, K.: Application of Learning Curve Based Simulation Model for Software Development to Industry. In: Proceedings of the 11th International Conference on Software Engineering and Knowledge, Kaiserslautern, Germany, pp. 283–289. World Scientific Publishing, Singapore (1999)
11. Hanakawa, N., Matsumoto, K., Torii, K.: A Knowledge-Based Software Process Simulation Model. Annals of Software Engineering 14, 383–406 (2002)
12. Henesey, L., Notteboom, T., Davidsson, P.: Agent-based simulation of stakeholders relations: An approach to sustainable port and terminal management. In: Proceedings of the International Association of Maritime Economists Annual Conference, Busan, Korea (2003)
13. Kellner, M.I., Madachy, R.J., Raffo, D.M.: Software process simulation modeling: Why? What? How? Journal of Systems and Software 46(2-3), 91–105 (1999)
14. Madachy, R.: Process Modeling with Systems Dynamics. In: 1996 SEPG Conference, Atlantic City, NJ. Software Engineering Institute, Carnegie Mellon University (1996)
15. Myers, G.: Software Reliability: Principles and Practices. John Wiley & Sons, Chichester (1976)

16. Parunak, V.D., Savit, R., Riolo, R.: Agent-Based Modeling vs. Equation-Based Modeling: A Case Study and Users Guide. In: Sichman, J.S., Conte, R., Gilbert, N. (eds.) MABS 1998. LNCS (LNAI), vol. 1534, pp. 10–25. Springer, Heidelberg (1998)
17. Rasch, R.H., Tosi, H.: Factors affecting software developers' performance: An integrated approach. MIS quarterly 16(3), 395 (1992)
18. Smith, N., Capiluppi, A., Fernández-Ramil, J.: Agent-Based Simulation of Open Source Evolution. Software Process: Improvement and Practice 11(4), 423–434 (2006)
19. Wickenberg, T., Davidsson, P.: On Multi Agent Based Simulation of Software Development Process. In: Sichman, J.S., Bousquet, F., Davidsson, P. (eds.) MABS 2002. LNCS (LNAI), vol. 2581, pp. 171–180. Springer, Heidelberg (2003)
20. Xiang, X., Kennedy, R., Madey, G.: Verification and Validation of Agent-based Scientific Simulation Models. In: Proceedings of the 2005 Agent-Directed Simulation Symposium (ADS 2005), San Diego, CA, pp. 47–55 (2005)
21. Yilmaz, L., Phillips, J.: The Impact of Turbulence on the Effectiveness and Efficiency of Software Development Teams in Small Organizations. Software Process: Improvement and Practice 12(3), 247–265 (2007)
22. Rotter, J.B.: Generalized expectancies of internal versus external control of reinforcements. Psychological Monographs 80(609) (1966)

Agent-Based Simulations with Beliefs and SPARQL-Based Ask-Reply Communication

Ion Mircea Diaconescu and Gerd Wagner

Institute of Informatics
Brandenburg University of Technology, Germany
{M.Diaconescu,G.Wagner}@tu-cottbus.de

Abstract. This paper presents the results of extending an agent-based simulation framework by adding a full-fledged model of beliefs and by supporting ask-reply communication with the help of the W3C RDF query language *SPARQL*. Beliefs are the core component of any cognitive agent architecture. They are also the basis of ask-reply communication between agents, which allows social learning. Our approach supports the conceptual distinctions between facts and beliefs, and between sincere answers and lies.

Keywords: cognitive agent simulation, beliefs, reasoning, RDF, SPARQL.

1 Introduction and Motivation

While allowing to model many complex simulation scenarios, today's agent-based simulation systems, such as SESAM [3], REPAST [5] or NetLogo [9], do not offer much support for modeling beliefs and ask-reply communication based on beliefs. The situation is different in the area of agent programming languages. For example, in [1] a solution for automated belief revision in the language AgentSpeak [7] is presented. A powerful Java-based interpreter for an extended version of AgentSpeak is provided also as an open source project under the name of JASON [2]. But unlike cognitive agent simulation systems, agent programming languages are not concerned with the important conceptual distinction between *facts* and *beliefs*.

This paper presents a solution for modeling agent beliefs related to itself or to other agents involved in the simulation scenario, along with the required support of a belief-based ask-reply agents communication protocol. *SPARQL* [6], the standard query language for the W3C RDF [4], is used to define the query part of the ask messages. The proposed solution is obtained as an extension of the open source *Agent-Object-Relationship (AOR) Simulation* framework[1], which is an ontologically well-founded agent-based discrete event simulation framework with a high-level rule-based simulation language, *AORSL*, together with an abstract simulator architecture and execution model.

AOR Simulation offers support for the distinction between facts and beliefs by maintaining both the objective and the subjective state of an agent in parallel

---

[1] Available from http://AOR-Simulation.org

G. Di Tosto and H. Van Dyke Parunak (Eds.): MABS 2009, LNAI 5683, pp. 86–97, 2010.

using the two classes *AgentObject* and *AgentSubject*. A fact about an agent is represented by means of a slot of the corresponding instance of the AgentObject class, while a belief about the agent (called a *self-belief* in AORSL) is represented by means of a slot of the corresponding instance of the AgentSubject class.

Beliefs about objects in the environment (including other agents) cannot be represented by simple *property-value slots*, like self-beliefs, but they need to be represented by *object-property-value triples*, also called "subject-predicate-object" triples in the jargon of RDF. Therefore, we have extended AORSL by adding a construct for defining *belief entity types* as part of the definition of an agent type. A belief entity type defines a number of belief properties for expressing belief triples about an object of some type.

The concept of belief entity types allows to represent all kinds of agent beliefs about its environment, no matter what vocabulary (or ontology) the agent is using. In this way, agents could either use a shared vocabulary, or they could use their own private vocabularies, which would have to be mapped to each other for successful communication. However, in this paper, we do not consider the problems of private vocabularies and ontology mapping. For simplicity, we assume that all agents are using a shared vocabulary, including shared identifiers for all objects of the simulation scenario.

2   Introduction to AOR Simulation

AOR Simulation was proposed in [10]. It supports both basic discrete event simulations without agents and complex agent-based simulations with (possibly distorted) perceptions and (possibly false) beliefs. A simulation scenario is expressed with the help of the XML-based *AOR Simulation Language (AORSL)*. The scenario is then translated to Java source code, compiled to Java byte code and finally executed, as indicated in Figure 1.

Fig. 1. From AORSL to Java byte code

A **simulation scenario** consists of a *simulation model*, an *initial state* definition and zero or more *view* definitions.

A **simulation model** consists of: (1) an optional *space model* (needed for physical objects/agents); (2) a set of *entity types*, including different categories of event, message, object and agent types; and (3) a set of *environment rules*, which define *causality laws* governing the environmental state changes.

An **entity type** is defined by means of a set of *properties* and a set of *functions*. There are two kinds of properties: attributes and reference properties.

Attributes are properties whose range is a data type; *reference properties* are properties whose range is another entity type.

An **agent type** is defined by means of: (1) a set of (objective) *properties*; (2) a set of (subjective) *self-belief properties*; (3) a set of (subjective) *belief entity types*; and (4) a set of *agent rules*, which define the agent's reactive behavior in response to events.

A **space model** is characterized by the parameters: (1) dimension (1D, 2D or 3D); (2) discrete/continuous; (3) geometry (Euclidean or Toroidal); and (4) space limits (xMax, yMax, zMax).

The upper level **ontological categories** of AOR Simulation are objects (including agents, physical objects and physical agents), messages and events, as depicted in Figure 2. Notice that according to this upper-level ontology of AOR Simulation, agents are special objects. For simplicity it is common, though, to say 'object' instead of the unambiguous term *non-agentive object*.

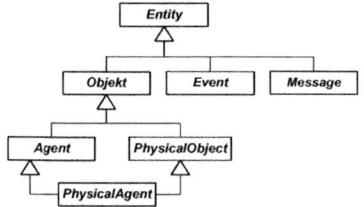

Fig. 2. Upper-level ontological categories

An elaborate ontology of **event types**, shown in Figure 3, has proven to be fundamental in AOR Simulation. Internal events are those events that happen *'in the mind'* of the agent. For modeling distorted perceptions, both a perception event type and the corresponding actual perception event type can be defined and related with each other via actual perception mapping rules.

Both the behavior of the environment (its causality laws) and the behavior of agents are modeled with the help of **rules**, thus supporting high-level declarative

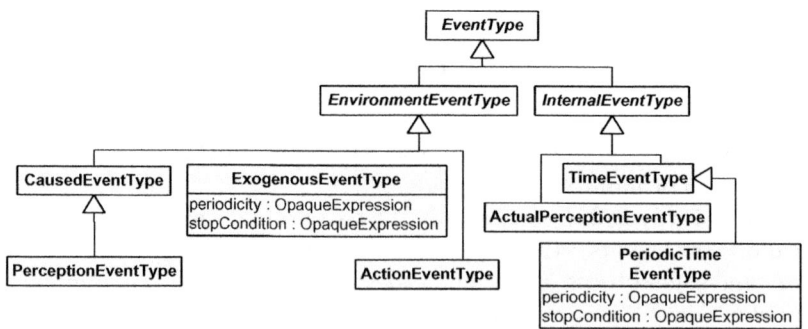

Fig. 3. Categories of event types

behavior modeling. An **environment rule** is a 5-tuple $\langle EvtT,\ Var,\ Cond,\ UpdExpr,\ ResEvtExpr \rangle$, where: (1) $EvtT$ denotes the type of event that triggers the rule; (2) Var is a set of variable declarations, such that each variable is bound either to a specific object or to a set of objects; (3) $Cond$ is a logical condition formula, allowing for variables; (4) $UpdExpr$ specifies an update of the environment state; and (5) $ResEvtExpr$ is a list of resulting events, which will be created when the rule is fired.

3   Modeling Beliefs

3.1   Self-beliefs

When defining an agent type, we can not only define its (objective) *attributes*, which are used to express fact statements about agents of that type, but we can also define its *self-belief attributes*, which are used to express belief statements of agents of that type about themselves. The following definition of an agent type *Foo* contains both kinds of attributes:

```
<AgentType name="Foo">
 <Attribute name="position" type="Float"/>
 <Attribute name="velocity" type="Float"/>
 <SelfBeliefAttribute name="position" type="Float"/>
 <SelfBeliefAttribute name="myFavoriteNumber" type="Integer"/>
</AgentType>
```

The agent type *Foo* is then implemented with the help of two classes, as shown in Figure 4:

1. The class *FooAgentObject* representing the objective state of Foo agents with the help of the attributes x (for *position*) and v (for *velocity*).
2. The class *FooAgentSubject* representing the subjective state of Foo agents with the help of the attributes x and *myFavoriteNumber*.

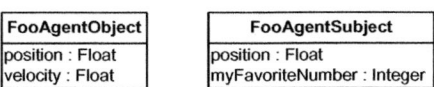

Fig. 4. An agent is divided into an object and a subject

Notice that according to this definition, Foo agents have a *position* and a *velocity*. They also have a self-belief about their position and another self-belief about their favorite number, but not about their velocity. A self-belief attribute that corresponds to an objective attribute need not have the same name. Instead of *position*, a Foo agent type definition could use another name, say *myPosition*, for expressing beliefs about their position.

In general, a fact about an agent is represented by means of a slot of the corresponding instance of the AgentObject class, while a self-belief about the agent is represented by means of a slot of the corresponding instance of the AgentSubject class.

3.2   Belief Entity Types

For defining the types of beliefs that an agent may have about the entities in its environment, *belief properties* applying to all entities of some type are grouped with the help of *belief entity types*. For instance, a belief entity type (`Castle`) may be defined for the agent type (`Knight`) in order to allow beliefs about the location of castles:

```
<PhysicalAgentType name="Knight">
 <BeliefEntityType name="Castle">
   <BeliefAttribute name="x" type="Integer"/>
   <BeliefAttribute name="y" type="Integer"/>
 </BeliefEntityType>
</PhysicalAgentType>
```

In AORSL, any entity type is defined as a class in the sense of the UML, as shown in Figure 5. Therefore, any entity type has a number of properties. Belief entity types specialize entity types, since they have a number of belief properties, which specialize properties by imposing the constraint that their domain (the entity type to which they belong) must be a belief entity type component of an agent type (called *believer type* in the metamodel shown in Figure 5). Self-belief properties specialize belief properties by imposing the constraint that their domain is the believer type (that is, they are properties of instances of the believer type).

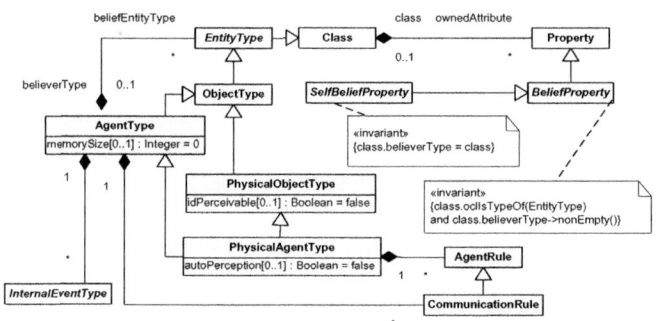

Fig. 5. Modeling agents with beliefs

3.3   Facts and Beliefs Are Represented by Triples

More precisely speaking, we do not deal with 'facts' and 'beliefs', but with *atomic fact statements* and *atomic belief statements*, each of them having the form of an *object-property-value triple*. For instance, the atomic fact statements that the positions of the Foo agents with identifiers "007" and "008" are given by x = 347.2, resp. x = 12.7, is expressed by the triples

(It's a fact that) 007 position 347.2
(It's a fact that) 008 position 12.7

while the atomic belief statement of agent "007" that its position is given by x = 346.9 is expressed by the triple

(Agent 007 beliefs that) 007 position 346.9

and the atomic belief statement of agent "007" that the position of agent "008" is given by x = 13.1 is expressed by the triple

(Agent 007 beliefs that) 008 position 13.1

In standard predicate logic syntax, such a triple corresponds to an atomic sentence where the property of the triple statement would be used as a predicate, and the object identifier and the properties value would be the arguments of this predicate, resulting in the expression:

(It's a fact that) position(007, 347.2)

As discussed below, AORSL supports the use of the W3C RDF query language SPARQL for expressing queries about the beliefs of other agents in Ask messages. RDF defines a language for expressing triples in multiple vocabularies.

3.4   Discrepancies between Fact Statements and Belief Statements

In general, we can have various types of discrepancies between fact and belief statements. The first issue is the possibility to use different languages to express statements about the same fact. Assuming that the same languages (i.e. the same names for entity types and properties and the same identifiers for individuals) are used, we still have the possibility of discrepancies between a fact statement and a corresponding belief statement with respect to the actual and the believed value of a property.

There are several types of possible discrepancies arising from different vocabularies being used. Agents may use different names for entity types and/or properties, and they may use different identifiers for individuals. There are also the issues of *partiality* and *non-correspondence*. Partiality refers to the possibility that not all 'real' entity types and properties (as defined objectively for the environment of a simulation model) have a corresponding name in the vocabulary of an agent. Non-correspondence refers to the possibility that some of the entity type and/or property names used by an agent do not correspond to a real entity type or property.

AOR Simulation allows modeling of all these kinds of discrepancies between fact and belief statements. However, we are still investigating the required inference capabilities of agents for being able to map the vocabularies of other agents to their own when they communicate with each other.

3.5   Belief Handling

An agent may create new beliefs, or it may change or destroy existing beliefs. The way an agent manages its beliefs is defined with the help of *agent rules*.

For instance, as in the scenario presented in next section, knights have beliefs about the castle and about magic objects found on the map. Since the prince may have already discovered some magic objects, when he asks a knight about the position of the next nearest magic object, he will first inform the knight about any magic objects already found. Moreover, the prince has to create new beliefs about any magic object found. The following example is an excerpt form an agent rule of the agent type Knight and a prince rule showing how beliefs may be created and destroyed.

```
<!-- the Prince creates beliefs about a discovered magic object -->
<UPDATE-AGT>
  <CreateBeliefEntity beliefEntityType="MagicObject">
    <BeliefEntityId language="Java">
      e.getPerceivedPhysicalObject().getId()
    </BeliefEntityId>
  </CreateBeliefEntity>
</UPDATE-AGT>

<!-- the Knight destroy beliefs about already discovered magic objects -->
<UPDATE-AGT>
  <DestroyBeliefEntity>
    <BeliefEntityRef beliefEntityType="MagicObject" language="Java">
      this.getBeliefEntityById(((Ask)e.getMessage()).getFoundMagicObjectId())
    </BeliefEntityRef>
  </DestroyBeliefEntity>
</UPDATE-AGT>
```

The communication between the prince and knight agent is message based. The prince sends his request via an *Ask* message and the knight replies by sending a *Reply* message. The generic Ask/Reply message types may be adapted for a specific problem domain, such as in this example, the message contains specific information about the magic object near the SPARQL query. The following example defines an *Ask* message type used by the prince when he asks a knight about the nearest magic object. The property `foundMagicObjectId` refers to the ID of an already discovered magic object:

```
<MessageType name="AskAboutMagicObject">
  <Attribute type="String" name="queryLanguage"/>
  <Attribute type="String" name="queryString"/>
  <Attribute type="Integer" name="foundMagicObjectId"/>
</MessageType>
```

One may raise the problem of IDs management for beliefs and respectively objects/agents. AORSL provides the support for expressing these IDs both as static value or via expressions. Therefore, the user does not need to remember the IDs that refers to entities involved into a simulation scenario.

4   The Simulation Scenario Test Case

A simulation scenario based on a *'quest game'* is used to exemplify and test capabilities discussed in this paper. This scenario was mainly used as a test case during this research. The used story is simple: a *Prince* wants to rescue the *Princess* kidnaped by the *Evil Demon*. First, the *Prince* has to improve his power by finding some *magic objects* on the map. Until the *Prince* has at least the same power level as the *Demon*, he will ask any found *Knight* about the position of the next *magic object*. When the power level is greater than the *Demon*'s power, he will start to ask about the position of the *Castle*.

A set of rules and axioms defines the simulation: (1) the prince has beliefs about the demon's power level; (2) while the demon's power is constant, the prince's one may be increased by finding some magic objects; (3) a constant number of magic objects providing additional power are available on the map; (4) knights are randomly distributed and they can provide the position of the castle or of the nearest magic object; (5) the map is a grid space, and the prince can move only one cell during each simulation step, in one of the four directions: E, W, S or N; (6) the prince sees a knight, a magic object, the castle or the demon when he enters in the same cell where this is placed; (7) the castle and the demon are in the same cell; (8) the prince rescues the princess only if at the moment when he discovers the castle his power level is greater than the demon's one. (9) the prince has basic learning capabilities. He tries to find *the best* moving direction when does not know yet, from a knight, where is the position of another magic object or where the castle is located.

The following scenarios are possible: (i) the castle is found before the prince has the requested power level; (ii) the prince does not find the castle before the stimulation steps are finished; (iii) the prince finds the castle, defeats the demon, rescues the princess and marries her.

5   An RDF-Based Representation for Agent Beliefs

In this section a solution to represent the beliefs of an agent as an RDF graph (a conjunction of triple statements) is presented. The main purpose of the RDF representation is to have a standard representation of beliefs, together with a standard query language (SPARQL). The main advantages of this approach are that it allows to: (1) use any SPARQL (or other RDF query answering) engine; (2) use RDF-based reasoning engines, such as Jena Rules [8] or ERDF [11] as a middleware layer between an agent's beliefs and the query level; (3) express Semantic-Web-based simulation scenarios (e.g. social networks simulations).

An AOR simulation model defines a `baseURI` attribute, with an URI value, used as a base URI for all defined RDF triples. Moreover, each `Entity` type has a unique `ID` during its life cycle. Two types of RDF triples are defined for beliefs:

1. type definition triples, (b rdf:type T), where:
   - $b = [baseURI] + "/" + [AgentType] + "/" + [BeliefType] + "/" + [ID]$;
   - $T = [baseURI] + "/" + [AgentType] + "/" + [BeliefType]$;
2. property value triples, (b prop val), where:
   - $b = [baseURI] + "/" + [AgentType] + "/" + [BeliefType] + "/" + [ID]$;
   - $prop = [baseURI] + "/" + [AgentType] + "/" + [BeliefType] + "/" + [prop\_name]$;
   - $val = Literal \quad OR \quad TypedLiteral \quad OR \quad URIRef$.

For example, having the `Castle{id=501, x=12, y=15}` beliefs for a `Knight` agent, and `baseURI = 'http://aor.org/KK'`, the following RDF triples are generated :

```
http://aor.org/KK/Knight/Castle/501 rdf:type http://example.com/KK/Knight/Castle;
                              http://aor.org/KK/Knight/Castle/x "12"^^xs:integer;
                              http://aor.org/KK/Knight/Castle/x "15"^^xs:integer.
```

6   Querying Beliefs with SPARQL

In this scenario, the `Prince` has to ask `Knights` about the position of a *magic object* or the position of the *Castle*. Ask/Reply messages are used for communication. The *request message* encapsulates the SPARQL query and the ID of the already found magic object. The *response message* contains the position of the requested onject, as known by the *Knight*.

```
<OutMessageEventExpr messageType="AskAboutMagicObject">
  <ReceiverIdRef language="Java">e.getPerceivedPhysicalObjectIdRef()</ReceiverIdRef>
  <Slot xsi:type="aors:SimpleSlot" property="queryLanguage" value="SPARQL"/>
  <Slot xsi:type="aors:SimpleSlot" property="queryString"
        value="SELECT ?x ?y WHERE {?c rdf:type :MagicObjectBelief;:x ?x;:y ?y.}"/>
  <Slot xsi:type="aors:SimpleSlot" property="foundMagicObjectId">
    <ValueExpr language="Java">prince.getBeliefEntityByType(0).getId()</ValueExpr>
  </Slot>
</OutMessageEventExpr>
```

The default (and built-in) namespace (expressed as `:`) represents the value of `baseURI` attribute and the agent type (e.g. `http://aor.org/KK/Knight/`).

The `Knight` replies with an *Reply* message containing the position of the nearest *Magic Object*.

```
<OutMessageEventExpr messageType="ReplyAboutTheMagicObject">
  <ReceiverIdRef language="Java">e.getSenderIdRef()</ReceiverIdRef>
  <Slot xsi:type="aors:OpaqueExprSlot" property="messageReference">
    <ValueExpr language="Java">(int)e.getMessage().getId()</ValueExpr>
  </Slot>
  <Slot xsi:type="aors:OpaqueExprSlot" property="answer">
    <ValueExpr language="Java">
    knight.computeAnswer(((Ask)e.getMessage()).getQueryString(),
                    ((Ask)e.getMessage()).getFoundMagicObjectId())
    </ValueExpr>
  </Slot>
</OutMessageEventExpr>
```

Queries are processed by calling the appropriate `executeQuery(queryString)` method. A `Map` that contains all query solutions is provided as result. Concrete values of a solution are extracted by using the corresponding keys, these being the names of the variables used in the SPARQL query. It is the decision of the programmer what to do with the results and what are the actions performed depending on them. There is a work in progress to automatically process standard message types and to automatically reply to them. These are provided as builtin rules for standard agents types.

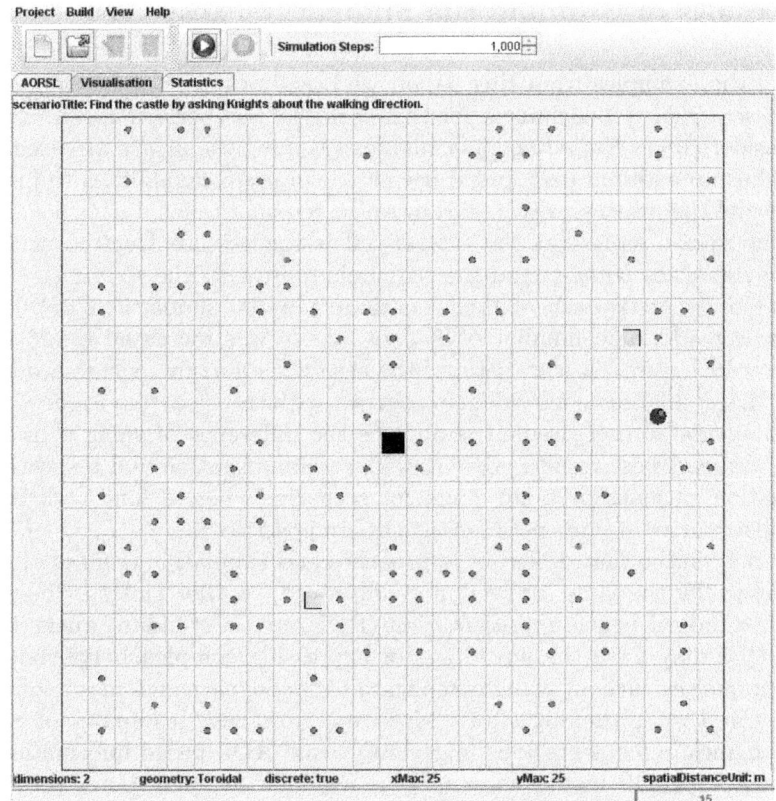

Fig. 6. Knights&Knaves visualisation

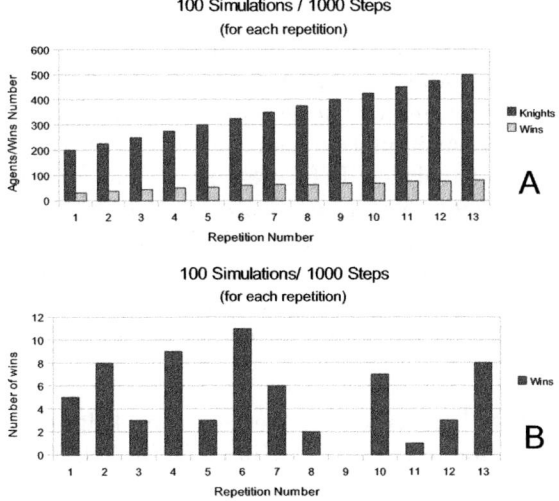

Fig. 7. Knights&Knaves Statistics - (A) With Knights; (B) Without Knights

7   Results of Running the Simulation Test Case

Most of the examples from this paper are based on the *Knights&Knaves* simulation scenario. A benchmark for this scenario was performed and two cases are considered: (1) *Knight* agents capable of helping the *prince* are used; (2) the *prince* has no external help and it uses it's own *basic* capabilities to find magic objects and the princess. Figure 6 shows a screen-shot taken during a simulation. The blue square represents the *Castle*, yellow squares are *Magic Objects*, green circles symbolizes *Knights* and the red circle represents the *Prince*.

A set of 13 tests, each of them consisting in 100 simulations of 1000 steps each, was made. The number of *Knight* agents was increased by 25 for each new test. In Figure 7A a statistic of the case when `Knight` agents are available during the simulation is provided, in contrast with the case from Figure 7B where `Knight` agents are not used. It is obvious the difference of game wins between the two cases. These results prove that the communication and respectively the information exchange is a key point for scenarios where a final task is defined and collaborative actions between agents are possible.

One may argue that, different approaches and simulation engines of this scenario may offer the same (or even more improved) results. This may be true, but using a standard beliefs representation (RDF) and a standard query language (SPARQL) may have the advantage of expressing complex belief models and complex queries without using complicate technologies which may require more learning and programming effort. Moreover, nowadays a number of SPARQL query engines implementations (e.g. ARQ[2]) and RDF based information representation (e.g. RDF models in Jena[3]) are available as open source projects.

8   Conclusions and Future Work

We have presented a solution for dealing with a full-fledged model of beliefs in agent-based simulation. Moreover, we have shown how the RDF query language SPARQL can be used for implementing a model of ask-reply communication between cognitive agents. A simulation scenario dealing with these new capabilities has been described and analyzed. In future work we will turn the Java-based communication code into more high-level constructs that extend the current version (0.7) of our simulation language AORSL. Another important step in our research is to integrate an inference engine as a middle layer between the RDF triples representation and SPARQL queries. This requires to define a representation of production and/or derivation rules as a further extension of AORSL.

Acknowledgments. Thanks to Jens Werner for his help provided to implement these improvements, and to Dr. Adrian Giurca for his helpful advice and support.

---

[2] ARQ Web Page - http://jena.sourceforge.net/ARQ/
[3] Jena Web Page - http://jena.sourceforge.net/

References

1. Alechina, N., Bordini, R.H., Hübner, J.F., Jago, M., Logan, B.: Automating belief revision for agentspeak. In: Baldoni, M., Endriss, U. (eds.) DALT 2006. LNCS (LNAI), vol. 4327, pp. 1–16. Springer, Heidelberg (2006)
2. Bordini, R.H., Hübner, J.F., Wooldridge, M.: Programming Multi-Agent Systems in AgentSpeak Using Jason. John Wiley and Sons, Ltd., Chichester (2007)
3. Kluegl, F., Puppe, F.: The Multi-Agent Simulation Environment SeSAm. In: Proceedings of Workshop Simulation in Knowledge-based Systems (Report tr-ri-98-194, Reihe Informatik, Universität Paderborn) (1998)
4. Klyne, G., Caroll, J.J.: Resource Description Framework (RDF): Concepts and Abstract Syntax. W3C Recommendation, February 10 (2004), http://www.w3.org/TR/rdf-concepts/
5. North, M.J., Howe, T., Collier, N., Vos, J.R.: The Repast Simphony Development Environment. In: Proceedings of the Agent 2005 Conference on Generative Social Processes, Models, and Mechanisms, ANL/DIS-06-5, pp. 159–166. Argonne National Laboratory and The University of Chicago (2005)
6. Prud'hommeaux, E., Seaborne, A.: SPARQL Query Language for RDF (November 2007), http://www.w3.org/TR/rdf-sparql-query/
7. Rao, A.S.: AgentSpeak(L): BDI agents speak out in a logical computable language. In: Perram, J., Van de Velde, W. (eds.) MAAMAW 1996. LNCS (LNAI), vol. 1038, pp. 42–55. Springer, Heidelberg (1996)
8. Reynolds, D.: Jena Rules experiences and implications for rule use cases. In: W3C Workshop on Rule Languages for Interoperability (2005)
9. Tisue, S., Wilensky, U.: NetLogo: Design and implementation of a multi-agent modeling environment. In: Proceedings of 8th Annual Swarm Users/Researchers Meeting, Ann Arbor, MI, May 9-11 (2004)
10. Wagner, G.: Aor modelling and simulation - towards a general architecture for agent-based discrete event simulation. In: Giorgini, P., Henderson-Sellers, B., Winikoff, M. (eds.) AOIS 2003. LNCS (LNAI), vol. 3030, pp. 174–188. Springer, Heidelberg (2004)
11. Wagner, G., Giurca, A., Diaconescu, I.-M., Antoniou, G., Analyti, A., Damasio, C.V.: Reasoning on the Web with Open and Closed Predicates. In: de Bruijn, J., Heymans, S., Pearce, D., Polleres, A., Ruckhaus, E. (eds.) Proceedings of the 3rd International Workshop on Applications of Logic Programming to the (Semantic) Web and Web Services (ALPSWS 2008), Udine, Italy (December 2008); CEUR Workshop Proceedings

Stigmergic Modeling of Hierarchical Task Networks*

H. Van Dyke Parunak[1], Theodore Belding[1], Robert Bisson[1], Sven Brueckner[1],
Elizabeth Downs[1], Rainer Hilscher[2], and Keith S. Decker[3]

[1] Vector Research Center, TTGSI, 3520 Green Court, Suite 250
Ann Arbor, MI 48105 USA
{van.parunak,ted.belding,robert.bisson,sven.brueckner,
liz.downs}@newvectors.net
[2] Altarum Institute, 3520 Green Court, Suite 300, Ann Arbor, MI 48105 USA
rainer.hilscher@altarum.org
[3] University of Delaware, 444 Smith Hall, Newark, DE 19716 USA
Decker@cis.udel.edu

Abstract. Stigmergy is usually used to model semantically simple problems
such as routing. It can be applied to more complex problems by encoding them
in the stigmergic environment. We demonstrate this approach by showing how
stigmergic agents can plan over a hierarchical task network, specifically a
resource-oriented dialect of the TÆMS language.

Keywords: Stigmergy, HTN, TÆMS, Planning, Scheduling, Interaction.

1 Introduction

Stigmergy, in which agents coordinate actions by making and sensing changes to a
shared environment, is often applied to routing problems. Agents deposit digital
markers analogous to insect pheromones in the environment. The environment aggre-
gates deposits from different agents (fusing information), propagates them to nearby
locations (coupling local actions with global objectives), and evaporates them (dis-
carding obsolete information). Agents base decisions on a function of nearby pheromone strengths. For example, an agent representing a network packet may climb a
pheromone gradient to find the most efficient path to its destination.

The semantics of route planning are fairly constrained, and stigmergy is usually
considered a low-level form of cognition [13]. But this semantic constraint really says
more about the nature of a flow network than of stigmergic interaction. In general,
stigmergy is applicable to any problem that can be represented as a topology in which
agents are localized. One can imagine using stigmergy to coordinate agent behaviors
on a network that embeds much more complex semantics. Stigmergy can transfer
cognition from the agents to the environment. A cognitively rich environment can
yield cognitively complex outcomes among relatively simple agents, as in Simon's
parable of the ant [15].

---

* This research was conducted with the support of the office of Naval Research (Contract #
N00014-06-1-0467). The results presented do not necessarily reflect the opinion of the
sponsor.

G. Di Tosto and H. Van Dyke Parunak (Eds.): MABS 2009, LNAI 5683, pp. 98–109, 2010.
© Springer-Verlag Berlin Heidelberg 2010

Higher cognition is usually considered necessary for coordinated execution of complex tasks. For example, the treatment plan for a hospital patient has both internal relationships (some tests must be done in a particular order or within certain time limits) and external relationships between treatment plans (only one MRI machine exists; certain ancillary hospital units prefer to run similar tests in batches to reduce set-up times, etc.) [5]. Another example is the coordination of pre-planned activities in dynamic environments such as military, law-enforcement, or disaster planning scenarios [3]. Several law-enforcement units may wish to surprise suspects simultaneously at different locations so they cannot warn each other. Besides coordinating the surprise itself, some units may require equipment or information whose delivery time is not known in advance. The structure of such tasks can be represented as a graph, specifically, a hierarchical task network or HTN.

The usual approach to such scenarios is to give complex agents an internal representation of their own plans (and how they relate to the plans of other agents). Examples include CSC agents [7], or unrolling each agent's view of the HTN into a Markov decision process [8], or translating it into a Simple Temporal Network [16]. We take a different approach. Rather than putting the HTN inside complex agents, we put stigmergic agents inside the HTN. Coordination is achieved, not by dialogs based on each agent's individual analysis of the HTN, but by means of interactions among the agents mediated by the structure of the HTN itself.

The motivation for this alternative approach to reasoning over HTN's is twofold. Theoretically, it shows how stigmergy can be applied to cognitively complex problems. Practically, by turning the problem inside out, stigmergy permits the analysis of HTN's that are much too large to be analyzed using classical approaches.

This paper demonstrates stigmergy on an HTN, in a dialect of the TÆMS task language [6]. Section 2 reviews TÆMS and the rTÆMS dialect, which emphasizes the importance of resources in coordination. Section 3 shows how to apply stigmergy to an rTÆMS graph (along the way analyzing some "obvious" approaches that do not work). Section 4 reports experiments that demonstrate this approach for single-agent planning. Section 5 discusses the relative virtues of stigmergic and more complex agents in reasoning over HTN's, and outlines future work. Section 6 concludes.

2   TÆMS and rTÆMS

A hierarchical task network (HTN) is a collection of events, with two kinds of relations among them: a hierarchical structure relating tasks to subtasks, and constraints on the order of execution among the tasks.

2.1   Introduction to TÆMS

Fig. 1 illustrates TÆMS on the dining philosophers problem.

- Ovals ("Argue," "Think$_1$") are *tasks* and *subtasks*. Tasks and subtasks may be associated with one or many agents, and can be further subdivided.
- Rectangles ("Eat$_1$") are *methods*, which are the lowest level of activity. Each method is associated with a single agent.

- Labeled arcs between methods ("Facilitates") are *non-local effects* (NLE's), which capture precedence constraints.
- Inverted triangles ("Forks") are *resources*, which methods produce and consume.

Curved lines show the subgraphs accessible to each agent, their *subjective* graphs. The overall graph, describing the complete problem, is the *objective* graph.

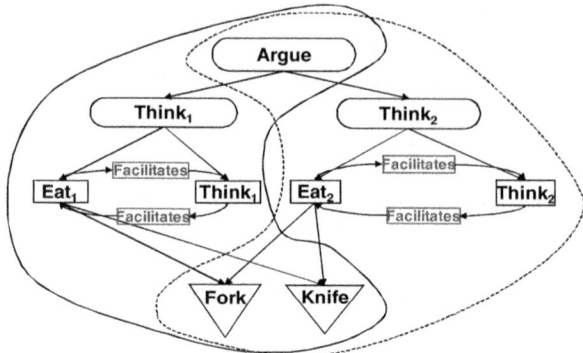

Fig. 1. Agents Interact through Resources. Both agents must access a knife and a fork in order to eat

A method's execution produces quality that flows up to its dominant subtasks and tasks. Each task or subtask has a Quality Accumulation Function (QAF), providing a more nuanced way to capture what other HTN's represent as AND and OR branches. For example, a Min QAF says that the quality of a task is the minimum of the incoming qualities, and thus remains at 0 until all subtasks or methods execute (an AND), while a Max QAF corresponds to an OR, yielding nonzero task quality as soon as any subtask succeeds. More complex functions are also possible.

The version of TÆMS in [6] explicitly represents dependencies between events and resources. C_TAEMS [1] does not represent resources.

Sometimes we need a more general vocabulary. Tasks, subtasks, methods, and resources are all *nodes* in a graph, whose *relations* are provided by non-local effects, resource dependencies, and QAF's. Tasks, subtasks, and methods all describe *events*.

Because HTN's are graphs, and because graphs are convenient stigmergic environments, could we use an HTN directly as an environment for stigmergic interaction? Perhaps the events in an HTN could serve as places of our environment where agents deposit and sense digital pheromones. On reflection, this approach poses a problem. Commonly, a single agent is responsible for each event (or at least each method), so different agents cannot interact through a single method.

However, even private events must access shared resources. So it is natural to use resources as the basis for coordination. Competition for resources is a form of stigmergic coordination [12], suggesting that resources are natural candidates for the places of a stigmergic environment.

2.2 rTÆMS (Resource TÆMS)

The intuition in the previous section is useful only if there are enough relations in a structure to mediate all the events that need to be coordinated. In [6], resources are only involved in some task relationships. Subtasking relations and NLE's do not involve resources, and [1] ignores them altogether.

But things that behave like resources are ubiquitous in TÆMS structures, and lie behind both subtasking and NLE's. We argue that a fully elaborated TÆMS structure is a bipartite graph, whose two components are events and resources.

Quality as a Resource.—Quality is central in TÆMS. It is produced by every event, and determines the sequencing of events. This behavior is reminiscent of a manufacturing job shop, where operations add successive features to parts that move between them. One operation might cut a bar of material to length, the next might drill a hole in it, and the next might tap the hole. TÆMS events are analogous to manufacturing operations, and TÆMS quality is analogous to features.

In a manufacturing system, the parts that move from one operation to the other are naturally modeled as resources, produced by one operation and consumed by the next. The actual resource would not be the bare part, but part-with-specified-features. Perhaps we can model quality as a (virtual) resource and capture its effects through resource relations. To verify this hypothesis, we need to explain how quality-as-resource can accommodate non-local effects (NLE's), the subtasking relation, and QAF's. We summarize this mapping. For a complete description, see [9].

Non-Local Effects (NLE's).—C-TÆMS defines four NLE's: *Enables*, *Facilitates*, *Disables*, and *Hinders*. Each has a source, a destination, and a delay. *Facilitates* and *Hinders* also have discrete distributions over quality, cost, and duration. The semantics of NLE's assume that the destination is a method, though they are often drawn between tasks as shorthand. We map each of these into a NLE method. This method has a duration equal to the specified delay, is limited by the quality produced by its source, and at the end of its duration[1], produces the same amount of quality as its input, and makes it available to its target. A NLE method requires some computational element to execute it. The natural candidate is the environment [17].

QAF's.—Some QAF's [6] (e.g., SeqMax, SeqMin) constrain sequencing among subtasks. These have disappeared in [1], and can always be handled using the apparatus of NLE's outlined above. The QAF's that remain are Sum, Max, Min, SyncSum, SumAnd, and ExactlyOne.

Subtasks produce their individual qualities, and sometimes additional resources. The supertask then combines individual qualities. The Task computes its quality by applying the appropriate function (Max, Min, Sum) to the qualities of its subtasks.

3   Stigmergy over rTÆMS

This section summarizes stigmergy, analyzes two approaches to applying it to HTN's that did not succeed, then describes one that does.

3.1   Basic Stigmergic Approach

Our approach is based on polyagents [11], which represent each entity in the real world with a set of agents. A single persistent avatar sends out a stream of ghosts that

---

[1] This is the DTT specification favored by Decker [4]. An alternative specification permits quality to accumulate as a method executes.

explore alternate routes through the environ-ment, recording their experiences by con-structing pheromone fields over that envi-ronment. These fields allow the ghosts to in-teract with the possible futures of other entities, exploring a much richer set of potential interac-tions than is possible

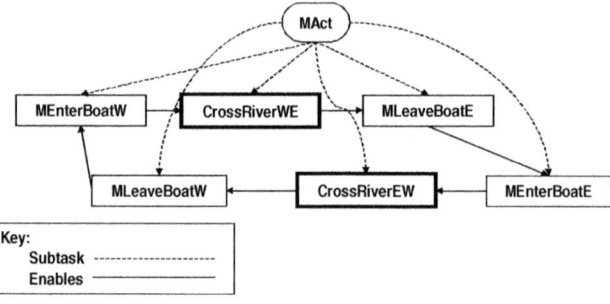

Fig. 2. Conventional TÆMS Graph for MC Problem

with single-trajectory simulations. The avatar picks its next step by consulting the pheromone fields generated by its ghosts.

3.2 The Resource Dual of a TÆMS Graph

A network of tasks and methods is a poor stigmergic environment because at least the methods, and often the tasks, belong to single agents. Resources, not tasks, are the locus of most coordination. By considering quality as a resource, we can represent any TÆMS graph as a bipartite graph whose nodes are resources and events.

It is possible to construct the resource dual of a TÆMS graph, containing only resources. Fig. 2 exhibits a resource-free TÆMS graph for a Missionary in the Mis-sionary-Cannibal problem, in the spirit of [10]. Relation types are encoded by line patterns (dashed for subtasks, solid for Enables). The bold methods are public meth-ods, those in which both Missionaries and Cannibals participate jointly. The technical memo [9] elaborates this structure into a full rTÆMS graph, then derives the resource dual, a hypergraph shown in Fig. 3. In this graph,

- The outer ring of qXXX quality resources captures the same structure as the ring of events in Fig. 2.
- The links among the population resources (mX, cX) and be-tween them and the quality resources capture important constraints on en-abled events.
- Eight nodes are shared with other agents, more loci for stigmergy than the two in Fig. 2.
- Paths of public nodes (bold outlines)

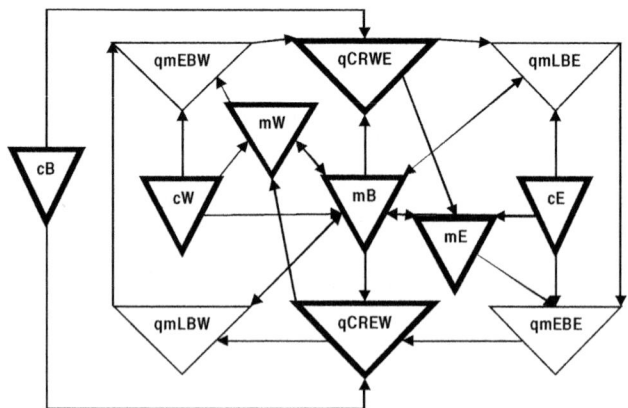

Fig. 3. Recurrent Core of the Resource Dual of Fig. 2

connect every pair of private nodes, providing paths through which agents can constrain one another's behavior.

In spite of its promise, we were unable to solve the missionary-cannibal problem by swarming on Fig. 2. By omitting events from the agents' environment, we lost important distinctions among different ways that resources could be replenished or consumed, leaving the ghosts with too little information to solve the problem.

3.3 Full rTÆMS Graph

Next we swarmed on a full rTÆMS graph. Ghosts deposit and sense pheromones on both resources and events. Pheromone on a *resource* enables the methods that require that resource. Pheromone on a *method* tells agents how desirable the method is for execution. Even if the method is enabled (that is, its resources have pheromones), an agent might still prefer an alternative method. As ghosts move out from their avatar to explore alternative futures, they deposit pheromone on the resources they encounter to enable the execution to unfold. On the way back, having reached the end of their exploration and evaluated the outcome, they deposit pheromone on methods to show the desirability of the path they followed. This pheromone field then guides not only other ghosts, but also the avatar when the time comes to execute the plan.

This approach was also unsuccessful. The dominant structure of the graph is a hierarchy. Ghosts moved up and down the hierarchy in order to move from one method to another. In the process, they bottlenecked at branch points in the hierarchy.

An HTN's hierarchy shows how methods and subtasks are organized into tasks, but does not highlight the causal flow. In a hierarchy, node proximity represents the logical structure of the task, not its temporal structure. In solving a planning or scheduling problem, agents need to attend to the temporal relations among events. The most important nodes for them to access at any moment are not superordinate and subordinate tasks, but the next nodes in the causal sequence. An entity executing a process is always on one method, looking for the next to visit. The entity's movement is from method to method, not from method to subtask to task and back down. Bottlenecking at branch points is a symptom of the inappropriateness of the hierarchical topology to the problem we are trying to solve.

3.4 Quality Graph vs. Execution Graph

Our current approach decomposes the graph into two parts, with different functions. We discuss first the decomposition, then how the avatars and ghosts explore it.

3.4.1 The Decomposed rTÆMS Graph
Any rTÆMS graph includes an execution graph and a quality hierarchy (Fig. 4).

The methods and the resources (physical or virtual) that constrain their sequencing form the *Execution Graph*. Polyagents live on the execution graph, not on the rTÆMS hierarchy. For clarity, the execution graph in the figure is incomplete, omitting the constraints implied by the two virtual resources higher in the hierarchy. In practice, we compile the rTÆMS graph to generate a complete activity graph. Current TÆMS dogma is that a method can be executed only once. An agent that internalizes the graph instantiates new schemata as needed, and in this case the execution graph will be a directed acyclic graph. It is more natural for agents that live within the graph to revisit a node, and we intend to support reentrant methods, since some problems (notably Missionary and Cannibals) cannot be solved with a bounded set of methods.

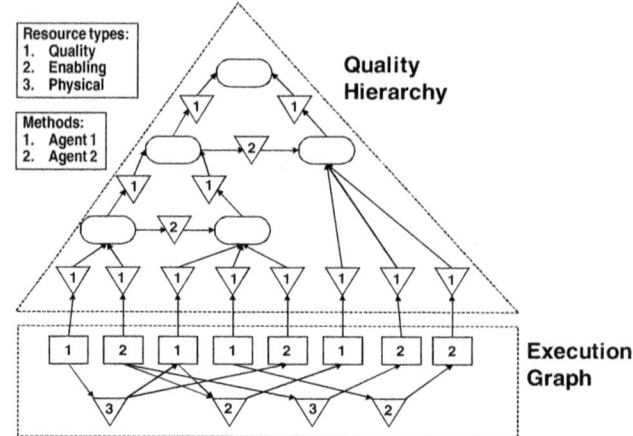

The subtask hierarchy computes and communicates the quality achieved by the system, so we call it the *Quality Hierarchy*.

Fig. 4. rTAEMS graphs merge quality, enablement, and execution dependencies

Compilation of the rTÆMS graph yields two functions that utilize this hierarchy.

One function propagates quality up the graph, keeping all subtasks notified of their current state of quality. This might support a human-meaningful interface, perhaps by shading each subtask with its current level of quality.

The other function uses the current state of quality to propagate method desirability back down the graph. The desirability of a method depends on its Quality Improvement Potential (QuIP), how much difference to the overall mission the quality it would produce would yield. For example, if two methods are OR'd into a subtask, the more quality has already accumulated at the subtask, the less difference additional quality would make, and the less desirable the execution of the methods is.

The distinction between the Execution Graph and the Quality Hierarchy (with its associated functions) illustrates two important functions of the environment in stigmergic reasoning. The environment *localizes* agents and their effects to reduce their computational burden. In addition, it is *active*, offloading some computation from the agents. (In routing systems, the aggregation, propagation, and evaporation of pheromones are examples of environmental action.) In this case, the Execution Graph provides meaningful localization by ensuring that an agent's neighborhood includes the most relevant methods for it to consider next, while the functions of the Quality Hierarchy extend the environment's actions to support the planning task.

3.4.2 Searching the Execution Graph

An entity's polyagent seeks an optimal path through the Execution Graph. If multiple entities execute concurrently in the same Execution Graph, their stigmergic interaction via shared resources will result in individual plans that are optimized conditional on one another, in other words, a coordinated plan. Our algorithm resembles the polyagent algorithm for manufacturing in [2], but with the addition of quality feedback from the Quality Hierarchy.

The polyagents use three pheromone flavors to coordinate their search for an optimal path through the Execution Graph. Avatars deposit *Execution* pheromone on methods that they have executed, to indicate that they do not need to be executed. (To handle the reentrant case mentioned above, we allow this pheromone to evaporate.) Ghosts deposit *Exploration* pheromone on methods as they visit them. In addition, after they complete their trajectories, they deposit *Desirability* pheromone proportional to the overall quality that they have achieved on all the nodes that they visited. Methods propagate both Execution and Exploration pheromones to the resources that they provision.

Each time a ghost is activated, it chooses among 1) sleep, 2) choose a new method and execute it, or 3) report and terminate.

The *sleep* behavior, chosen by flip of a coin, allows the system to explore alternative orderings of method execution.

If a ghost's lifetime is not exhausted, it *chooses and activates a method.* It identifies the subset of its avatar's methods with no Execution or Exploration Pheromone, but with Execution or Exploration Pheromone on each incoming resource. It scores each such method with a weighted sum of the Desirability Pheromone deposited on that method by previous ghosts, and the quality improvement potential (QuIP) propagated to the node by the quality hierarchy. The QuIP represents the increase in quality that would be realized *at the root of the tree* if the method were chosen. Then it selects a node with a roulette wheel whose segments are weighted by the scores of each method. It moves to the node, and sleeps for a period of time corresponding to the node's execution duration.

If a ghost's lifetime is exhausted, or if there are no methods left for it to visit, it assesses the quality of its overall trajectory, *reports* this quality by depositing Desirability Pheromone on each method in its trajectory, and *terminates.*

At any moment, an avatar is situated on some method in the execution graph, modeling the execution of that method. When execution is complete, it deposits Execution Pheromone on the method to indicate that it has been executed. Then it selects from those methods that do not yet have Execution Pheromone, based on the Desirability Pheromone deposited by the ghosts.

In this approach, the Execution Graph provides agents with a topology in which nearby nodes are also the most relevant ones to the execution of the process in its current state, while the Quality Hierarchy uses the overall task structure to update the desirability of each method based on the current quality of the higher-level tasks.

4 Experimental Performance

We demonstrate our method on the rTÆMS graph of Fig. 5 This graph does not represent any specific problem, but is constructed to capture two different kinds of constraints that can emerge in a HTN: precedence constraints among methods (captured in the Execution Graph), and the subtask structure represented by the Quality Hierarchy. For clarity, we omit the resources that in fact occupy each link.

We compare our algorithm to two simpler algorithms, on Fig. 5 and two simpler graphs, for 3 x 3 = 9 experimental configurations, each replicated 25 times.

The three algorithms are:

A1. A random baseline selects methods randomly, ignoring both their enablement in the Execution Graph and their contribution of quality root in the Quality Hierarchy.

If a method chosen is not in fact enabled, it remains eligible for later selection. If it is enabled, it is executed and removed from the pool of methods, and other methods dependent on it are enabled. Thus the random method can take arbitrarily many steps to select all methods. In

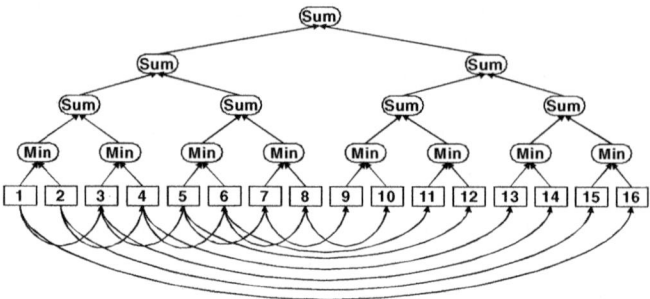

Fig. 5. Test HTN for Experiments

the mean field limit, this process can be modeled as a cumulative advantage process [14], a form of preferential attachment, but the probabilities involved in fact change as selections take place, due to the non-uniform nature of precedence links among the methods.

A2. A version of our algorithm that ignores QuIP and selects methods based only on enablement and desirability, yielding a process similar to that described in [2].

A3. Our full algorithm, with selection among enabled methods based on QuIP.

The three versions of the network are:

N1. A single task from which all methods descend directly, with no physical resources or non-local effects among them.

N2. N1 with the addition of precedence constraints among the methods.

N3. N2 with the addition of subtasks (and associated Quality Accumulation Functions) between the root task and the methods.

We monitor two dependent variables: how rapidly quality accumulates, and the variation among different runs. Fig. 6 shows quality vs. time for each configuration. The maximum quality available is 16 units (one for each method), except in N3, where the use of *Min* QAF's reduces it to 8. A2 and A3 reach maximum quality in 16 steps. A1 does so only in N1. Its average time to reach maximum quality in N2 is 47.3 ± 12.6 steps, and in N3, the statistically identical 46.4 ± 14.8 steps.

The rate of quality accumulation shows a strong correlation between the nature of the network and the effectiveness of the various algorithms. When the network is unconstrained (N1), all algorithms perform the same. Addition of precedence constraints gives A2 and A3 an advantage over A1, but they perform comparably to one another. When we introduce considerations of quality accumulation imposed by the Quality Hierarchy, A3 accumulates quality more rapidly than the other two.

This result highlights two different kinds of complexity in an HTN, one due to precedence constraints among methods, the other to the task structure through which methods deliver their quality. One could characterize HTN's by their location in this two-dimensional space, and distinguish solution strategies by the dimension(s) they address. This distinction, obvious from our inside-out approach to HTN's, is likely to be important for classical AI reasoners as well.

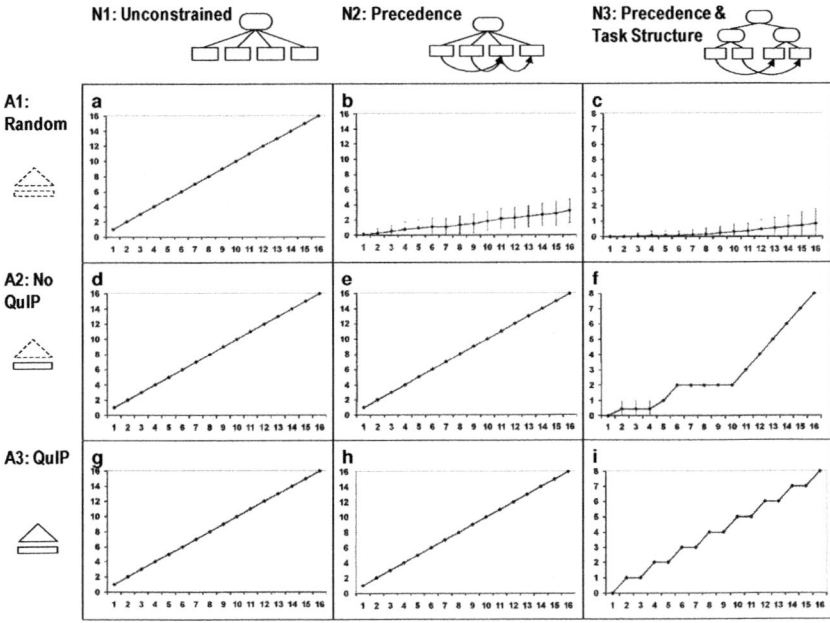

Fig. 6. Experimental Results. Abscissa is cycle #, 1-16 in all graphs. Ordinate is avatar quality, with maximum of 16 in left and center columns, 8 at right.

Now consider the variance in the various graphs. As problem complexity increases, the more sophisticated algorithm has less variance. This difference is an important advantage for our methods. Each run of the system represents an actual execution of the problem by a physical entity guided by an avatar, which does its planning guided by swarming ghosts. Real-world agents do not have the luxury of solving the problem 25 times and taking the best result, and high variance means that the simpler methods impose a risk of unacceptably low performance.

5 Next Steps

We are planning to extend this work in a number of ways.

To validate the claim of execution efficiency made in the introduction, we are executing our algorithm on larger graphs, and on scenarios for which benchmark results from classical approaches are available.

Our current experiments focus on a single avatar. We will explore coordination among multiple polyagents.

The methods in our current experiments do not include several features that are needed in solving realistic problems. These features, which can be accommodated with straightforward extensions, include deadlines, task quality that degrades with the passage of time, a quality threshold below which no quality is generated, reentrant methods, conservation of physical resources, and respect for resource capacity limits.

Stigmergy in general, and polyagent simulation of multiple futures in particular, are heuristics. Like all heuristics, they need to balance simplification against accuracy of results. One simplification that invites more careful study has to do with the ergodicity of causal sampling. Consider two methods, one of which (A) generates a resource needed by another (B). Under our current system, the future explored by one ghost might visit A, thus provisioning its resource and enabling B, but it might not visit B. Another ghost finds B enabled and visits it, but never visits A. Neither future is in fact feasible for the avatar. Our current approach is based on the hypothesis that averaged over a large number of ghosts, such anomalies will be dominated by valid futures, but more detailed experimentation is needed to verify this. The problem can be addressed by ghosts that make more careful use of the trajectory stacks that they are already building, but at the expense of their execution speed.

6   Conclusion

Stigmergy can be applied to semantically complex problems (such as planning) by embodying the semantics in the environment over which the agents swarm. It offers significant advantages over methods that apply more complex reasoning methods to the entire plan representation. For one thing, stigmergic processes can be scaled by distributing them over multiple processors. For another, conventional approaches encode specific constraints (NLEs or QAF's) in heuristics, and are brittle in the face of introducing new classes of constraints, but the rTÆMS vocabulary of virtual resources can easily be configured to capture any constraint as a graph structure over which our agents swarm naturally.

Our exploration of this approach on HTN's has led to several important lessons.

- A representation must have locations that are shared among agents in order to support stigmergy. A TÆMS graph with only physical resources, or (as in C-TÆMS) with no explicit resources, does not satisfy this requirement, but can be made to do so by adding virtual resources to form a bipartite graph.
- Though shared nodes (in this case, resources) are necessary to support stigmergy, they are not sufficient. The information in the rest of the graph is also needed.
- Having the agents swarm over all kinds of nodes is not necessarily the best way to give them this information, as our experiments in Section 3.3 showed. Some parts of a graphical representation of a domain may be useful to localize the agents, while other parts can support actions on the part of the environment.
- The topological neighborhood of the agents must be relevant to the task that the agents need to perform.
- HTN's exhibit two qualitatively different kinds of complexity (reflected in precedence constraints and subtask hierarchy), which yield to different aspects of our algorithm. This distinction is probably relevant for other HTN reasoners as well, and methods to characterize an arbitrary HTN along these two dimensions would be useful in selecting appropriate solution tactics.

References

1. Boddy, M., Horling, B., Phelps, J., Goldman, R.P., Vincent, R., Long, A.C., Kohout, B., Maheswaran, R.: C_TAEMS Language Specification, Version 2.02. DARPA, Arlington, VA (2006)
2. Brueckner, S.: Return from the Ant: Synthetic Ecosystems for Manufacturing Control. Thesis at Humboldt University Berlin, Department of Computer Science (2000)
3. Chen, W., Decker, K.: The Analysis of Coordination in an Information System Application–Emergency Medical Services. In: Bresciani, P., Giorgini, P., Henderson-Sellers, B., Low, G., Winikoff, M. (eds.) AOIS 2004. LNCS (LNAI), vol. 3508, pp. 36–51. Springer, Heidelberg (2005)
4. Decker, K.: Environment Centered Analysis and Design of Coordination Mechanisms. Thesis at University of Massachusetts, Department of Computer Science (1995)
5. Decker, K., Li, J.: Coordinating mutually exclusive resources using GPGP. Journal of Autonomous Agents and Multi-Agent Systems 3(2), 133–158 (2000)
6. Horling, B., Lesser, V., Vincent, R., Wagner, T., Raja, A., Zhang, S., Decker, K., Garvey, A.: The Taems White Paper. Multi-Agent Systems Lab, University of Massachusetts, Amherst, MA (2004), http://dis.cs.umass.edu/research/taems/white/
7. Maheswaran, R.T., Szekely, P., Becker, M., Fitzpatrick, S., Gati, G., Jin, J., Neches, R., Noori, N., Rogers, C., Sanchez, R., Smyth, K., Vanbuskirk, C.: Predictability & Criticality Metrics for Coordination in Complex Environments. In: Proceedings of Seventh International Joint Conference on Autonomous Agents and Multi-Agent Systems, AAMAS 2008 (2008)
8. Musliner, D.J., Durfee, E.H., Wu, J., Dolgov, D.A., Goldman, R.P., Boddy, M.S.: Coordinated Plan Management Using Multiagent MDPs. In: Proceedings of AAAI Spring Symposium on Distributed Plan and Schedule Management (2006)
9. Parunak, H.V.D.: HTN-Induced Stigmergic Environments. VRC division of TTGSI, Ann Arbor, MI (2008),
   http://www.newvectors.net/staff/parunakv/rTAEMS_TechMemo.pdf
10. Parunak, H.V.D., Brueckner, S.: Ant-Like Missionaries and Cannibals: Synthetic Pheromones for Distributed Motion Control. In: Proceedings of Fourth International Conference on Autonomous Agents (Agents 2000), pp. 467–474 (2000)
11. Parunak, H.V.D., Brueckner, S.: Concurrent Modeling of Alternative Worlds with Polyagents. In: Antunes, L., Takadama, K. (eds.) MABS 2006. LNCS (LNAI), vol. 4442, pp. 128–141. Springer, Heidelberg (2007)
12. Parunak, H.V.D., Brueckner, S., Fleischer, M., Odell, J.: A Preliminary Taxonomy of Multi-Agent Activity. In: Proceedings of Autonomous Agents and Multi-Agent Systems (AAMAS 2003), pp. 1090–1091. ACM, New York (2003)
13. Parunak, H.V.D., Nielsen, P.E., Brueckner, S., Alonso, R.: Hybrid Multi-Agent Systems. In: Brueckner, S.A., Hassas, S., Jelasity, M., Yamins, D. (eds.) ESOA 2006. LNCS (LNAI), vol. 4335, pp. 1–14. Springer, Heidelberg (2007)
14. de Price, D.S.: A General Theory of Bibliometric and Other Cumulative Advantage Processes. Journal of the American Society for Information Science 27(5-6), 292–306 (1976)
15. Simon, H.A.: The Sciences of the Artificial. MIT Press, Cambridge (1969)
16. Smith, S.F., Gallagher, A., Zimmerman, T., Barbulescu, L., Rubinstein, Z.: Distributed Management of Flexible Times Schedules. In: Proceedings of Sixth International Conference on Autonomous Agents and Multi-Agent Systems (AAMAS 2007), IFAAMAS, pp. 472–479 (2007)
17. Weyns, D., Parunak, H.V.D., Michel, F., Holvoet, T., Ferber, J.: Multiagent Systems, State-of-the-Art and Research Challenges. In: Weyns, D., Van Dyke Parunak, H., Michel, F. (eds.) E4MAS 2004. LNCS (LNAI), vol. 3374, pp. 1–47. Springer, Heidelberg (2005)

The Impact of Naive Agents in Heterogeneous Trust-Aware Societies

Amirali Salehi-Abari and Tony White

School of Computer Science, Carleton University,
1125 Colonel By Drive, Ottawa, Ontario, K1S 5B6, Canada
{asabari,arpwhite}@scs.carleton.ca

Abstract. Autonomous agents require trust and reputation concepts in order to identify communities of agents with which to interact reliably in ways analogous to humans. Agent societies are invariably heterogeneous, with multiple decision making policies and actions governing their behaviour. Through the introduction of naive agents, this paper shows empirically that while learning agents can identify malicious agents through direct interaction, naive agents compromise utility through their inability to discern malicious agents. Moreover, the impact of the proportion of naive agents on the society is analyzed. The paper demonstrates that there is a need for witness interaction trust to detect naive agents in addition to the need for direct interaction trust to detect malicious agents. By proposing a set of policies, the paper demonstrates how learning agents can isolate themselves from naive and malicious agents.

1 Introduction

The concept of trust is crucial in driving decision making and relationships in human and artificial societies. According to Jarvenpaa et al.[5], trust is an essential aspect of any relationship in which the trustor has no control over the actions of a trustee, the decision is important, and the environment is uncertain.

Agents make use of trust and reputation models in deciding how, when and who to interact with in a specific context [7]. Stated another way, an agent must be able to model trustworthiness of potential interaction partners and make decisions based on that model. It is a commonly held position that the main utility of trust and reputation models is minimizing the risk of interacting with others by avoiding interacting with malicious agents. With this view in mind, the principal objective of such models is the detection of untrustworthy agents.

The majority of computational trust and reputation models are designed and evaluated based on the assumption that the agent society only comprises two types of agents: trust-aware and malicious. It is our view that an agent society should include another type of agent called *a naive agent*. Naive agents are naive in terms of deciding how, when and who to interact with while always cooperating with other agents. The effects of naive agents on trust-aware individuals and the whole of society have not been analyzed to date. This observation motivates the work reported in this paper. Agents types represented in this paper have extremely limited cognitive properties modeled with simple policies. This

G. Di Tosto and H. Van Dyke Parunak (Eds.): MABS 2009, LNAI 5683, pp. 110–122, 2010.

is deliberate as we wish to understand the importance of agent heterogeneity in societal dynamics. Our research goal is the understanding of self-organization of agents into trusted communities.

This paper makes the following contributions: the introduction of the concept of a naive agent; analyzing the impact of this agent class on agent societies using a game-theoretic model on a simulation platform, and a strategy proposal for trust-aware agents to deal with them. While ART [3] aims to provide a unified platform for trust model evaluation it does not consider variables that are central to the evaluation proposed in this paper. Therefore, in order to evaluate our model, we design our own testbed which is described in Section 4.

The remainder of this paper is organized as follows. After describing related work in Section 2, we discuss naive agents and the environment model of agents in Sections 3 and 4 respectively. We describe the proposed agent model in Section 5, and experiments in Section 6. Finally, conclusions and future work are explained in Section 7.

2 Related Work

The body of research on trust and reputation models is substantial; a review of which can be found in [7] and [9]. In this paper our discussion is limited to models that incorporate, or discuss, multiple information sources.

Regret [8] is a decentralized trust and reputation system which takes into account three different sources of information. The direct trust, witness reputation, neighborhood reputation and, system reputation are introduced in Regret. Except for the direct trust module, the rest of the model is not readily applicable here because it is unclear how each agent can build the social network.

Yu and Singh proposed a social reputation management system in which they represented an agent's trust ratings regarding another agent as a scalar and combined them with testimonies [14]. Yu et al. have proposed the trust model in large-scale peer-to-peer systems in which each peer has its own a set of acquaintances [13]. The acquaintance's reliability and credibility are included in this model but are not used to drive the selection of new acquaintances as proposed here. However, the trust model strongly influenced the model described in Section 5.

Huynh et al. introduce a trust and reputation model called FIRE that integrates a number of information sources to estimate the trustworthiness of an agent [4]. Specifically, FIRE incorporates interaction trust, role-based trust, witness reputation, and certified reputation to provide a trust metric. FIRE does not consider malicious witness providers because it assumes honest agent information exchange. The research reported here explicitly deals with inaccurate witness providers.

In the Social Interaction Framework (SIF) [11], agents are playing a Prisoner's dilemma set of games with a partner selection phase. Each agent receives the results of the game it has played plus the information about the games played by a subset of all players. An agent evaluates the reputation of another agent based on observations as well through other witnesses. However, SIF does not describe how to find witnesses, which the model reported here does.

There are few trust models which consider the existence of an adversary in providing witness information and present solutions for dealing with inaccurate reputation, essentially the problem of naive agents of interest here. TRAVOS [12] models an agent's trust in an interaction partner. Trust is calculated using probability theory that takes account of past interactions and reputation information gathered from third parties while coping with inaccurate reputations. Yu and Singh [15] is similar to TRAVOS, in that it rates opinion source accuracy based on a subset of observations of trustee behavior.

Most recently, Salehi-Abari and White [10] have empirically shown that exploitation resistance is important for trust and reputation models. They declared that exploitation resistance "implies that adversaries cannot take advantage of the trust model and its associated systems parameters even when they are known or partially known to adversaries."

3   Naive Agent

We define a naive agent in the following way: a naive agent is incapable of properly deciding how, when and with whom to interact. As such, it fails to detect and stop interacting with untrustworthy agents due to its inability to properly assess other agents. Such agents are optimistic; they consider all other agents to be completely trustworthy and always cooperate with every member of the society. Naive agents usually do not have any malicious intention.

Examples of naive agent can be seen in many places. On eBay, sellers receive feedback (+1, 0, -1) in each auction and their reputation is calculated as the sum of those ratings over the last six months. It has been observed that there are many users (buyers) who do not receive satisfactory goods or services but they rate the sellers highly and even continue interacting with them. In other words they fail to "complain". We see these users as naive users.

4   Environment Model

The majority of open distributed computer systems can be modeled as multi-agent systems (MAS) in which each agent acts autonomously to achieve its objectives. Autonomy is represented here by the evaluation of pre-determined policies that cause changes in agent trust and reputation models and subsequent changes in societal structure. Our model incorporates heterogeneous agents interacting in a game theoretic manner. The model is described in the following 3 subsections.

4.1   Interactions

An agent interacts with a subset of all agents. Two agents are *neighbors* if both accept each other as a neighbor and interact with one another continuously.

An agent maintains the *neighborhood* set which is dynamic, changing when an agent is determined to be untrustworthy or new agent interactions are required. Agents have bounded sociability as determined by the maximal cardinality of the neighborhood set. Agents can have two types of interactions with their neighbors: *Direct Interaction* and *Witness Interaction*.

Direct Interaction. Direct interaction is the most frequently used source of information for trust and reputation models [9,7]. Different fields have their own interpretation of direct interaction. For example, in e-commerce, direct interaction might be considered to be buying or selling a product.

Witness Interaction. An agent can ask for an assessment of the trustworthiness of a specific agent from its neighbors and then the neighbors send their ratings of that agent to the asking agent. We call this asking for an opinion and receiving a rating, a ***Witness Interaction***.

4.2   Games: IPD and GPD

Direct and witness interactions are modeled using two extensions of the Prisoner's Dilemma. The Prisoner's Dilemma is a non-zero-sum, non-cooperative, and simultaneous game in which two players may each "cooperate" with or "defect" from the other player. In the iterated prisoner's dilemma (IPD) [1], the game is played repeatedly. As a result, players have the opportunity to "punish" each other for previous uncooperative play. The IPD is closely related to the evolution of trust because if both players trust each other they can both cooperate and avoid mutual defection. We have modeled the direct interaction using IPD[1].

Witness Interaction is modeled by the Generalized Prisoner's Dilemma (GPD). GPD is a two-person game which specifies the general forms for an asymmetric payoff matrix that preserves the social dilemma [2]. GPD is compatible with client/server structure where one player is the client and the other one is the server in each game. The decision of the server alone determines the ultimate outcome of the interaction.

4.3   Cooperation and Defection

We define two kinds of **Cooperation** and **Defection** in our environment: (1) Cooperation/Defection in Direct Interaction (CDI/DDI) and (2) Cooperation/Defection in Witness Interaction (CWI/DWI).

CDI/DDI have different interpretations depending on the context. For example, in e-commerce, defection in an interaction can be interpreted as the agent not satisfying the terms of a contract, selling poor quality goods, delivering late, or failing to pay the requested amount of money to a seller [7]. CWI means that the witness agent provides a reliable rating for the asking agent regarding the queried agent. In contrast, DWI means that the witness agent provides an unreliable rating for the asker agent regarding the queried agent.

---

[1] Our work is different from the well-known trust game appeared in the game theory literature.

5   Agent Model

This section presents two types of trust variables that assist agents in determining with whom they should interact. Furthermore, three policy types will be presented: direct interaction policy, witness interaction policy, and connection policy which assist agents in deciding how and when they should interact with another agent.

5.1   Trust Variables

Based on the aforementioned cooperation/defection explained in section 4.3, two modeled dimensions of trust are proposed. The motivation for having two trust variables is that we believe trustworthiness has different independent dimensions. For instance, an agent who is trustworthy in a direct interaction is not necessarily trustworthy in a witness interaction.

Each trust variable is defined by $T_{i,j}(t)$ indicating the trust rating assigned by agent i to agent j after t interactions between agent i and agent j, with $T_{i,j}(t) \in [-1, +1]$ and $T_{i,j}(0) = 0$. One agent in the view of the other agent can have one of the following levels of trustworthiness: *Trustworthy, Not Yet Known,* or *Untrustworthy.* Following Marsh [6], we define an upper and a lower threshold for each agent to model different levels of trustworthiness. The agent i has its own upper threshold $-1 \leq \omega_i \leq 1$ and lower threshold $-1 \leq \Omega_i \leq 1$. Agent j is *Trustworthy* from the viewpoint of agent i after t times of interactions if and only if $T_{i,j}(t) \geq \omega_i$. Agent i sees agent j as an *Untrustworthy* agent if $T_{i,j}(t) \leq \Omega_i$ and if $\Omega_i < T_{i,j}(t) < \omega_i$ then the agent j is in the state *Not Yet Known.*

Direct Interaction Trust (DIT). Direct Interaction Trust (DIT) is the result of CDI/DDI. Each agent maintains $DIT_{i,j}(t)$ variables for the agents with which they have had direct interactions. We used the following trust updating scheme motivated by that described in [14]:

$$DIT_{i,j}(t+1) =$$
$$\begin{cases} DIT_{i,j}(t) + \alpha_D(i)(1 - DIT_{i,j}(t)) & DIT_{i,j}(t) > 0 , CDI \\ (DIT_{i,j}(t) + \alpha_D(i))/(1 - min(|DIT_{i,j}(t)|, |\alpha_D(i)|)) & DIT_{i,j}(t) < 0 , CDI \\ (DIT_{i,j}(t) + \beta_D(i))/(1 - min(|DIT_{i,j}(t)|, |\beta_D(i)|)) & DIT_{i,j}(t) > 0 , DDI \\ DIT_{i,j}(t) + \beta_D(i)(1 + DIT_{i,j}(t)) & DIT_{i,j}(t) < 0 , DDI \end{cases}$$

Where $\alpha_D(i) > 0$ and $\beta_D(i) < 0$ are positive evidence and negative evidence weighting coefficients respectively for updating of the direct interaction trust variable of agent i. The value of $DIT_{i,j}(t)$, ω_i^{DIT} and Ω_i^{DIT} determine that the agent j is either *trustworthy, Not Yet Known* or *Untrustworthy* in terms of direct interaction from the perspective of agent i.

Witness Interaction Trust (WIT). Witness Interaction Trust (WIT) is the result of the cooperation/defection that the neighbors of an agent have with the agent regarding witness interaction (CWI/DWI). Agent i maintains a $WIT_{i,j}(t)$ variable for the agent j from whom it has received witness information. The updating scheme of $WIT_{i,j}(t)$ is similar to the one presented for $DIT_{i,j}(t)$ but CDI and DDI should be replaced by CWI and DWI respectively and $\alpha_D(i) > 0$ and $\beta_D(i) < 0$ is replaced with $\alpha_W(i) > 0$ and $\beta_W(i) < 0$ respectively. Where $\alpha_W(i) > 0$ and

$\beta_W(i) < 0$ are positive evidence and negative evidence weighting coefficients respectively for updating of the witness interaction trust variable of agent i. The value of $WIT_{i,j}(t)$, ω_i^{WIT} and Ω_i^{WIT} determine that the agent j is either *Trustworthy*, *Not Yet Known* or *Untrustworthy* in terms of witness interaction from the perspective of agent i.

5.2 Agent Policy Types

The perceptions introduced above allow agents to determine the trustworthiness of other agents. Policies make use of agent perceptions, trust and reputation models in order to decide upon the set of agents with which they will interact and in what ways they will interact. Policies may cause the agent interaction neighborhood to change, for example. While the testbed is extensible, several policy classes have been defined for the research reported here; they are explained in the following subsections.

Direct Interaction Policy (DIP). This type of policy assists an agent in making decisions regarding its direct interactions.

Witness Interaction Policy (WIP). This type of policy assists an agent in making two categories of decisions related to its witness interactions. First, agents need to decide how to provide the witness information for another agent on receiving a witness request. Should they manipulate the real information and forward false witness information to the requester (an example of defection) or should they tell the truth? The second decision is related to when and from whom the agent should ask for witness information.

We defined two sub witness interaction policies: Answering policy (AP) and Querying policy (QP). The former covers the first category of decisions mentioned above while the latter is for the second category.

Connection Policy (CP). This policy type assists an agent in making decisions regarding whether it should make a request for connection to other agents and whether the agents should accept/reject a request for a connection.

Disconnection Policy (DP). DP aids an agent in deciding whether it should drop a connection to a neighbor or not.

5.3 Experimentally Evaluated Policies

This section described policies that were evaluated experimentally.

Direct Interaction Policies. Three kinds of DIPs used in our experiments are: Always Cooperate (AC), Always-Defect (AD), and Trust-based Tit-For-Tat (TTFT). Agents using the AC policy for their direct interactions will cooperate with their neighbors in direct interactions regardless of the action of their neighbor. In contrast, agents using the AD policy will defect in all neighbor interactions. Agents employing TTFT will start with cooperation and then imitate the neighbors' last move as long as the neighbors are neither trustworthy nor untrustworthy.

Algorithm 1. Connection Policies

{CRQ is a queue containing the connection requests}
if CRQ is not empty **then**
　j = dequeue(CRQ)
　connectTo(j)
end if
if $size(neighborhood) < ST$ **then**
　j = get unvisited agent from list of all known agents
　if $\exists j \neq null$ **then**
　　requestConnectionTo(j)
　end if
end if

If a neighbor is known as untrustworthy, the agent will defect and if a neighbor is known as trustworthy, the agent will cooperate with it.

Connection Policies. Three kinds of connection polices are used in our experiments: Conservative (C), Naive (N), and Greedy (G). Each of these policies has a property called the Socializing Tendency (ST). ST affects decisions for making a connection request and the acceptance of the connection request. All three connection policies use Algorithm 1 with different ST values.

According to Algorithm 1, any connection request from another agent will be accepted regardless of the value of ST but the agent will acquire unvisited agent IDs if its number of neighbors is less than ST. In our experiments the value of ST is 5, 15, and 100 for Conservative, Naive, and Greedy connection policies respectively. The motivation for these values is that malicious agents will tend to be greedy and try and exploit a large number of agents; trust-aware agents, like their human counterparts, will tend to have a small circle of trusted agents.

Witness Interaction Policies. Three kinds of answering policies are modeled: Honest (Ho), Liar (Li), and Simpleton (Si). All these sub-policies use the pseudo-code presented in Algorithm 2 while differentiating in the assignment of opinion variable (refer to * in Algorithm 2). The asterisk should be replaced by $DIT_{i,j}(t)$, "$-1 * DIT_{i,j}(t)$", or 1 for Honest, Liar, or Simpleton policy respectively. An agent employing the Liar policy gives manipulated ratings to other agents by giving high ratings for untrustworthy agents and low ratings for trustworthy ones. The Simpleton policy ranks all other agents as trustworthy but the Honest policy always tells the truth to everyone. CWI/DWI will be sent based on whether the forwarding opinion agrees with the internal trust value of an agent or not. If the difference between them is less than the Discrimination Threshold (DT), an agent will send CWI otherwise DWI is sent. We can therefore say that: Liar always defects, Honest always cooperates, and Simpleton sometimes defects (by rating high untrustworthy agents) and sometimes cooperates (by rating low trustworthy agents) in providing the witness information. In the experiments reported here DT is set to 0.25.

Algorithm 2. Answering Policy

---

if receiving a witness request about j from k **then**
   $opinion = *$
   send opinion to k
   if $|opinion - DIT_{i,j}(t)| < DT$ **then**
      Send CWI to k after T_W time steps
   else
      Send DWI to k after T_W time steps
   end if
end if

By use of the querying policy presented in Algorithm 3, the agent asks for witness information from its neighbors regarding one of the untrustworthy agents which has already interacted with the given agent. As a result, the agent can understand which neighbors are capable of detecting untrustworthy agents.

Algorithm 3. Querying Policy

{BlackList: a list of known untrustworthy agents in terms of direct interactions}
if BlackList is not empty **then**
   $j =$ select randomly j from BlackList
   Ask for witness information about j from all neighbors
end if

Disconnection Policies. We have experimentally evaluated three kinds of disconnection policies: Lenient (Le), Moderate (Mo), and Strict (St). An agent will never drop a connection when using the Lenient policy. An agent that uses the Moderate policy will disconnect from the neighbor known as an untrustworthy agent in terms of direct interaction. An agent employing the Strict connection policy disconnects from the neighbor which is known to be untrustworthy either in direct interactions or in witness interactions.

6   Experiments

We have empirically analyzed our agent types at both microscopic and macroscopic levels. On the macro level, we studied how society structure changes over the course of many interactions. On the micro level, the utility of agents is examined. $\overline{U_{AT}(i)}$, the average of utilities for agents with the type of AT at time step i, is calculated by: $\overline{U_{AT}(i)} = \frac{\sum_{a \in AT} U_{Avg}(a,i)}{N_{AT}}$, where $U_{Avg}(a,i)$ is the average of utility of agent a over its interactions at time step i and N_{AT} is the total number of agents in the society whose type is AT. The utility of each interaction is calculated as follows: If agent i defects and agent j cooperates, agent i gets the Temptation to Defect payoff of 5 points while agent j receives the Sucker's payoff of 0. If both cooperate each gets the Reward for Mutual Cooperation payoff of 3 points, while if both defect each gets the Punishment for Mutual Defection payoff

Table 1. Agent Types and Specifications

Name	Naive	Malicious	Trust-Aware(TA)	Trust-Aware$^+$ (TA^+)
Trust	–	–	DIT	DIT&WIT
DIP	AC	AD	TTFT	TTFT
CP	N	G	C	C
DP	Le	Le	Mo	St
AP	Si	Li	Ho	Ho
QP	–	–	–	QP

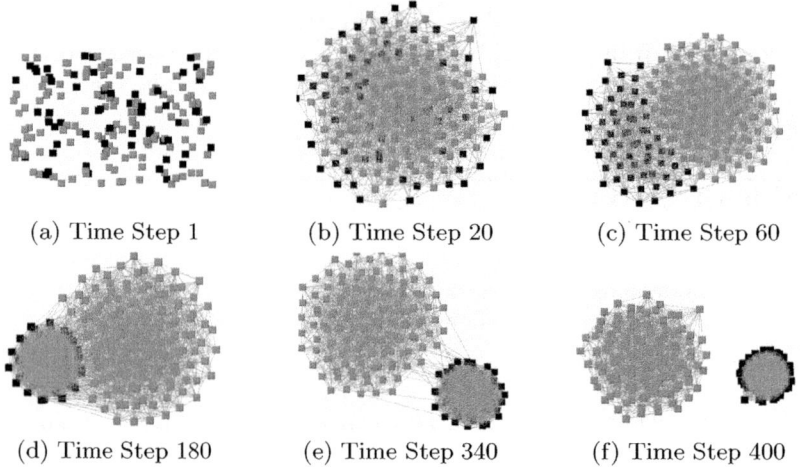

(a) Time Step 1   (b) Time Step 20   (c) Time Step 60

(d) Time Step 180   (e) Time Step 340   (f) Time Step 400

Fig. 1. Structural changes of Agents Society in Experiment 1

of 1 point. We have used the agent types presented in Table 1 for all experiments. In this paper, we use the same experimental values for our trust models as used by Yu and Singh in [14].

Experiment 1. We run the simulation with the population size of 200 agents where TA agents cover 66% of population and the rest are Malicious agents. The objective of this experiment is to understand whether cooperation emerges between TA agents while they isolate themselves from Malicious agents.

Different stages of this simulation are depicted in Figure 1, where TA agents and Malicious agents are in green (light gray in white-black print) and in black respectively. Starting from an initially unconnected society (Figure 1a) Malicious agents are quickly discovered (Figure 1c) and are completely isolated by time step 400 (Figure 1f).

Experiment 2. We run 200 agents where 55%, 11% and 34% of population are TA, Naive and Malicious agents respectively. The structure of the agent society after 400 time steps is presented in Figure 2a. Malicious and Trust-Aware agents are shown with the same colors of the previous experiment and blue squares with white "+" represent Naive agents. With the introduction of Naive agents, we could not achieve separation of Malicious and TA agents seen in Experiment 1. Since TA agents perceived Naive agents as trustworthy agents in direct interaction so they maintain their connections with Naive agents. On the other hand, since Naive agents accept all connection requests and do not drop any connections, they will be exploited by Malicious agents. As illustrated in Figure 2a, TA agents are connected indirectly to Malicious agents by means of Naive agents. Figure 2b shows Naive agents acting a buffer between the 2 other agent communities for a 30 agent simulation.

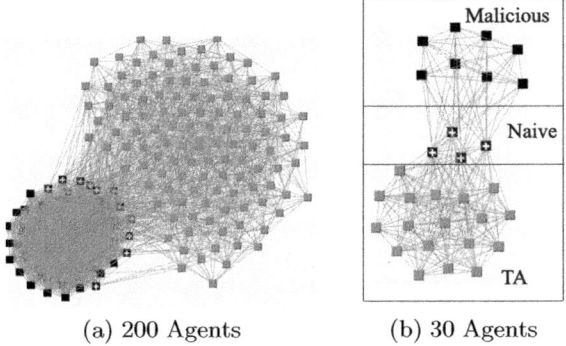

(a) 200 Agents   (b) 30 Agents

Fig. 2. The Final Society Structure in Exp. 2

Figure 3 shows the $\overline{U}$ of each agent type over the course of the simulation. $\overline{U}_{TA}$ increases over the simulation with small fluctuations. The more $\overline{U}_{TA}$ gets close to 3, the higher the proportion of interactions of TA agents are mutual cooperation. $\overline{U}_{Malicious}$ is increasing due to connecting to more Naive agents. The $\overline{U}_{Naive}$ drops over the course of simulation since the number of their connections with Malicious agents increases. All three graphs stabilize before time step 350, which is the result of not establishing new connections by any agents. Not requesting any connections can be the result of reaching the ST threshold (e.g., Naive and Trust-Aware) or scanning all of the agents (e.g., Malicious agents).

Experiment 3. This experiment intends to show the effect of a varying proportion of Naive agents. We have run five simulations of 200 agents with different proportions of Naive and Trust-Aware agents while maintaining Malicious agents unchanged as shown in Table 2.

Figure 4 presents $\overline{U}$ of each agent type at time step 400 for each of the runs. By increasing the proportion of Naive agents, $\overline{U}_{Malicious}$ increases considerably although the proportion of Malicious agents is unchanged. $\overline{U}_{TA}$ in all runs stays at 3 indicating that the proportion of Naive agents does not influence $\overline{U}_{TA}$. $\overline{U}_{Naive}$ increases slightly because Malicious agents have more choices to connect to Naive agents and to satisfy their ST threshold. For Pop5, the $\overline{U}_{Malicious}$ exceeds that of TA agents. In such societies, where malicious agents are unbounded in terms of their ability to exploit other agents, there is no incentive to be a Trust-aware agent

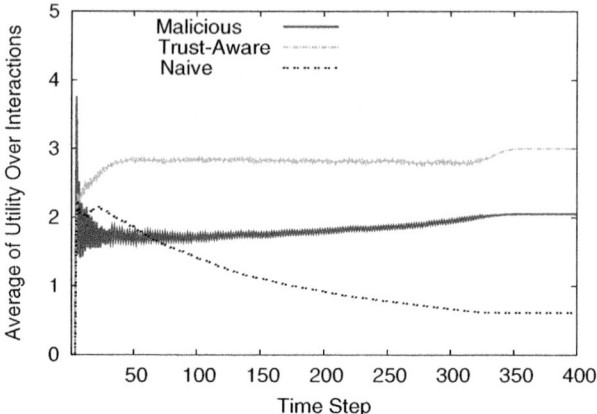

Fig. 3. $\overline{U}$ of agent types over simulation

Table 2. Population Distributions of Experiment 3

Agent Type	Population				
	Pop1	Pop2	Pop3	Pop4	Pop5
Malicious	34%	34%	34%	34%	34%
Naive	0%	11%	22%	33%	44%
Trust-Aware	66%	55%	44%	33%	22%

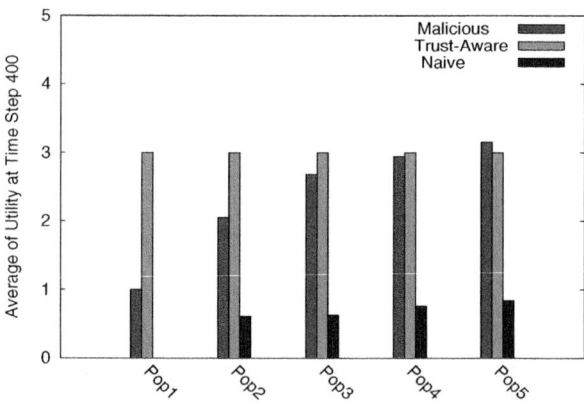

Fig. 4. $\overline{U}$ for five runs of Exp. 3

since Malicious agents have better utility. That is all the outcome of having a high proportion of Naive agents in the society.

Experiment 4. We run 200 agents where 55%, 11% and 34% of the population are Trust-Aware[+] (TA[+]), Naive and Malicious agents respectively. The structure of the agent society at three points in the simulation are presented in Figure 5.

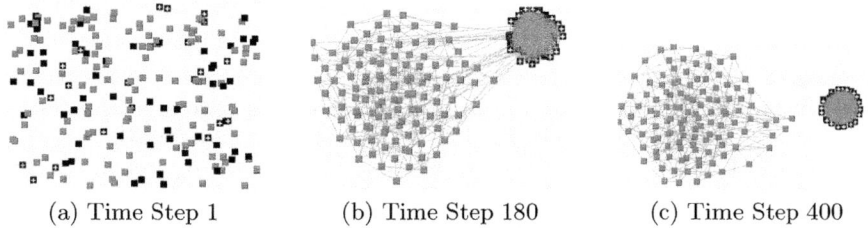

(a) Time Step 1 (b) Time Step 180 (c) Time Step 400

Fig. 5. Structural changes of Agents Society in Experiment 4

Malicious and Naive agents are shown with the same colors of previous experiments and TA$^+$ agents are presented in green. It is interesting to observe that Naive and Malicious agents are isolated from the TA$^+$ agents. By using multidimensional trust (DIT and WIT) and the Strict disconnecting policy, TA$^+$ agents could identify both Malicious and Naive agents to isolate them from their community. Naive agents are detected based on their failure to provide the appropriate witness information while Malicious agents are recognized by their defections in direct interactions.

7   Conclusion and Future Work

The isolation of untrustworthy agents from a society of agents is considered one of the main objectives of trust models [14]. Experiment 1 demonstrates that malicious agents can be isolated using DIT when naive agents are absent. Experiments 2 and 3 demonstrate how the proportion of naive agents affects the utility of malicious agents and society structure. When this proportion exceeds some threshold, malicious agents have the best utility in the society and consequently there is no incentive for trust-aware agents to stay trustworthy. In contrast, they are motivated to be malicious to exploit naive agents too. As shown in experiment 3, it is important for a society to limit the ability of any agent to exploit another agent. Experiment 4 shows how adding WIT allows naive agents to be detected. In this sense, TA$^+$ agents assessed the ability of their neighbors in detecting malicious agents. Those agents which fail in this assessment turn out to be naive agents.

Naive agents strongly degrade the value of DIT in trust-aware agent societies. Our results demonstrate that naive agents help malicious agents survive by cooperating with them directly (by providing good services) and indirectly (by giving a good rating for them). The proposed model demonstrates that trust-aware agents need multi-dimensional trust models to separate malicious and naive agents from the trustworthy community and would benefit from maintaining networks for each dimension of trust.

We plan to extend the proposed trust model for other sources of information such as observed interactions and modeling agents that are naive in observing the results of interaction. It would be interesting to see the effect of naive agents in reputation variable (systems) where the ratings regarding the specific agents will be gathered from naive neighbors.

References

1. Axelrod, R.: The Evolution of Cooperation. Basic Books, New York (1984)
2. Feldman, M., Lai, K., Stoica, I., Chuang, J.: Robust incentive techniques for peer-to-peer networks. In: EC 2004, pp. 102–111. ACM, New York (2004)
3. Fullam, K.K., Klos, T.B., Muller, G., Sabater, J., Schlosser, A., Topol, Z., Barber, K.S., Rosenschein, J.S., Vercouter, L., Voss, M.: A specification of the agent reputation and trust (art) testbed: experimentation and competition for trust in agent societies. In: AAMAS 2005, pp. 512–518. ACM, New York (2005)
4. Huynh, T.D., Jennings, N.R., Shadbolt, N.R.: An integrated trust and reputation model for open multi-agent systems. Autonomous Agents and Multi-Agent Systems 13(2), 119–154 (2006)
5. Jarvenpaa, S.L., Tractinsky, N., Vitale, M.: Consumer trust in an internet store. Inf. Technol. and Management 1(1-2), 45–71 (2000)
6. Marsh, S.: Formalising trust as a computational concept (1994)
7. Ramchurn, S.D., Huynh, D., Jennings, N.R.: Trust in multi-agent systems. Knowl. Eng. Rev. 19(1), 1–25 (2004)
8. Sabater, J., Sierra, C.: Regret: A reputation model for gregarious societies. In: Fourth Workshop on Deception Fraud and Trust in Agent Societies, pp. 61–70 (2001)
9. Sabater, J., Sierra, C.: Review on computational trust and reputation models. Artif. Intell. Rev. 24(1), 33–60 (2005)
10. Salehi-Abari, A., White, T.: Towards con-resistant trust models for distributed agent systems. In: IJCAI 2009: Proceedings of the Twenty-first International Joint Conference on Artificial Intelligence, pp. 272–277 (2009)
11. Schillo, M., Funk, P., Rovatsos, M.: Using trust for detecting deceitful agents in artificial societies. Applied Artificial Intelligence, Special Issue on Trust, Deception and Fraud in Agent Societies 14(8), 825–848 (2000)
12. Teacy, W.T.L., Patel, J., Jennings, N.R., Luck, M.: Coping with inaccurate reputation sources: experimental analysis of a probabilistic trust model. In: AAMAS 2005, pp. 997–1004. ACM, New York (2005)
13. Yu, B., Singh, M.P., Sycara, K.: Developing trust in large-scale peer-to-peer systems. In: IEEE First Symposium on Multi-Agent Security and Survivability, August 30-31, pp. 1–10 (2004)
14. Yu, B., Singh, M.P.: A social mechanism of reputation management in electronic communities. In: Klusch, M., Kerschberg, L. (eds.) CIA 2000. LNCS (LNAI), vol. 1860, pp. 154–165. Springer, Heidelberg (2000)
15. Yu, B., Singh, M.P.: Detecting deception in reputation management. In: AAMAS 2003, pp. 73–80. ACM, New York (2003)

HUME$_{1.0}$ - An Agent-Based Model on the Evolution of Trust in Strangers and Division of Labour⋆

Oliver Will

University of Bayreuth
Department of Philosophy
95440 Bayreuth
Germany
oliver.will@uni-bayreuth.de

Abstract. David Hume delivered an informal theory of how humans managed their way from a rather poor life in small groups to comparatively big wealth based on division of labour in large groups of people that are distant from each other. The dynamic is driven by two antagonistic forces: on the one hand specialisation entails incentives for division of labour but on the other hand the interaction structure of exchange regimes is that of a social dilemma. In this paper, an agent-based model is introduced that formalises important elements of Hume's theory. The main concepts that capture Hume's ideas are described and first results are presented.

Keywords: agent-based modelling, social dilemma situations, division of labour, trust game.

1 Introduction and Motivation

In *Of Morals*—that is part III of his *Treatise of Human Nature* [4]—David Hume delivers a rich theory of the origin of virtue and government. According to Hume, *both* are human *inventions* that evolved and emerged in a long process. Virtue and government enabled humanity to form large societies that are comparatively wealthy due to division of labour and specialisation.

Key components in Hume's ideas on the spread of virtue are:

1. an *original human nature* that causes serious trouble in large groups (a systematic short-sightedness in particular);
2. the invention of *artificial virtues*, especially justice (i.e. respecting property, transferring property only by consent, and keeping promises), that are acquired by a 'moralizing' character transformation;
3. *division of labour* with a corresponding development of special capabilities[1].

⋆ In this paper, HUME$_{1.0}$ is described for a special scenario. See collaborative work with Rainer Hegselmann [3] for a more fundamental and comprehensive account.

[1] Though the term 'division of labour' is coined by Adam Smith the general idea is already discussed in Hume's work (cf. [2, p.24]).

G. Di Tosto and H. Van Dyke Parunak (Eds.): MABS 2009, LNAI 5683, pp. 123–134, 2010.
© Springer-Verlag Berlin Heidelberg 2010

Hume delivered an informal theory and in the last decades many scholars did a lot of work on that conception[2]. The agent-based model that this paper is concerned with, $HUME_{1.0}$, is a first step towards a formalisation of Hume's theory. A *first* step since it focusses on the evolution of virtue and leaves that of government to future research. Different from what Hume has done, $HUME_{1.0}$ has precisely defined assumptions. Parameters that are involved will be explicit and can be varied in order to analyse *systematically* under what assumptions— in which parameter regions (more factual or more contra-factual ones)—virtues, specialization, and wealth prosper and how robust or how sensitive these processes are when parameters and/or mechanisms are varied.

In the following, the model is introduced in some technical detail. A description of the structure of agent interaction is given and the spatial scenario is characterised. Afterwards, a mechanism that models how agents classify potential partner according to their trustworthiness is presented and the matching procedure of $HUME_{1.0}$ is explained. Having described how agents learn in the model, I end with some first results and concluding remarks.

2   Interaction Structure and Specialisation

The dynamic suggested by Hume's theory is affected by two antagonistic forces: on the one hand, agents have different levels of competence in solving certain problems that change via practice, innovation etc. Thus there is an incentive for specialisation and division of labour. On the other hand, the interaction structure of exchange regimes is that of a social dilemma. This will become more clear in the remainder of this section.

The interaction structure that $HUME_{1.0}$ focusses on is the *trust game* (*TG*), a simple 2-person game that plays a central role in Hume's theory[3]. In a *TG*, two players could gain from mutual co-operation. One of them, $player_1$, has to choose on whether to contribute or not in advance (*trust*). *Afterwards*, $player_2$ chooses whether he contributes as well (*reward*) or not (*exploit*). $Player_2$ gets a higher payoff if he exploits than in case he rewards and for $player_1$ being exploited is worse than distrusting. Thus it can be seen by backward induction that for *rational* players the *noniterated, one-shot TG* has only one solution: anticipating that $player_2$ will go for exploitation, $player_1$ decides not to trust. This outcome is inefficient since both players would be better off in mutual co-operation. The interaction structure captured by the trust game is the very core of $HUME_{1.0}$ but it is incorporated into an *enriched setting*.

Key ingredients of this setting are:

1. In each iteration, half of the agents have one of K special problems. Those with a problem are referred to as *P-agents* the others are called *S-agents*.

---

[2] For detailed analysis, reconstruction, and elaboration of Hume's theory see e.g. [5], [6], [11], [1], [7], and [2].
[3] For reviews of research in the field of models on trust see [9] [10].

2. Agents have a competence vector with K entries that represent their competence in solving the respective problem. By working on a certain problem, agents become better in solving that problem. However, at the same time their other competencies *deteriorate*. Formally, this is realised by adding a certain Δ to the component in question and afterwards re-normalising the whole competence vector in such a way that $\sum_{k=1}^{K} c_{i,k} = 1$ holds again.
3. The more competent an agent is in solving a problem k, the less are his costs of producing a solution and the higher is the quality and thus the value added.
4. Agents can solve their problems either on their own or look for more competent agents that can solve it in a cheaper and better way.
5. Pairs of agents result from a *matching* process in which the competence and trustworthiness of agents plays an important role (see section 5).
6. If a match is established, the P-agent has to do some *prepayment*. Only afterwards, the S-agent that was 'hired' to solve the problem, starts working on the solution—*or not*. Prepayment of the P-agent and the resulting *temptation* for the S-agent to keep the prepayment without delivering the solution, makes the setting strategically analogous to the trust game described above[4] Figure 1 illustrates the interaction structure. The payoff structure is the same as in the simple trust game: a P-agent likes the outcome from trusting a rewarding S-agent best, that from distrusting second best, and is worst off if he trusts and the S-agent exploits. For the S-agent, the highest outcome results from exploiting a trusting P-agent, followed by rewarding a trusting P-agent. S-agents that are not trusted earn nothing at all. This payoff structure is fixed. Total payoffs depend on the S-agent's competence in solving problem k, parameters concerning functions of costs and value, and the share of the value added[5] that is earmarked for the S-agent[6].

3   The Spatial Scenario

HUME$_{1.0}$ analyses the trust game in different spatial scenarios (cf. [3]). Here, I will concentrate on only one: the **partition** and **market** based scenario (PM-scenario). In this scenario, agents are distributed among an exogenously given number of partitions. They search for partners either within their partition or on a central market. The decisive structural details are[7]:

---

[4] See [3] for a motivation of the chosen and a discussion of other plausible *exchange regimes* for HUME$_{1.0}$.

[5] That 'value added' is the difference between the value and production costs of a solution.

[6] Determined by the exogenous parameter β.

[7] The PM-scenario has structural similarities with the Macy-Sato-model ([8], [12], [13]) but in HUME$_{1.0}$ the probability for rewarding on the market can be different from the probability for rewarding locally. An endogenous mechanism of mobility between partitions is planned to be implemented in future versions of the model.

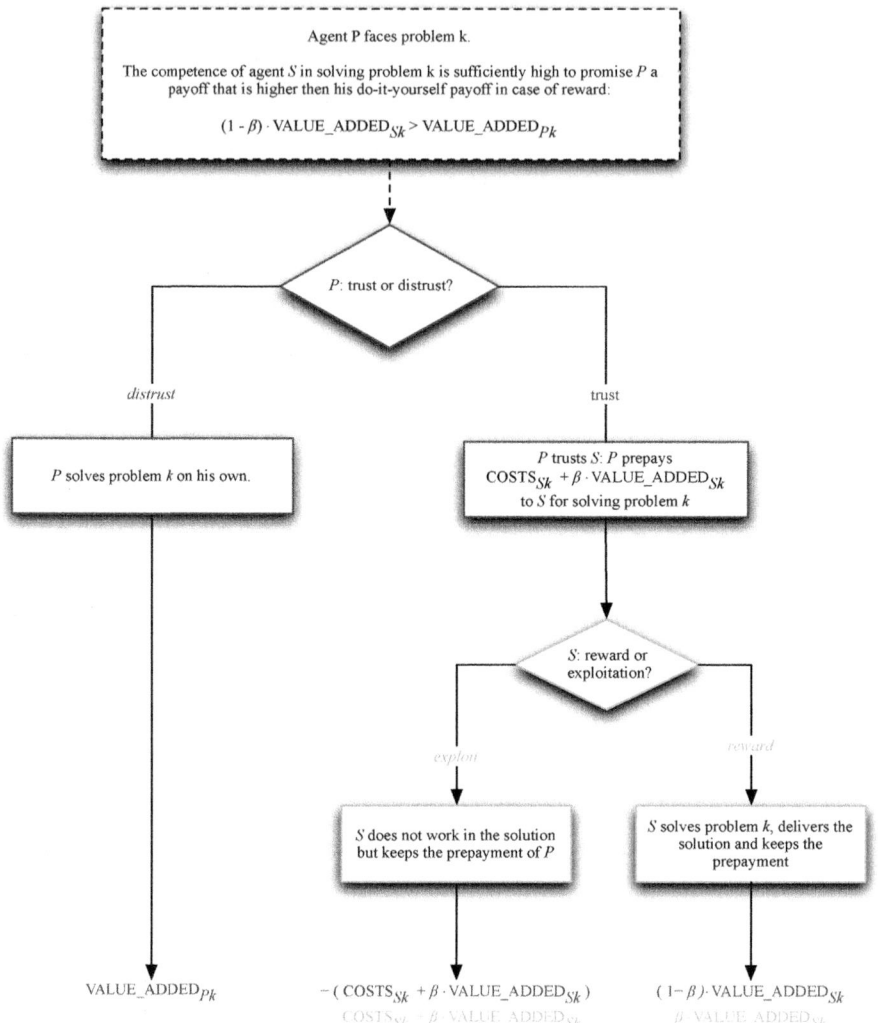

Fig. 1. The trust game in HUME$_{1.0}$. The matching algorithm ensures that the S-agent is sufficiently competent. At the first node the P-agent decides whether he trusts the S-agent or not. If the P-agents trusts, the S-agents decides whether or not he delivers a solution or not. Upper payoffs are those of the P-agent, lower payoffs refer to the S-agent.

1. With an individual, dynamic probability, $p_i^{P \to market}$, P-agents look for a partner to solve their problem at the market. They search for partners that are trustworthy and as competent as possible with regard to the problem they have. Correspondingly, with probability $p_i^{local}(t) = 1 - p_i^{market}(t)$ P-agent i looks for a trustworthy and competent S-agent within his partition. Analogously, S-agents have an propensity, $p_i^{S \to market}$, to go for the market.

2. S-agents reward with a certain individual and dynamic probability: With
probability $p_i^{reward\_market}(t)$ agent i rewards in *market*-interaction; with
probability $p_i^{reward\_local}(t)$ i rewards in case he is involved in interaction
in the *local* group.

4 Classification of Potential Partners

In HUME$_{1.0}$, agents are assumed to have a certain knowledge of each others
trustworthiness that might stem from sources like reputation, signalling, and past
experience. One of the questions that we want to tackle, is how much knowledge
of each others trustworthiness has to be assumed for division of labour in large
groups to evolve. Therefore, we are not interested in *how* these mechanisms work
but only *that* they work with a precision that we can keep under control. Thus,
we do not model them explicitly. It is furthermore assumed that the agents'
knowledge of each others trustworthiness becomes less precise the larger the
social distance between them gets.

A classification mechanism based on the agents trustworthiness, i.e. their
probability to reward, is implemented in HUME$_{1.0}$. The main component of
this mechanism is a function that maps from actual trustworthiness of the S-
agent to the trustworthiness perceived by the P-agent. Since knowledge about
other agents' trustworthiness depends on social distance, there are indeed two
functions: one for interaction within the partitions and another one for market
interaction.

Indicators of trustworthiness are assumed to work at least to a certain degree.
Thus the classification functions should assign greater values of perceived trustworthiness to greater values of actual trustworthiness. This way of modelling
allows for the implementation of several assumptions on the agents' behaviour.
One could, for example, implement the assumption that 1) agents distrust whenever their perceived trustworthiness is below and 2) trust whenever it is above a
certain threshold (dashed grey line in figure 2). Currently, simulations are done
in which agents are sceptical about their partners' trustworthiness. They are furthermore assumed to be more sceptical in interactions with people they do not
know. Thus, for the functions mapping from actual to perceived trustworthiness
that are currently implemented (example in figure 2) it holds true that:

1. they underlie the 45 degree line (which represents the case in which actual
   and perceived trustworthiness are identical), i.e. agents are sceptical, and
2. the function for interactions on the market underlies that for interactions
   within partitions, i.e. agents are less sceptical with partners they know.

If a P-agent trusts his partner, he could end up in two different situations.
Either his partner rewards and he gains a positive payoff or he is left with a
negative payoff because the S-agent exploits (see figure 1). A P-agent's expected
probability of a reward is given by his perceived trustworthiness of the respective
S-agent. The complementary probability is the expected probability of an exploit.

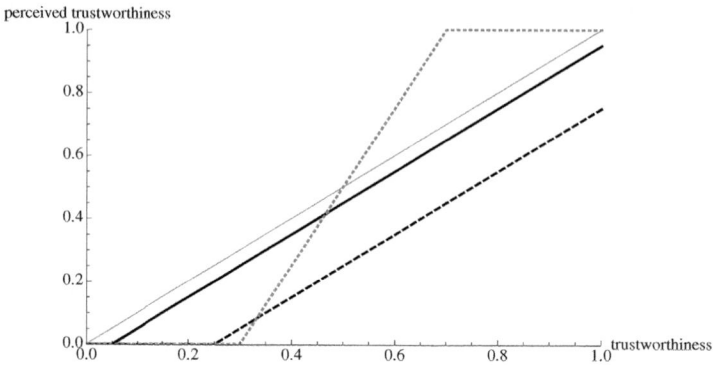

Fig. 2. Mapping from actual trustworthiness of S-agents to perceived trustworthiness of sceptical (graphs are below the grey 45 degree line) P-agents in partitions (solid black) and on the market (dashed black). More complex assumptions will be analysed in future experiments (dotted grey).

The agent's expected payoff can be calculated from these probabilities plus his payoff in case of reward, π_{reward}, and exploit, π_{reward}:

$$\pi_{expected} = p_{trust_{perceived}}\pi_{reward} + (1 - p_{trust_{perceived}})\pi_{exploit} \tag{1}$$

A P-agent is assumed to trust if and only if the expected payoff from interacting with the respective S-agent is positive. Figure 3 shows an example of a mapping from perceived trustworthiness to expected payoff for given payoffs in case of reward or exploit. The slope of the equation for the graph is

$$\pi_{expected} = \pi_{exploit} + p_{trust_{perceived}}\pi_{reward} + |\pi_{exploit}| \tag{2}$$

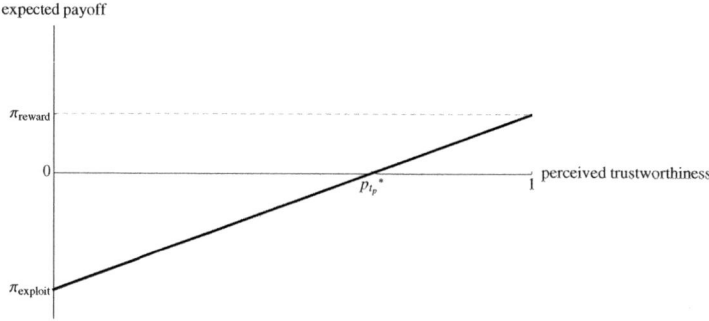

Fig. 3. Expected payoff, depending on perceived trustworthiness and payoffs in case of reward and exploit. pt^* is the value of perceived trustworthiness above which the P-agent's expected payoff is greater than zero, i.e. above which the P-agent trusts.

Now, the critical perceived trustworthiness, $P^*_{trust_{perceived}}$, can be calculated from

$$P^*_{trust_{perceived}} = -\frac{\pi_{exploit}}{\pi_{reward} + |\pi_{exploit}|} \tag{3}$$

Thus to determine whether a P-agent is trusting a S-agent in the current time step, we have to take the payoffs for reward and exploitation, calculate the critical perceived trustworthiness and compare it with the perceived trustworthiness. Only if the trustworthiness perceived by the P-agent is greater than the critical perceived trustworthiness, the P-agent trusts the S-agent.

5   Matching Agents

The matching procedure of HUME$_{1.0}$ is *not* an explicit model of how agents search for partners. It is a random-based mechanism that is designed to make pairs that agents—with all the limitations concerning cognitive abilities, information, and time restrictions—would or could plausibly have brought about by their activities. The effects that the matching procedure should produce, can be translated into the following requirements (R1 to R5):

R1 in all pairs, P- and S-agent are in each other's pool of possible partners,
R2 all P-agents that have a partner think that this partner is trustworthy,
R3 all pairs are economically reasonable in a sense that is described below,
R4 two agents' probability to be matched is positively correlated with the payoff they expect from an interaction[8], and
R5 the matching does neither constitute privileges for P-agents nor for agents of S-type.

The matching procedure is a two-stage mechanism that takes as input the set of all possible pairs of a P- and a S-agent. In the first stage, the subset of *plausible* pairs is identified. A pair is *plausible* if it meets the demands of requirements 1 to 3. In stage two, the actual pairs of the current time step are drawn at random from the set of plausible pairs. To fulfil requirement 4, the probability of a pair to be drawn depends on the payoff expected by the involved P- and S-agent.

5.1   Identifying the Set of *Plausible* Pairs (R.1 to R.3)

Let $\mathcal{P}$ be the set of all P-agents and $\mathcal{S}$ that of all S-agents. Then $\mathcal{P} \times \mathcal{S}$ is the set of all possible pairs of a P- and a S-agent. In the PM-scenario there are spatial reasons why some of these pairs are implausible (R.1). Only those pairs in which P- and S-agent are located in the same partition and at the same time search for a partner within the partition and those in which both agents search for a partner on the global market are plausible and the subset of those pairs is denoted by $(\mathcal{P} \times \mathcal{S})_{spatial} \subseteq \mathcal{P} \times \mathcal{S}$.

---

[8] The positive correlation reflects the agents ability to find partners that fit well in terms of competence.

The second step of our matching algorithm reduces the set of plausible pairs to those spatially plausible pairs in which the P-agent classified the S-agent as a trustworthy partner (R.2). Details of the classification mechanisms that can be implemented are discussed in section 4. $(\mathcal{P} \times \mathcal{S})_{trusted} \subseteq (\mathcal{P} \times \mathcal{S})_{spatial}$ denotes the subset of pairs in which the P-agent trusts the S-agent.

Requirement 3 concerns *economic reasonability*. In $\mathrm{HUME}_{1.0}$, P-agents can solve their problems on their own. Thus only pairs in which the S-agent's competence is high enough to ensure that the P-agent's payoff in case of reward exceeds his payoff in case of solving his problem on his own are plausible in terms of *economic reasonability*. The matching procedure finds the subset of pairs, $(\mathcal{P} \times \mathcal{S})_{competent} \subseteq (\mathcal{P} \times \mathcal{S})_{trusted}$, that contains all such pairs.

We end up with a subset of pairs that are plausible with regard to spatial reasons, trustworthiness and competencies. Thus we have a set of pairs that fulfil requirements 1 to 3 and which is therefore a set of *plausible* pairs, $(\mathcal{P} \times \mathcal{S})_{plausible}$, as it was defined in the beginning of this section. Now, that this set is determined we can step forward to the second stage of the matching mechanism.

5.2   Finding the Pairs of the Current Time Step (R.4 and R.5)

In the second stage of the matching process, we take the set of plausible pairs and randomly determine the actual pairs of the current time step. This process cannot be random in the sense that all pairs have the same chance of being drawn. Requirement 4 demands this process to be assortative to a certain degree: the probability of a pair to be drawn for the current time step must be positively correlated with the payoff expected from the respective P- and S-agent. To fulfil requirement 5, the process must be assortative without implying type privileges, i.e. it should neither favour P- over S-agents nor the other way round.

The determination of the pairs of the current time step starts with listing all P- all S-agents that occur in plausible pairs. Two lists result: a list of all P- and a list of all S-agents in plausible pairs. To avoid any risk of effects caused by the sequence in which the agents appear on the lists, random permutations of these lists are generated. Afterwards the drawing of pairs begins. This drawing procedure consists of a number of steps in which elements are deleted from the two lists. It is repeated until either the list of P- or the list of S-agents is empty.

1. A random number between zero and one is drawn to **determine whether a P- or a S-agent's perspective is taken**. To keep the process *neutral*, we take on a P-agents perspective if and only if the random number is smaller than the ration of P- and S-agents, i.e. if $random\text{-}number < \frac{\#list\text{-}of\text{-}p\text{-}agents}{\#list\text{-}of\text{-}s\text{-}agents}$.
2. We **get a *chosen agent*** by taking—depending on the perspective decided in step 1— the first entry on the list of P- or S-agents. This *chosen agent* is the agent for whom a partner is drawn in this run.
3. **The chosen agent's expected payoffs with all his partners in plausible pairs are calculated.** For a P-agent this means that we calculate the reward payoffs since the set of plausible pairs does not contain a pair in which the P-agent expects the S-agent to exploit. In case of the chosen agent

being a S-agent, the expected payoffs depend on whether or not the chosen agent intends to reward or to exploit.

4. **A vector of the chosen agent's expected payoffs is formed.**
5. **The elements of the vector of expected payoffs are normalised to unity**, i.e. each value of expected payoff is divided by the sum of the expected payoffs from all the chosen agent's partners in plausible pairs.
6. **The chosen agent's *actual* partner is determined using a random number between zero and one.** This is done by consecutively summing up the values in the vector of expected payoffs until this sum exceeds the drawn random number. That chosen agent's possible partner to which the expected payoff relates that was the last one added to the sum is the chosen agent's actual partner in the current time step.
7. **The chosen agent and his actual partner are removed from the lists of P- and S-agents.** This ensures that a paired agent cannot appear as a chosen agent afterwards.
8. **All plausible pairs that contain either the chosen agent, his partner or both are removed from the set of plausible pairs** to ensure that agents that are already paired do not appear as a chosen agent's possible partner afterwards.

At the end of step 8 we go back to step 1 and draw the next pair of agents for the current time step. This process is repeated until one of the lists is empty in which case no plausible pairs are left and our matching for the current time step is complete.

6 Learning

Agents develop their competencies by working on problems. Besides this technical learning agents learn on how to decide in certain situations. First, they have to choose on whether they search for a partner on the market or in partition. Since they could be either in a P- or a S-agent's position they have two propensities to go for the market: $p_i^{P \rightarrow market}$ and $p_i^{S \rightarrow market}$. Second, S-agents decide on whether or not they reward their partner and they differentiate between market interaction and interaction in the partitions. Thus for this decision two further propensities are needed: $p_i^{reward\_market}$ and $p_i^{reward\_local}$. These four propensities constitute the agents' *decision vector*.

The transformation of an agent's decision vector is always *success driven*, i.e. it is assumed that morality (the propensities to reward) cannot evolve if it is a *loser strategy*. Thus in HUME$_{1.0}$ trust and trustworthiness *erode* if agents that use it have lower payoffs than those who do not. The same is true for their propensities to go for the market. This idea is implemented using a kind of role model learning. For each agent i in the population it works as follows:

1. The pool of agents from which agent i selects his role model is determined by randomly drawing a exogenously given number of agents that inhabit the same partition as agent i.

2. Given that there is an agent in agent i's learning pool whose sum of payoffs exceeds that of agent i, that agent with the greatest sum of payoffs in the pool is agent i's role model in the current time step[9]. If agent i's sum of payoffs exceeds that of all agents in his learning pool, agent i does not have a role model and therefore does not change his decision vector.
3. Each value in agent i's decision vector is replaced by the corresponding value in the decision vector of his role model with a probability given by an exogenous parameter[10].

Besides this learning mechanism agents' propensities change due to some random mutation. In every time step each component of each agent's decision vector changes with a certain probability that is given by an exogenous parameter. A further parameter determines to what amount the component changes.

7   First Results

There are lots of parameters in $HUME_{1.0}$ and a systematic exploration of the parameter space is not yet completed. Nevertheless, there are some first results that are interesting to look at.

Figure 4 shows how the mean value of the agents' highest competence develops over time. It can be seen that the evolution of specialisation—as Hume thinks of it—is not a linear but rather stepwise process. Having reached a first level after around 2000 time steps, higher levels of specialisation are achieved suddenly around time steps 8500 and 13000. Many of the simulation runs that were conducted until today and in which a substantial level of division of labour evolves show similar courses.

A further interesting finding that appears in many of the simulation runs concerns the relation between local an market interaction. The graphs in

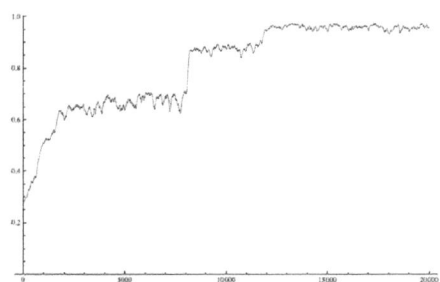

Fig. 4. A plot that display the development of the mean highest value of agents' competencies. Specialisation evolves step-wise in this and many other runs.

---

[9] Actually the sum of payoffs is discounted by an exogenously given discount rate.
[10] Note that this does not mean that either all or none of the components in agent i's decision vector are changed but rather that all, none, or some could be changed.

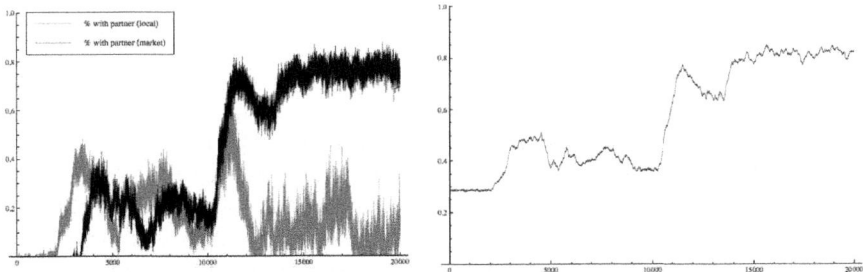

Fig. 5. A run in which local interaction prepares the ground for market interaction and the society ends up on a high level of division of labour. The plot on the right shows how the agents' mean highest competencies develops over time.

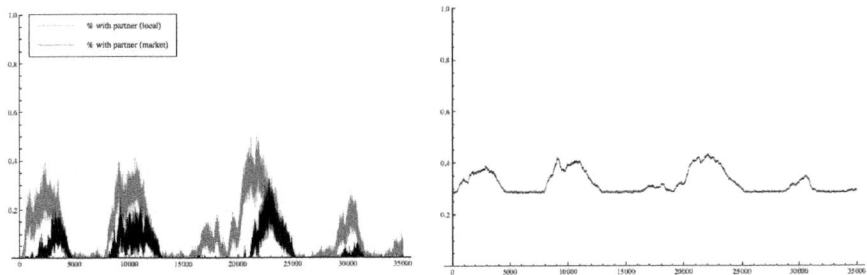

Fig. 6. A run in which repeatedly local interaction enables interaction on the market and both collapse

figure 5 show the development of the share of agents that successfully searched for a partner in a partition (grey) and on the market (black) and that of the agents' mean highest competence.

Looking a the left plot, we can hardly see any market interaction until local interaction reaches a substantial level at around time step 3000. This indicates that the evolution of market interaction can only develop if there is a certain level of local interaction. The right plot gives an explanation: local interaction leads to an increase in specialisation and only after it reaches a certain level, market interaction can come into place. Since after 12000 time steps market interaction is very successful and only few interaction take place in the partitions, we can conclude that once market interaction is established, it does no longer depend on local interaction.

We can also find runs in which local interaction leads to some market interaction but no further improvement of the society's situation develops. Figure 6 is an example of such runs: repeatedly, local interaction prepares the ground for interaction on the market but after some time both collapse.

8 Conclusion

The early results indicate that $HUME_{1.0}$ captures Hume's main ideas and raise hopes that a systematic exploration of the parameter space will lead to interesting results. Most important is to identify which of the many parameters are most important for the evolution of trust in strangers and division of labour. A further question concerns the stepwise evolution of specialisation that is described above. So far, the results indicate that the dynamic *is* stepwise but it is not clear *why* these jumps appear after thousands of time steps in which no substantial change in the level of specialisation happened. Furthermore, there are plausible alternatives to many of the components presented in the previous section[11]. Their effects on the results have to be analysed.

References

1. Binmore, K.: Game Theory and the Social Contract - Playing Fair, vol. 1. MIT Press, Cambridge (1994)
2. Hardin, R.: David Hume: Moral and Political Theorist. Oxford University Press, Oxford (2007)
3. Hegselmann, R., Will, O.: Modelling Hume's moral and political theory: The design of $HUME_{1.0}$. In: Baurmann, M., Brennan, G., Goodin, R., Southwood, N. (eds.) Norms and Values. The role of social norms as instruments of value realisation, Nomos, Baden-Baden (forthcoming)
4. Hume, D.: A Treatise of Human Nature. In: Norton, D.F., Norton, M. (eds.) Oxford University Press, Oxford (2007)
5. Kliemt, H.: Moralische Institutionen - Empiristische Theorien ihrer Evolution. Alber, Freiburg (1985)
6. Kliemt, H.: Antagonistische Kooperation. Alber, Freiburg (1986)
7. Lahno, B.: Versprechen - Überlegungen zu einer künstlichen Tugend. Oldenbourg, München (1995)
8. Macy, M., Sato, Y.: Trust, cooperation and market formation in the US and Japan. PNAS 99, 7214–7220 (2002)
9. Sabater, J., Sierra, C.: Review on computational trust and reputation models. Artif. Intel. l. Rev. 24, 33–60 (2005)
10. Sarvapali, D.R., Huynh, D., Jennings, N.R.: Trust in multi-agent systems. Knowl. Eng. Rev. 19, 1–25 (2004)
11. Sugden, R.: The Economics of Rights, Co-operation and Welfare, 2nd edn. Palgrave Macmillan, New York (2004)
12. Will, O., Hegselmann, R.: A Replication That Failed. JASSS 11(3), 3 (2008), http://jasss.soc.surrey.ac.uk/11/3/3.html
13. Will, O.: Resolving a Replication That Failed: News on the Macy & Sato model. JASSS 12(4), 11, http://jasss.soc.surrey.ac.uk/12/4/11.html

---

[11] See [3] for a discussion of some alternatives.

Mentat: A Data-Driven Agent-Based Simulation of Social Values Evolution

Samer Hassan[1], Luis Antunes[2], and Juan Pavón[1]

[1] GRASIA: Grupo de Agentes Software, Ingeniería y Aplicaciones, Departamento de Ingeniería del Software e Inteligencia Artificial, Universidad Complutense de Madrid, Madrid, 28040, Spain
{samer,jpavon}@fdi.ucm.es
[2] GUESS: Group of Studies in Social Simulation, LabMAg, Universidade de Lisboa, Campo Grande, 1749-016 Lisboa, Portugal
xarax@di.fc.ul.pt

Abstract. This work presents an agent based simulation model dealing with the evolution of social values in a 20 year period of the Spanish society, approaching it from Inglehart's theories on the subject. Surveys are taken as input to build the model by following a data-driven approach. This has been formalised in a methodology for introducing microsimulation techniques and importing data from several sources. It handles thousands of heterogeneous agents, which have a life cycle, reproduction patterns and complex social relationship dynamics. Its output is consistent with respect to the ideological, religious and demographic parameters observed in real world surveys. Moreover, several extension modules were designed: fuzzy logic for a smoother behaviour; natural language biographies generation; data mining for pattern finding. Thus, Mentat is proposed as a framework for exploring complexity at different levels in the social process.

Keywords: agent-based model, data-driven modelling, demography, social values, multi-agent based social simulation.

1 Introduction

Agent-based social simulation has proven to be a useful tool for the study of complex social phenomena, as it facilitates a bottom-up approach for the analysis of macro behaviour in societies of interacting entities [1]. This aggregate behaviour is called emergent, as the collective and even individual behaviours could not be predicted or expected from the initial settings of the simulation [2].

As this technology gets mature, new approaches are needed for bringing it closer to the real world, and therefore with an increased potential of being useful for social sciences researchers. With this purpose, an Agent-Based Model (ABM) was developed, aiming at analysing the evolution of social values in the postmodern Spanish society during 20 years. The particularity of this model, coined Mentat and based on the prototype of one of the authors [3], is that it tries to cope with several issues that are commonly neglected by a big part of the community of this field. In particular, most ABMs in literature tend to be

G. Di Tosto and H. Van Dyke Parunak (Eds.): MABS 2009, LNAI 5683, pp. 135–146, 2010.

overly simple, following the Keep It Simple, Stupid (KISS) principle. However, recently other works [4] claim for a substantial increase on the complexity of the models, taking real data more into consideration.

In this line, Mentat applies a data-driven approach that tries to draw a new methodology for injecting empirical data into Agent-Based Simulations. Specifically, Mentat has been intensively fed with surveys. Besides, several sociologists have been involved in the design of the system, strongly basing the modelling decisions in sociological literature, and even giving some empirically-based equations that support the demographic dynamics.

Mentat also handles complex friendship dynamics, which lead to the emerging of a robust social network. The links of this network evolve over time, both topologically (breaking and creating links) and in strength (strong and weak links can be identified). This process has been implemented with fuzzy logic techniques to obtain the smooth and continuous behaviour characteristic of typical friendship.

Another goal of this model is to provide ways to facilitate the analysis of different views of the system, with the ability to enable and disable different factors/aspects in the model, so that a social scientist can analyse either their impact in isolation or the mutual influence of some factors. Thus, a framework was used where it was possible to integrate, in a controlled way, several modules representing different social processes, and different artificial intelligence techniques, obtaining hybrid systems with richer outputs. Models of social processes are described along the paper, and the introduction of fuzzy logic is addressed in 4.2. Other AI techniques in Mentat fell out of the purpose of this paper. Nevertheless, section 7 goes through some of them: natural language processing for agent-biographies; data-mining for hidden pattern finding and validation; social network analysis for extracting and tracking structural variables.

The discussion of the sociological problem in section 2 provides more insight on the motivation for this work and the issues at stake. Section 3 presents several innovative methodological issues. The following two sections describe the micro and macro levels of Mentat. Section 6 discusses the output of the simulation, comparing it with the collected data. The paper finishes with some concluding remarks and future research lines that are being explored nowadays.

2   The Sociological Problem

Many sociological problems are difficult to be addressed properly with traditional analytical and statistical techniques, due to the diversity and great number of factors involved (e.g. evolution of culture), complicated dynamics (e.g. social networks), non-measurable social processes (e.g. psychological processes, world-size phenomena). Those problems are likely to be handled under the scope of complex systems theory. In this scope, agent-based systems have proved to be a proper framework to model and simulate these social processes [5].

To illustrate these issues with a specific example, this work has undertaken the analysis of the evolution of social values, together with other interrelated factors, in a specific space and time. In particular, we take an existing sociological research [6] on the Spanish society between the years 1980 and 2000. This Spanish period is interesting for social research, due to the big shift on moral values that the society underwent then. At the time of the re-instauration of democracy in 1975, the country was far from Europe in all the progress indicators, including the predominant social values and modernisation level. However, the observed trends of the social values evolution since then are analogous to those found in its EU partners [7]. Furthermore, the change in Spain has been developed with a special speed and intensity during the studied period. The problem faced is to study the shift in values and mentality of this society, in this period.

This issue has two main faces: the intra-generational changes (horizontal influence) and the inter-generational changes (demographic dynamics). R. Inglehart theories on modernisation [8] support that the change of values is driven mainly by inter-generational dynamics and the socialisation process (the assimilation of values in youth, mainly from the family). Thus, adult values would be stable over their course of life, with minor changes produced by intra-generational effects. According to this hypothesis, such elements should be enough to explain the magnitude of mentality change in modern Spain. Thus, this work attempts to model the shift of values taking into account just Inglehart's main factors: the demographic dynamics (i.e. the death of elders, carriers of the most traditional and conservative values, and the arrival of youngsters, bearers of emerging values) and a limited socialisation process (inheritance of values from the parents).

Thus, individuals social values remain constant, as they are not interfered by external influences. However, there are social dynamics (emerging and strengthening of friendships, couples), together with demographical changes (aging, deaths, reproduction). As a result, the values aggregation in the whole society evolved over time. This reflects the mentioned inter-generational changes, but not the intra-generational ones. However, this isolation is the only way to analyse and appreciate Inglehart's predictor effect of the demographic dynamics [9].

The source for modelling and initialization of agents attributes has been the European Values Survey (EVS). This is performed every ten years (1981, 1990, 1999) in all European countries [10], and thus provides a representative sample of the Spanish population. Moreover, as the EVS offers a wide source of quantitative information and periodical results (once every 10 years), it can be used for validation of the simulation model: initialising with EVS-1980, simulating 20 years, comparing with EVS-2000. Besides, for the design of the model and the selection of the relevant attributes, we have counted with the help of an expert in the field and several research studies [9].

The individual attributes that were taken into account have been selected according to their high influence in the subject. Thus, we considered: a general characterisation of the agents, like gender, age, education and economic level; social values-related attributes like ideology, religiosity, or tolerance to sensitive subjects like divorce, abortion or homosexuality; social relationships such as acquaintances, close friends, parents, spouse or children.

3   Methodological Stance: Deepening the Data-Driven Approach

Along this research project, we had the opportunity of devoting some thought to how social simulation is conducted and how it should be conducted to enhance the confidence in the obtained results. The search through the space of possible designs of the agents involved in the simulations, as well as their organisation (society) and the experimental set up (the simulations themselves) must be conducted with some guiding principles in mind.

Our starting point was Gilbert's "logic of simulation" [5], in which a target phenomenon is modelled, and simulation data are validated against collected data. We have advocated that when data are available from the real phenomenon, there are more steps in the simulation process that can be informed by their judicious use. In particular, data should be used instead of idealised theoretical random distributions, in an effort to bring the model closer to the real phenomenon. Another use of data is to inform the design and calibration of the model (cf. [11]).

In the search for the appropriate modelling stance, namely in terms of abstraction level and accuracy to the target phenomenon, a common approach is to keep the models as simple as explanation purposes demand (the KISS [1] principle: *Keep it simple, Stupid!*). Another approach, KIDS [4] (*Keep it descriptive, stupid!*) argues that too much simplicity yields useless models, so models should be as close to the real target as possible, and then progressively remove things deemed not essential for the model. The move from KISS to KIDS can be based on more intensive use of data that helps remove the many arbitrary assumptions and abstract simplifications of KISS models.

However, both approaches seem quite unrealistic in terms of the purposes we envisage for social simulation: explanation of phenomena at both micro and macro levels to the point that they can be used for accurate prediction of real world phenomena, and finally used to prescribe policy measures to accomplish desired political outcomes. Starting from Gilbert's principles, Antunes and colleagues have proposed a methodology for multi-agent-based exploratory simulation that proposes series of models designed to progressively tackle different aspects of the phenomena to be studied [12]. This new approach coined 'Deepening KISS,' amounts to start from a KISS model, following Sloman's prescription of a 'broad but shallow' design [13]. Then, through the use of evidence and especially data, a collection of models can be developed and explored, allowing for the designer to follow the KIDS prescription without really aiming at more simplicity or abstraction. This exploration of the design space allows to pick the best features of each model in the collection to design a stronger model, and the process is iterated. Deepening KISS with intensive use of data can be placed middle way in terms of simplicity versus descriptiveness, whilst it acknowledges the role of the experimenter as guide the search for the adequate models to face the stakeholders purposes [11].

4   Zooming in: The Micro Level

4.1   Autonomous Individuals

As we mentioned above, the multi-agent system Mentat was developed using agents with a wide collection of attributes related to the society under study. Most of the attributes are loaded from the EVS (except for social relationships, which do not appear in the survey). But while some are used mainly to be controlled in the final aggregated output (in the form of graphics and statistics), others constitute the key to the micro-behaviour in the demographic dynamics: age, gender and their relationships (together with the position and the neighbourhood, but those are completely random). Friendship dynamics is fed with the aggregation of all the characteristics, as explained in the next section.

The population in the motionless agent society evolves demographically: individuals are subject to life cycle patterns. Thus, they are born inheriting the characteristics of their parents (including the social values following the mentioned socialisation process); they relate to other people that may become their close friends; they can find a couple, reproduce and die, going through several stages where they follow some intentional and behavioural patterns. Therefore, every agent can be child, adult or elder, and, for instance, a child cannot have a spouse, only adults can reproduce, and elder will die at some point.

4.2   Neighbourhood Interaction

Understading Friendship. The most fundamental part of the agents' micro-behaviour is the set of social processes they develop. Each agent can communicate with their extended Moore neighbourhood, and depending on their rate of one-to-one similarity, occasionally arrive to a friendship relationship. Reaching to a certain period of their lives, the agents can search for a couple among their friends, and if they succeed, they can have children. However, the friendship choice and evolution is a complex process (deeply explained in [14]).

Principles of meeting and 'mating' by which strangers are converted to acquaintances, acquaintances to friends, and possibly even into spouse, follow the same rules of the important homophily principle in social networks of [15]. Meeting depends on opportunities alone (that is, to be in the same place at the same time); instead, mating depends on both opportunities and attraction. How readily an acquaintance is converted to close friendship depends on how attractive two people find each other and how easily they can get together. This is well synthesised in the 'proximity principle,' which states that the more similar people are, the more likely they will meet and become friends [16].

Friendship Evolution. We should note that similarity, proximity or friendship are vague or blurry categories. For this reason, a formal model of friendship dyads was developed using the general framework presented above, but considering similarity and friendship as continuous variables. Besides, because friendship occurs through time, we have considered our model in dynamical terms. In order to model formally the friendship evolution a specific logistic function [17] is used:

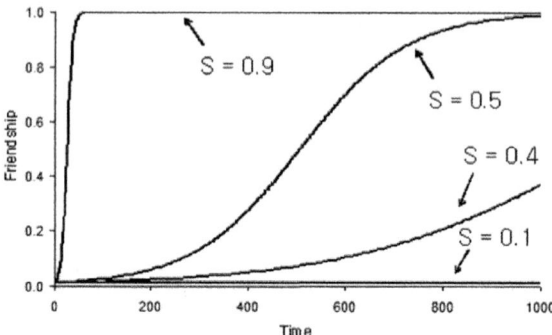

Fig. 1. The evolution of friendship function, for several one-to-one similarity values

$$\frac{dF}{dt} = rF(t)\left(1 - \frac{F(t)}{K}\right) \tag{1}$$

At each point in time, $F(t)$ defines the minimum degree of friendship that is given as an initial condition ($0 < F(t) < K$); K is the maximum degree of friendship that agents can reach (K can be understood as the level of 'close friends'), and finally r defines the growth rate of friendship. However, this equation does not include the 'proximity principle' described above. We can include this principle in equation 1 by modifying the growth rate r and stating it as follows: the more similar in social characteristics two individuals are, the higher the growth rate of their friendship is (we need to make r sensitive to the similarity value). Further equations of r and an analysis of the values in each formula can be found in [14].

Fuzzy logic in a fuzzy environment. In order to model the uncertainty of similarity and friendship more accurately, fuzzy logic has been used. Fuzzy logic is oriented at modelling the imprecise modes of reasoning in environment of uncertainty and vagueness, an usual feature in the social sciences realm [18].

Therefore, fuzzy sets over each agent attribute have been defined, as well as a fuzzy similarity operator that influences friendship emergence and partner choice. Such operator is defined as follows:

$$R_{similarity}(ind_A, ind_B) = OWA(\forall \mu_i \in ind, N(d(\mu_i(ind_A), \mu_i(ind_B)))) \tag{2}$$

This function would express the similarity among two agents in contact, aggregating the similarity in each of their attributes through an Ordered Weighted Averaging (OWA) [19]. E.g. for the attribute Economy, a fuzzy set is defined in both agents, each one with different degrees of membership (let's say 0.8 and 0.1). The distance among them would be 0.7 (as it is defined as a difference), and the fuzzy strong negation of such distance, a 0.3 (1-d). Thus, those agents would be similar in a 0.3 concerning economic level.

The friendship relation is turned into a fuzzy relation, evolving through the logistic function (with $K=1$), and letting it influence the partner choice as much as the similarity rate (through another OWA). This fuzzification of the operators improves the proximity of results to the qualitative assessments of the theory, achieving a smooth global behaviour. For an insight of the process check [14].

5   Zooming Out: The Macro Level

5.1   A Stable Environment: Some Technical Details

Due to the relative simplicity of the agents, the system can manage thousands of them, reaching the necessary amount for observing an emergent behaviour that results from the interactions of individuals, leading to the appearance of social patterns than can be studied [1]. Thus, Mentat handles 3000 agents in a grid of 100×100 cells. Agents are spread randomly (uniform distribution) around the space. So, with a resulting density of one agent per 3.3 cells, and an extended Moore radius of 6, each agent can communicate with about 35 agents. This number is consistent with the research on the average personal network sizes (with strong and medium-strength ties) [20]. The time scale is *one year = 50 steps*, so the total simulation time is 1000 steps (20 years).

The model has several configurable parameters: length of warming-up, agent density, Moore radius, linkage probabilities (randomly and if-similar) and similarity threshold (different if fuzziness is enabled). Such parameters were fixed after performing a sensitivity analysis over a subset of the possible range of values, determined by a domain expert in accordance to social theory. The rest of the choices have been empirically grounded (such as the chances for a Spanish 42 years old woman to have children, or how many children she may have), using data from several institutional sources. In order to explore the model space and for testing purposes, it is possible to enable/disable multiple model stages (such as fuzzy friendship or empirical initialisation).

The model has been implemented using the Repast framework, importing the EVS spreadsheets and generating a collection of graphs (which reflect the evolution of the main attributes of the social system) and aggregated statistics. Note that as the system is non-deterministic, the graphical results have some variations at each execution: the outcome should not be taken as a static output. In every execution the trends were very similar, even though the exact data have some small comparison errors. That is, the system has structural similarity [5].

5.2   Demographic Dynamics

It must be pointed out that, as long as Mentat analyses the evolution of moral values and socio-cultural phenomena during a long period of time (20 years), it becomes a need to implement an analog demographic pattern of the Spanish one. These demographic dynamics are synthesised here, more and more deepened following the methodology explained in section 3, and carefully detailed in [9].

Mentat is initialised with the Spanish section of the EVS-1980. However, there is an structural problem: children do not make surveys, but the ABM needs 1980's initial children. Those children would grow in the simulation and maybe reproduce, and so altering the output. In 1980 there was 30% of children in the country, so 700 new agents have been introduced, together with the 2300 of the EVS, hence filling this important gap. Those agents were generated by a domain expert crossing data from the youngest individuals available in the EVS-1980, as it is expected the missing ones will be similar to them.

A second structural change has been carried out because of another EVS issue: the lack of information related to the links among people. A proper simulation of 1980's behaviour should consider that back then some people *were already linked*. A simulation that begins with isolated people that must find their 'first friends' makes no sense. Therefore, a new stage was introduced in the simulation: a warming-up stage, where the individuals have time to relate to each others, but the 'timer' does not count (there is no aging and current year is always 1980). When it is considered 'enough' (the stage length is a free parameter) the actual simulation begins, but with initial friendships and marriages.

A third important point in the demography is that Mentat was first tested with Normal distributions for the typical demographic decitions (life expectancy, birth rate, age for having first child...). However, it was improved replacing them with empirically based probability equations.

With these demographic dynamics, as time goes by, agents will die and be born. Even if there is no horizontal influence (intra-generational changes), the deaths of the elder ones and the new children of certain couples will reveal a change in the global aggregations of the main parameters in the model (inter-generational changes). This change will be further explained in section 6.

5.3   Social Networks: Family and Friendship

Typically, in MABS models, complex networks emerge from the micro agent rules. Mentat's case is not different, and a robust social network can be observed emerging from the micro-interactions of individuals. There are two types of links (visually coloured) and therefore two related dynamics: friendship and family.

Each agent continuously compares itself with its neighbours, by using the fuzzy similarity function. The more similar two individuals are, the bigger are the chances that they become 'friends', i.e. create a friendship binary link between them. However, the intensity of the link matters, and friendship will become stronger depending on two factors: again similarity among them and time that went by. The logistic function described in section 4.2 represents this evolution: as time goes by, the bigger the similarity/likeliness, the faster the growth on friendship intensity. Thus, some people will always be acquaintances, while others will quickly become very close friends.

On the other hand, each agent, in a certain period of their lives, can try to find a spouse. The list of 'candidates' consists of its adult single friends of the opposite sex. The more 'compatible' among them will be chosen, with compatibility defined as the aggregation of the friendship degree and the similarity value. When a spouse is finally found, there is a chance of having children. Those children will be born spatially close to their parents, and as the couple, children and brothers are all connected through family links, family nuclei are built all over.

Big concentrations of families and the 'hubs' (agents with lots of friends) are deeply interrelated, as the more friends an agent has, the bigger the probability it will build a family. And the more families a sector has, the more populated it will become and more friends will its inhabitants have.

6 Results and Discussion

As further analysed in [9], the system's output can be compared with two validation points: the EVS of 1990 and 1999/2000, with respect to several indicators. The aggregated measures, such as ideology or religiosity, evolve over time due to the inter-generational demographic changes: i.e. the death of elders, carriers of the most traditional and conservative values, and the arrival of youngsters, bearers of emerging values. Besides, there are more births than deaths, so the population grows and the means and percentages change continuously.

The measures of Table 1 have been extracted from the three different EVS of the indicated years, together with the statistical calculations (over multiple executions) in Mentat for those years. All variables are calculated by considering only the individuals over 18 years, so that they can be directly compared with the EVS. For the sake of readability only a restricted collection of indicators (mostly means) are shown. Even so, the system calculates more than a hundred statistical measures. The high stability of Mentat has simplified the analysis, so it can be assessed that these values have a minimum error among executions.

The analysis of results can begin with simple parameters like the elderly percentage. It can be observed how the system follows a good projection till the 90's. However, as expected, it cannot predict that since 1990 Spain gradually received a young immigration that decreased the percentage of old people in the total population. Therefore, Mentat shows an approximation of the percentage that the Spanish society would have without that increase of immigration.

The percentage of single individuals is a factor related to the social network. A single individual a) does not have any single adult opposite-sex friend to have as a couple, or b) it does not want to have a couple (for example, because it is a child). In the beginning, the main cause of single agents is (a), but with time the network should grow in complexity and cohesion, so the predominant cause is (b). We can see that the singles amount should remain quite stable near 30%.

However, in the start-up Mentat shows N/A (or 100% of singles) because every agent is isolated before the warming-up. Obviously, the size of the warming-up is crucial: the more time they interact, the more couples will emerge. After that, the social network acquires consistence and approaches a lot the ideal value of 30%. It has been measured that the model reaches such ideal after 1500 steps. Taking into account that a year is 50 steps, with a warming-up of 500 steps the ideal is reached by the end of the simulation, but with a warming-up of 1000, it is reached in just 10 years. After the ideal is reached, the percentage remains stable: that is, the situation where the cause (b) is the widely dominant.

On the other hand, the warming period length has another logical effect: the more couples we have, the more children will be born. Anyway, as the most part

Table 1. Comparison between the results of the Mentat agent-based model and the European Values Survey three waves: EVS-1980 was used for initialisation, while 1990 and 1999 are validation points

	EVS waves			Mentat ABM		
	1981	1990	1999	1981	1990	1999
>65 years	16%	18%	21%	15%	19%	23%
Single agents*	28%	29%	29%	N/A	34%	30%
Single agents**	28%	29%	29%	N/A	29%	28%
Population Growth*			8%			8.6%
Population Growth**			8%			10%
Ideology						
Left	29%	33%	31%	29%	33%	36%
Centre	18%	19%	23%	18%	18%	17%
N/A	30%	25%	24%	30%	29%	27%
Right	22%	23%	21%	23%	22%	20%
Religious Typology						
Ecclesiastical	33%	25%	22%	33%	29%	25%
Low-Intensity	22%	26%	23%	22%	23%	22%
Alternatives	14%	17%	19%	14%	16%	16%
Non-religious	31%	32%	35%	31%	34%	37%

*,**: Warming-up of 500 or 1000 steps, respectively.

of the young couples find always someone, it does not have a big influence in the population growth. As we can check in the end of the table, the side effect of the extra 1000 steps yields a bigger error here. It has to be mentioned that there are no other important side effects, so we have not shown the other variables with other sizes different than the usual one of 100 steps.

The political ideology follows a similar trend but with some more slope, in the means and in the different percentages. This is due to several facts. First, we have not modelled the intra-generational changes, so the agents main attributes remain static over time (and these variables are quite sensible to those influences). Second, the simulation is not able to display the slight move to the right that occurred in the Spanish society during the conservative governments (1996-2004). But that would be too much to ask from a simulation drawn from 1981 data, while Spain was still in the period of democratic transition.

One of the best indicators for the evolution of values that we have available here is the religious typology, strongly based on them. As we can see in Table 1, the values are predicted with a pretty good accuracy, especially concerning the different curves that each of the four types follow: rapid fall, hill, smooth rising and smooth growing, respectively. This is supporting Inglehart's hypothesis [8] that religious evolution is deeply related with inter-generational evolution, and not with the horizontal influence along life. Other values are more volatile than these ones: e.g. a 30 years old woman may increase her tolerance against homosexuals, but it is very difficult that she will stop believing (or begin to believe) in her religion.

7   Concluding Remarks

This paper has described an Agent-Based Simulation Model of the evolution of social values across 20 years in the postmodern Spanish society. We have explained the wide sociological underground on which it is based, and the data-driven methodological approach that it follows and encourages. This approach facilitates the construction of the model by using data from surveys (for the initial agent attributes) and equations from social theory (for the demographic dynamics), and it is deeply interrelated with several sociological theories.

Mentat is proposed as a modular framework where each stage can be enabled or disabled so it can be studied in isolation, *ceteris paribus*. Thus, the system can disable the empirical initialisation and test the output with random agent attributes [21]. Or enable/disable the fuzzy logic module to check the improvement in the compatibility of the couples [14]. Each improvement, each new stage, can be enabled/disabled and therefore compared with the other versions, exploring the model space [9].

A sociological analysis showed that Mentat highlights the importance of demography in the twist in social values that happened in the Spanish society, supporting Inglehar's theories [8]. The high correlation of the output with observable data may appear counter-intuitive, as it does not take into account the horizontal influence in values among people (intra-generational evolution).

As open issues for Mentat, we are considering technical extensions of the framework by integrating other Artificial Intelligence techniques, like ontologies, data-mining (DM), natural language processing (NLP), or complex social network analysis. On the other hand, it would be interesting to complement Mentat with another ABM simulating the same shift of values but from the intra-generational approach, using opinion dynamics applied to social values.

Acknowledgments. We acknowledge support from the project *Agent-based Modelling and Simulation of Complex Social Systems (SiCoSSys)*, supported by Spanish Council for Science and Innovation, with grant TIN2008-06464-C03-01. We also thank the support from the *Programa de Creación y Consolidación de Grupos de Investigación UCM-BSCH, GR58/08*.

References

1. Axelrod, R.: Advancing the art of simulation in the social sciences. Complex 3(2), 16–22 (1997)
2. Conte, R., Castelfranchi, C.: Cognitive and Social Action. UCL Press, London (1995)
3. Hassan, S., Pavon, J., Arroyo, M., Leon, C.: Agent based simulation framework for quantitative and qualitative social research: Statistics and natural language generation. In: Amblard, F. (ed.) Fourth Conference of the European Social Simulation Association (ESSA 2007), Toulouse, France, pp. 697–707 (2007)
4. Edmonds, B., Moss, S.: From KISS to KIDS - an 'Anti-simplistic' modelling approach. In: Davidsson, P., Logan, B., Takadama, K. (eds.) MABS 2004. LNCS (LNAI), vol. 3415, pp. 130–144. Springer, Heidelberg (2005)

5. Gilbert, N., Troitzsch, K.G.: Simulation for the Social Scientist. Open University Press, Stony Stratford (1999)
6. Pavón, J., Arroyo, M., Hassan, S., Sansores, C.: Agent-based modelling and simulation for the analysis of social patterns. Pattern Recogn. Lett. 29, 1039–1048 (2008)
7. Inglehart, R.: Modernization and postmodernization: Cultural, economic, and political change in 43 societies. Princeton University Press, Princeton (1997)
8. Inglehart, R.: Culture shift in advanced industrial societies. Princeton University Press, Princeton (1991)
9. Hassan, S., Antunes, L., Arroyo, M.: Deepening the demographic mechanisms in a data-driven social simulation of moral values evolution. In: David, N., Sichman, J.S. (eds.) MAPS 2008. LNCS (LNAI), vol. 5269, pp. 167–182. Springer, Heidelberg (2009)
10. EVS: European values survey, http://www.europeanvalues.nl
11. Hassan, S., Antunes, L., Pavon, J., Gilbert, N.: Stepping on earth: A roadmap for data-driven agent-based modelling. In: Fifth Conference of the European Social Simulation Association (ESSA 2008), Brescia, Italy (2008)
12. Antunes, L., Coelho, H., Balsa, J., Respicio, A.: e*plore v.0: Principia for strategic exploration of social simulation experiments design space. In: Advancing Social Simulation: The First World Congress, pp. 295–306 (2006)
13. Sloman, A.: Explorations in design space. In: Proc. of the 11th European Conference on Artificial Intelligence (1994)
14. Hassan, S., Salgado, M., Pavón, J.: Friends forever: Social relationships with a fuzzy agent–based model. In: Corchado, E., Abraham, A., Pedrycz, W. (eds.) HAIS 2008. LNCS (LNAI), vol. 5271, pp. 523–532. Springer, Heidelberg (2008)
15. McPherson, M., Smith-Lovin, L., Cook, J.M.: Birds of a feather: Homophily in social networks. Annual Review of Sociology 27, 415–444 (2003)
16. Verbrugge, L.M.: The structure of adult friendship choices. Social Forces 56, 576–597 (1977)
17. Blanchard, P., Devaney, R.L., Hall, G.R.: Differential Equations, 2nd edn. Brooks Cole, Pacific Grove (2002)
18. Smithson, M.J., Verkuilen, J.: Fuzzy Set Theory: Applications in the Social Sciences: 147. Sage Publications, Inc., Thousand Oaks (2006)
19. Yager, R.R.: Families of OWA operators. Fuzzy Sets Syst. 59(2), 125–148 (1993)
20. Hamill, L., Gilbert, N.: Social circles: A simple structure for Agent-Based social network models. Journal of Artificial Societies and Social Simulation 12(2), 3 (2009)
21. Hassan, S., Pavon, J., Gilbert, N.: Injecting data into simulation: Can agent-based modelling learn from microsimulation? In: World Congress of Social Simulation 2008 (WCSS 2008), Washington, D.C. (2008)

Author Index

GPSR Compliance

*The European Union's (EU) General Product Safety Regulation (GPSR)
is a set of rules that requires consumer products to be safe and our
obligations to ensure this.*

*If you have any concerns about our products, you can contact us on
ProductSafety@springernature.com*

In case Publisher is established outside the EU, the EU authorized
representative is:

Springer Nature Customer Service Center GmbH
Europaplatz 3
69115 Heidelberg, Germany

Batch number: 09478804

Printed by Printforce, the Netherlands